Windows NT User Administration

Windows NT User Administration

Ashley J. Meggitt and Timothy D. Ritchey

O'REILLY™

Cambridge · Köln · Paris · Sebastopol · Tokyo

Windows NT User Administration
by Ashley J. Meggitt and Timothy D. Ritchey

Published by O'Reilly & Associates, Inc., 101 Morris Street, Sebastopol, CA 95472.

Editor: Robert Denn

Production Editor: Jane Ellin

Editorial and Production Services: Benchmark Productions, Inc., Boston, MA

Printing History:

October 1997:   First Edition.

ISBN: 1-56592-301-4   [3/98]

Table of Contents

Preface

Why a Book On Users

So, we stand in the computer section of the bookstore for the hundredth time slurping hot mocha with extra cream and stare at shelf upon shelf of books on Windows NT. For the hundredth time we notice that no one is addressing, in detail at any rate, the question of user management, and for the hundredth time we ask ourselves why not? Surely the purpose of putting together a Windows NT network and wrestling with its idiosyncrasies is so that the baying pack of users can get on with their work in a more efficient and hopefully more confident manner. It may be that the network is used to help turn a larger profit, administer the college more effectively, or prove that at the center of a black hole is in fact a singularity and not simply a hot jug of blue mountain coffee. The point here is that users are the final and most important element of the system, yet so many books give nothing more than a cursory nod at their management.

For this reason we decided to write a book, and the following is the product of our efforts. The book is not intended to simply collect together answers to what are common user management questions, but to try and demonstrate that you can improvise, given the appropriate tools, on many of the management themes. Managing users is a dynamic exercise and needs constant massaging in order to keep you as the administrator from having too much stress and the users from frustration, anger, and possibly a turn behind bars for grievous bodily harm.

Who This Book Is For

This book is aimed at the full spectrum of NT administrators—whether you are just getting started with NT, or have been using it for some time. Those of you who are new to it will hopefully get a feeling for the importance of user management as well as a jump start on the road to developing your own tools and forming your own philosophy. Those of you who are already up and running may well find some useful ideas for management that you can adapt to your own situation. Either way we feel this book has something for everyone. While we do think a beginning NT administrator will get much from this book, you should already be familiar with a working NT system.

Contents of the Book

The primary difficulty in writing a book on Windows NT user administration is figuring out exactly what that is supposed to mean. It is easier perhaps to figure out what it is not. It is not about installing NT on a particular hardware platform, connecting NT to a network, figuring out TCP/IP, optimizing NT's performance, setting up a RAID platform—and a whole host of other topics that are better served by other books. Our primary goal here is the support of users on a system, and the resources and tools available for that task. This means that we assume many things about NT in this book. Where aspects of NT's underlying construction are important to understanding a topic we will cover it in more detail—such as the Registry and Domain models. However, this book is primarily about the day-to-day user maintenance of an already functioning system.

Chapter 1, *Getting Started*, gives an overview of the issue of user management. It also introduces the Perl language and aims to give enough detail to allow a reader without any Perl knowledge to be able to follow the various scripts found within the book. If you are already a Perl addict then you may want to skip this one. However, it does talk about and the Win32 version of Perl.

Chapter 2, *Creating Users*, takes you through the process of adding users. It starts with a discussion on the basics of user creation such as the issues of usernames and passwords and goes on to demonstrate how to create a user account through the built-in graphical tool and the command line. It also touches on bulk user creation and discusses aspects of user maintenance.

Chapter 3, *Windows NT Groups and Security*, starts with a discussion on security and goes on to show how groups can be used to implement a security policy. It also demonstrates how to add users to groups *en masse*. Groups are a fundamental unit used within Windows NT to ease an administrator's burden, and a thorough understanding of this topic is important.

Chapter 4, *Managing Users Through Scripts*, demonstrates some aspects of user management through scripts. This includes information on logon scripts and takes a detailed look at the process of adding and removing users in bulk. Scripting is perhaps the most powerful tool an administrator has in their arsenal of utilities, and you will find them scattered throughout the book.

Chapter 5, *Managing Domain Users*, broadens the discussion of user management to take into account the prospect of managing users within the multiple domain environment. The chapter talks about the common domain models and applies each of these models in turn to a real world situation.

Chapter 6, *NT Internals and Managing Users*, tackles aspects of the Registry that relate to the user. It describes the purpose of the keys and values that are associated with a user and shows how these items can be modified through the appropriate graphical tool. It also talks about Perl and the Registry giving a simple example of how Perl can be used to access Registry information.

Chapter 7, *Controlling the User*, deals with user control. It details ways of both restricting the user in order to stop malicious action and as a way of generating a friendly user environment. It looks at how to make use of the built-in control tools as well as how to develop individual user profiles to help achieve your control goals.

Chapter 8, *Auditing and Windows NT*, tackles the issue of auditing. It talks about the audit policy, how auditing is set up, and explains the format of the individual audit records. It also describes the graphical tool used to look at the audit records as well as how to create a simple script that adds information to the audit logs.

Chapter 9, *Auditing with Perl*, details a number of useful scripts used for auditing purposes. Its purpose is to show the flexibility you can achieve by the use of Perl and a bit of flare.

We'd Like to Hear from You

We have tested and verified all of the information in this book to the best of our ability, but you may find that features have changed (or even that we have made mistakes!). Please let us know about any errors you find, as well as your suggestions for future editions, by writing to:

O'Reilly & Associates, Inc.
101 Morris Street
Sebastopol, CA 95472
1-800-998-9938 (in US or Canada)
1-707-829-0515 (international/local)
1-707-829-0104 (FAX)

You can also send us messages electornically. To be put on the mailing list or request a catalog, send email to:

nuts@oreilly.com (via the Internet)

To ask technical questions or comment on the book, send email to:

bookquestions@oreilly.com (via the Internet)

Conventions

The following typographic conventions are used in this book:

Italic

> is used for hostnames, URLs, filenames, and command names. It is also used to define new terms when they first appear in the text.

`Constant Width`

> is used in examples to show the text that you enter literally, and in regular text to show operators, variables, command-line options, Registry keys, and the output from commands or programs.

`Constant Italic`

> is used in examples to show variables for which a context-specific substitution should be made. The variable `filename`, for example, would be replaced by some actual filename.

Acknowledgments

Many people have encouraged us in the writing of this book and the following have helped us in ways that they may not have realized: Stephen Walcott, Racheal Scott, Dave Ingrams, Robert Feakes, Paul Alexander, Alex Perkins, and Rhona Watson—for the supply of tea and biscuits. Thanks also to our technical reviewers Erik Olson, Eric Pearce, and Jon Forrest.

There are a few people who deserve a special mention: Charlie Moore, for the constant encouragement and late night whiskey; the senior tutor of the College, Ian DuQuesnay, for supporting everything computing with such force that it couldn't possible go wrong; Rob Hopwood for his critical comments, his constant encouragement, and above all his humor; and Frank Zappa for the brilliant "Joe's Garage."

Thanks must also go to EDS, SUN, Hewlett-Packard, and 3COM for supplying the equipment we worked on and of course Jesus College Cambridge for giving us the opportunity to write the book in the first place.

AJM:

On a personal note I would like to thank the following for so many reasons that I can't begin to document here. They are: my brother Justin Meggitt, my parents Brenda and Bernard Meggitt, Sandra Last, and Jerry Toner.

I would also like to thank John Darlington for contributing absolutely nothing.

Finally the greatest thanks must go to my wife Jane Meggitt for simply everything.

TDR:

In addition to those already mentioned by Ashley, I would also like to thank the following: Steve Howard and Sara Wilson—congratulations! Steve Waterhouse and Phoebe White; Colin Shell, for his support and patience in my PhD; Don and Elizabeth Schilson for their encouragement in everything; Don Schilson, Jr.; and Ian Sheeler. My parents Jim and Bonnie Ritchey. Finally, thanks to Kristin Brannon, who has the eternal patience and love to put up with me.

Both Ashley and I would also like to thank everyone at O'Reilly & Associates for their help in this project. There were those working diligently behind the scenes that we never got to know, including Jane Ellin, the project manager, Robert Romano, the illustrator, Mike Sierra, who converted the files, Edie Freedman and Nancy Priest who did the design, Claire LeBlanc who organized the packager, and Sheryl Avruch for sanity control. Our thanks go especially to our editor Robert Denn for his patience, encouragement, and prodding at just the right times.

Dedication

To my children Ben and Lucie—*AJM*

To Michelle and Steve Ritchey—*TDR*

1

Getting Started

Trying to define the limitations of user administration can be somewhat difficult. It could be argued that computers are pretty much worthless without users, so all administration is ultimately user administration. A certain set of tasks that an administrator routinely performs can be seen as directly related to user management, and other tasks that are peripheral. We have divided the day-to-day roles of user administration into three broad areas:

Resource Management

deals with the problems of defining user resources such as workstations, printers, disk space, and applications, and granting or denying access to these resources based on the role of users within the organization.

Auditing

can be seen as the tasks that deal with monitoring users, both internal and external to an organization. Monitoring entails the proper setup and use of logging facilities available within Windows NT.

User Customization

concerns the tools and procedures for providing each user with his or her own custom environment where he or she can work—from desktop wallpaper to drive mappings.

In addition to these routine jobs, there are the basic tasks of user and group account creation. Although creating accounts occurs less often, this function has a great influence on how effectively an administrator can carry out day-to-day tasks.

Just as computers do not work well without users, by its very nature, user administration does not exist within a vacuum. If you are still considering installing NT, if you are in the middle of setting it up, or if you already have a system running, you must understand how users fit into the overall deployment of an NT system.

As you select hardware, software, and future upgrades, you must ensure that the work you carry out today is just as valid two to five years from now. In the fast-paced world of computing, this is a difficult proposition.

In addition to the tools provided with NT, many other resources are available from Microsoft and third-party developers. Many of these specifically address user administration tasks; others, such as Perl, are more generally adaptable to almost any functions you need to carry out regularly. Although this book mostly concerns itself with an "out-of-the-box" installation of NT and additional free utilities, you should know about the available tools if you have the means to get them. In some cases, unless you are running a small site or are strapped for cash, additional utilities such as Microsoft's Resource kits could be considered a necessity. Apart from free utilities, we do not make any assumptions about additional software you would need to purchase to follow the examples in the book.

Resource Management

Many movements within the computer industry over the years have affected the overall functional model of computing within business. First, out of the large mechanical era came the mainframes, or big iron. Computing resources were so scarce that users sat at dumb terminals, time-sharing the limited processor cycles and disk space of a central computer. In some cases, expensive UNIX workstations were used to provide limited mainframe-type power to individual users. These were (and still are, in most cases) expensive solutions—limiting their widespread acceptance. With the advent of the PC, computing resources began to become decentralized and affordable, providing resources on users' desks. The proliferation of computing resources had begun in earnest. Resources, though, were still considered in terms of processor cycles and hard disk size.

There were two problems with the new desktop model of computing resources. First, for most businesses, information exchange is the name of the game. Having isolated computers that could not communicate limits their usefulness. The necessity to communicate spawned the expansion of local area networks, wide area networks, and ultimately, the Internet. Investment in infrastructure then began to entail not only computing resources such as memory or processor speed, but also resources such as bandwidth. Adding networking resources increased the burden on limited budgets.

The second problem with the desktop model was that no matter how little computing you needed, the smallest quantum you could get was the PC itself. Even if you needed to use your computer only a few times a week, the company still had to invest several thousand dollars on a box that might sit idle most of the time. With increased costs of networking to defray, controlling and monitoring resource usage, possible under mainframes, became necessary. Controlling computing resources has lately seen the advent of network computers, where most of the computing resources can be centrally located and controlled.

No matter which of these resource models you end up deploying, defining your requirements, setting up your shares, and granting or denying access will be central to its implementation. Of course, most of this work can be seen as somewhat more organizational than user based because the requirements of the work done are on the computers, the sensitivity of the data, and the demarcation of duties are highly dependent on each individual situation.

In general, though, you will need to divide your computing resources into categories based on several objectives:

Optimum resource usage

Seemingly, no matter how much computing power you have, your users will always want more. At the same time, the days of behemoth companies are gone. Instead, management's focus is typically lean and mean: lean budgets and mean employees. The expense to install and maintain computer networks is an easy target, and matching limited supply to unlimited demand requires the flexibility to move storage, processor, and bandwidth resources between functional groups as needed.

Working convenience

To benefit most from networked computers, your users should be able to share data easily. This means organizing data storage and availability along departmental lines so that as new users are added or removed from groups or the system itself, they are automatically attached to the data most relevant to their jobs.

Data security

At the same time that data availability aids productivity, the security risks associated with such open systems have been exposed by increased usage and awareness of the Internet. Because many corporate networks, or intranets, are based on the same technologies as the Internet, making sure that sensitive data is safe from both outside hackers and inquisitive or malicious employees is imperative.

Creating users and groups that make these tasks as easy as possible requires thorough examination of the work to be done and the available infrastructure. This includes an analysis of not only the functional model the corporate computing will take, but the domain model that the corporate network will implement. Chapter 2, *Creating Users*, and Chapter 3, *Windows NT Groups and Security*, discuss the intricacies of user and group creation. In addition, Chapter 7, *Controlling the User*, discusses domain models and trust relationships.

Controlling Users

Of course, you would never have to do anything to a system if only there were no users. Unfortunately, the folks in Redmond haven't come up with a solution for that (yet). Until then, the administrator will always face the two-edged sword that is the user. A computer system is worthless without users, but often, users make the system pointless.

Controlling users can be divided into two main categories:

- Limiting the ability of users to access or change the system

- Providing an environment where users can set up their own preferences

Providing the right balance of freedom and control over user activities and preferences can mean the difference between happy and disgruntled users. You will never be able to fulfill every wish, but providing for the majority is still difficult enough. It is important to see how these two kinds of control provide a more stable working environment and, therefore, a more stable network.

Controlling users by limiting their ability to get at resources on the system is the first line of defense. Most system failures or breaches do not occur because of external hackers; instead, they occur when valid users either accidentally or intentionally mess about with their computers. Because of the overall complexity of NT and application support, determining exactly what users should and should not be able to do is difficult. For example, simply locking down the *%systemroot%* directory (which you might be tempted to do if you come from a UNIX background) might stop applications from running or create an unusable system altogether. This means that as an administrator, you must decide what elements of the system to leave open and what elements to lock down.

The two primary methods for limiting user access are *ACLs* and system policies. *ACLs*, or Access Control Lists, are the settings that limit the kind of activities that can be carried out on an object. File ACLs, for example, provide the traditional limitations of read, write, and execute that are familiar to users of any multiuser system. Additional resources such as printers and the registry have their own associated ACLs. These ACLs are customized to the activities related to the underlying object. Printers, for example, have *print* and *manage printers* options for their ACLs.

In addition to locking down system objects with ACLs, administrators can define *system policies* followed by the operating system applications such as the explorer shell. These policies can limit access to programs or settings, such as programs available through the Start menu or options available for setting desktop options. By choosing specific values for policies, it is possible to create limited environments that restrict users to specific activities. These policies can be based on computer, user, or group organizations. This approach allows fine-tuning of environments for different levels of ability and/or needs.

One misconception in controlling users is that it exclusively involves limitations. In fact, supporting custom environments for users is just as valid a method for controlling them. At the simplest level, this might mean providing custom shortcuts, drive mappings, and scripts for specific jobs. Because users have to deal with only those elements of the system that are directly related to their work, the chance that they might inadvertently change settings, which would require administrative assistance to correct, is reduced.

In addition to using custom user environments for control, allowing each user to customize his or her working environment—even if the customization is as simple as changing the background wallpaper—often gives a feeling of control. It is when users begin to feel too constrained by their environment that they start thinking of what they can do elsewhere. UNIX is a perfect example of an operating system that, in fact, severely limits what users can do and provides an environment where even the most demanding users can get their jobs done. NT supports these same multiuser features. In your never-ending quest for system security, remember that it is your own users who have the most power to damage the system—don't give them cause to wield that power if you don't have to.

Chapter 3, while ostensibly about creating groups, takes a view of group creation from the security standpoint, beginning with an overview of ACLs in NT, and discussing how groups can be used to more easily organize and control user access to resources. Chapter 5, *Managing Domain Users*, extends control of users through scripts, while Chapter 6, *NT Internals and Managing Users*, and Chapter 7 discuss more low-end details such as the registry, user profiles, and system policies. Together, we consider these tasks *controlling the user*.

Auditing Users

Auditing users is an important aspect to keeping a system running properly. In a previous section, we considered the deployment of a computing system in terms of proper resource allocation. Once such a system is set up, the activities of users will generate millions of requests on the system for access to these resources, be it executable files to run, database files for information, printers for creating hard-copy, fax servers, remote access servers, or Internet access—the list goes on and on. As you can well imagine, it would be impossible to keep track of all this activity manually. Instead, we must depend on the auditing services built into NT itself to be our eyes and ears. This means setting up a logging system to record events for us.

Even with a computer, keeping track of things is still daunting. The computer doesn't intuitively know when something is going wrong—if it did, then presumably it could stop it. For this reason, we must be prepared to look for suspicious activity that by itself could be harmless, but in combination with other events might lead to possible breaches in security. This means developing the tools to search through the copious information Windows NT will generate for us if asked. Therefore, implementing a proper auditing system entails a combination of choosing *what* to audit and determining *when* an event merits closer scrutiny.

Security breaches should not, however, be considered the only reason for auditing a system because breaches are only one kind of resource misuse. Overuse is just as valid a reason for auditing the system. By closely monitoring the usage level of resources by different groups, as well as the performance of the system in servicing requests, you can head off imminent breakdowns, which might require a reshuffling of the system. Things to consider then when evaluating auditing are these:

- What resources are critical to the system in maintaining security?
- What resources are critical to maintaining usability?
- What activities might be construed as malicious?
- What events indicate imminent overload or breakdown?
- How can these events, once recorded, be effectively searched?

Many administrators find it extremely difficult to dig themselves out of the day-to-day chores associated with running large-scale systems. Lack of sufficient auditing requires more intensive monitoring, and thus more time spent at the keyboard. By implementing a balanced auditing policy, it is possible to spot trouble before it begins or to more quickly determine what the problem is if one does occur. Chapter 8, *Auditing and Windows NT*, and Chapter 9, *Auditing with Perl*, discuss auditing and users, as well as using Perl to automate auditing tasks.

Perl

Perhaps the most important tool we will cover in this book is the Perl language. Although probably not as well known as some other languages, Perl has for some time been the main tool in many UNIX administrator toolboxes. As of Windows NT 4.0, Microsoft began supporting the use of Perl on NT, supplying it with the Resource Kit CD.

Why a new scripting language? There are a few obvious reasons:

- Windows NT is challenging the traditional turf of UNIX boxes. If Microsoft was going to appeal to this crowd, it needed to make sure that the most important utilities entrenched administrators used were available. This makes the argument for "NT as UNIX" that much stronger.

- Most of the existing languages available were either too low or too simple. Languages like C++, Java, or Pascal require compilation/linking stages and low-level understanding that add unneeded complexity when you want to get something done quickly. Other batch languages are simply not deep enough to be generally useful in and of themselves.

- When it comes to getting something done, there is rarely a quicker (or dirtier) way to do it than in Perl.

Almost all of the chapters in this book use Perl in one way or another. This reflects its constant use on our system. It did not start out this way. In fact, there was no plan at the beginning to use ANY Perl at all in our day-to-day administrative tasks. Perl, even by its creator's admission, is not a pretty language, and certainly it was not our first choice. After looking at most of the options out there, you have to keep coming back to Perl for both its simplicity in getting a job done quickly and its enormous depth when tasks require more than the quick fix. As the Perl language began to play an ever more important role in the development of our network, its importance in the book increased as well. In the end, we decided to forgo almost all other languages, and when scripting is required, we will use Perl in the examples throughout the book.

The rest of this chapter is a brief run-through of Perl as used in the examples in this book. This is by no means meant as a tutorial, and many fine books are out on the subject. If you don't already know the rudiments of Perl, you should pick up the Gecko book[*] for a quick introduction or the Camel book[†] for more complete coverage.

What we present assumes a basic understanding of Perl, so you should consider picking up one of these books. If you don't know Perl at all, check out the section, "The Basics," later in the chapter so that you can read the scripts without getting lost. You can also check out these web resources:

Perl for Win32 FAQ:
  http://www.endcontsw.com/people/evangelo/Perl_for_Win32_FAQ.html

CPAN:
  http://www.perl.com/CPAN/

FAQs:
  http://www.perl.com/docs/FAQs/

There is one important caveat to all of this: Perl is a very young language on NT. Even though it has been around for some time on UNIX and has had time to

---

[*]*Learning Perl on Win32 Systems,* by Randal Schwartz, Erik Olson, and Tom Christiansen, O'Reilly & Associates, Inc., 1997.

[†]*Programming Perl,* 2nd ed., by Larry Wall, Tom Christiansen, and Randal Schwartz, O'Reilly & Associates, Inc., 1997.

mature, the port to Win32 is an evolving package with constant change. We have tried to keep the examples up to date by using the very latest builds; however, these will obviously be out of date by the time you read this. In moving such a large program from UNIX to NT, the odd problem is inevitiable. Primarily, these problems exist in the native Win32 API calls that have been integrated into the Win32 port, or as functions that exist in UNIX without an equivalent in NT. We have tried to steer clear of as many of these as possible, and we have even written our own user administration module to carry out functions we found necessary that were either nonexistent or not working properly. As time goes on, though, Perl will only become more stable and more functional. The code you see in the book is a combination of standard functions and workarounds to some of the problems we encountered with the current version of Perl.

Where to get it

Although the NT resource kit does come with a copy of the Perl distribution, this version, as expected, is somewhat out of date. The current build of Perl is available from the ActiveState web site at:

> *http://www.activestate.com*

As of writing, this is build 306, although this changes quite rapidly. In addition to the basic Perl distribution, versions of Perl are available as a scripting language (PerlScript) and as a dynamic library for Microsoft's Internet Information Server. We will deal with only the basic Perl package in this book. Installation is straightforward. For Intel machines, the Perl distribution comes as a self-extracting archive—simply double-click the executable file. For the Alpha release, you will need to unpack the distribution with an unzipping program. Simply unpack the distribution into the directory where you want it to reside (i.e., *root*). Make sure you uncompress it into its original directory structure, and it automatically creates a *perl* directory with the correct subdirectories. Once Perl is extracted, change to the *root\perl\bin* directory, then run the installation script *perlw32-install.bat*. This script will create the proper path and registry changes to run Perl from the location to which it was extracted.

NOTE   Perl build 5.004 was just released during the final editing of this book, and it will build under NT. Build 306 of Perl for Win32 by ActiveState was based on the older 5.003 version of Perl, which did not. There are known incompatibilities with the Win32 Perl from ActiveState and the standard 5.004 Perl, so you may find that the scripts will require some modifications to run under the newer version. However, you should have no problems if you use the ActiveState Win32 version of Perl.

The Basics

Perl is not what most people would consider traditional in its syntactic choices, which can often lead to some difficult times pondering code. The first thing to remember is that if there is one way to do it in Perl, then there are a million ways; or, as the authors of the *Programming Perl* book say it:

"There is more than one way to do it."

The following is intended to run through some of the basic features of Perl, especially those that seem intent on causing the most grief possible.

Variables

First, variables in Perl come in three flavors: scalar, array, and hash. These are easy to spot because they are always prefixed by a dollar sign ($), at sign (@), and percent sign (%), respectively (usually). Scalar variables can hold any kind of data, including numbers, characters, strings, and references. Arrays are collections of scalars indexed by number, starting at zero. Hashes are similar to arrays; however, instead of being indexed by number, they are indexed by a string key. The following all make assignments to scalars, arrays, and hashes:

```
$name = "Ashley Meggitt";
$age = 32;
@children = ("Ben", "Lucy");
%address = {"street", "Jesus Lane", "city", "Cambridge", "zip",
"CB58BL"};
```

For the hash example, the list of strings is broken down into pairs, with the first string acting as the key and the second string acting as the value. You could additionally create a hash in the following manner, which might be more obvious:

```
%address = {
    "street" => "Jesus Lane",
    "city" => "Cambridge",
    "zip" => "CB58BL"
};
```

In this case, the string on the left side of the => operator is the key, and the right string is the value. In order to reference variables, you do the following:

```
$who = $name;
$daughter = $children[1];
$hometown = $address{"city"};
```

Notice that when referring to a scalar value within the array or hash, the prefix changes to a dollar sign.

Special variables

Perl uses special variables throughout, and you will often see programmers making use of these, especially when using regular expressions. The two most important are $_ (or @_) and $!. Often, functions in Perl seem to be acting on nothing. In fact, they are acting on the $_ variable. Methods by default take as arguments and return into the $_ or @_ variable. This means that functions can be strung together without any visible connection. For example, the following two code examples are equivalent:

```
foreach $child(@children) {
    print $child;
}

foreach (@children) {
    print;
}
```

The `foreach` statement loops through the block for every element in the array provided (in this case, @children). In the first case, each element is placed in the scalar variable $child, while in the second, the hidden $_ is assumed. You will often see regular expressions seemingly standing by themselves—almost always the $_ is around somewhere.

The $! variable is used to return information about errors that occur in a function call. Traditionally, functions return true if they are successful and false when they are not. In order to get any more information about problems when something has gone wrong, the functions often place additional information into the $! variable. This means you can include the $! variable in any output, such as:

```
print "$!: error occurred in backlog script";
```

Command-line arguments

An additional special variable is the @ARGV array. This array holds the values passed into the script from the command line. Each space-separated word is placed in its own array element in order of appearance on the command line. If you want a longer string (with spaces) to be taken as a single argument, you must surround it with quotes. The following made-up call to the *hello.pl* script passes in both /v and "hello there" as single arguments:

```
D:\perl\scripts\>perl hello.pl /v "hello there"
```

Often, you will see the Perl `shift` command used in conjunction with the @ARGV variable. This grabs the element from the front of the array (i.e., location [0]) and pushes the remaining elements down one location. For example, the following code takes in each of the command-line arguments and checks to see if they match known parameters:

```
while($_ = shift @ARGV) {
    if(m!/v!) {
        $verbose = true;
    } elsif (m!/c!) {
        $create_automatically = true;
    }
}
```

Quotes

As with everything in Perl, there are as many different kind of quotes as you would like. In fact, in some cases you can define almost *anything* to be a quote. However, you will run across two most often: the single (') and double ("). The single quote is considered the literal quote. Its value is exactly what it surrounds (with the traditional rules about backslash escape sequences used for characters such as tabs (\t) and new-lines (\n), etc.). The double quote is literal as well, but in this case, any variables found inside the string are interpolated. For example, the following code:

```
$there = 'Frank';
$string1 = 'hello $there';
$string2 = "$string1, wish you could stay";
print $string2;
```

produces the string:

```
hello $there, wish you could stay
```

In addition to the single and double quotes, regular expressions use the slash character (/) as delimiters around the expression. Because one of Perl's greatest strengths is in its ability to use regular expressions, you will often be staring at lines of slashes, backslashes, and other weird assorted constructions.

One additional quote character is the backtick (`). This is not, as it may seem, a single quote; instead, it is a character in its own right. When a line is surrounded by backticks, Perl executes the enclosed string as if it were issued on the command line. For example, the following line issues a *mkdir* command:

```
$user = 'kab24';
`mkdir d:\users\$user`;
```

Notice that the backtick operation interpolates any variables inside the quotes. The results of the command are returned as either a scalar string or list, depending on the context. You will see this command used either when there is not an equivalent Perl built-in function for carrying out the action or when you need additional information not supplied by a function call.

All quotes have generic versions that are often more readable, depending on what they are doing in the code. The following lines show equivalent traditional and generic quotes:

```
'hello'                   q/hello/
"This will $interpolate"  qq/This will $interpolate/
`cacls $filename`         qx/cacls $filename/
```

In fact, any nonalphanumeric character can be used for the slash character in the generic quotes, so you might often see constructs like this one:

```
qx(net group $groupname /add)
q!Jean-Luc intones, "make it so, Number One"!
```

Pattern matching

Perhaps Perl's greatest strength is its ability to work with strings. This is why it is often used in CGI scripts, where programs must generate HTML text on the fly. One part of this strength is Perl's innate ability to handle regular expressions, which are standard methods for describing general string patterns. You are undoubtedly familiar with the wildcard character (*) used on most command lines to replace any possible character sequence. The wildcard is just one of the many options available in Perl. For more information on regular expressions, the book *Mastering Regular Expressions,* by Jeffrey Friedl (O'Reilly & Associates, Inc., 1997), will teach you everything you ever wanted to know about regeps. Although regular expressions and Perl's string abilities are often touted for CGI programming, they also offer utility script writers a way to extract information from the command line. This allows you to script together collections of existing utilities to get jobs done. In the case of the user administration examples in the book, when functions did not exist in the language, it was almost always possible to call a command-line program and grab its output. Taking this output and parsing into a usable form were the responsibility of the regular expressions we used.

Running command-line programs

As an example of using regular expressions, we can take the string output of the *net user* command:

```
D:\perl\scripts>net user

User accounts for \\JC-CC-05

-------------------------------------------------------------------------
Administrator            Guest                    IUSR_JC-CC-05
tdr20                    srw1001                  ajm39
rjh45                    kab24
The command completed successfully.
```

Knowing the structure of the output, we can extract the usernames from the system. First, notice that the lines of output that begin with "User," "---," and "The" can all be thrown away. The words on any lines that are left must be usernames.

The following block of code first takes the output from the **net user** command and places it into a list (with each line of the output taking up a list element). The **foreach** loop then takes each of these lines and places it into the **$line** variable. For each **$line** variable, the **split** operator is used to break each line into its component words. The next three lines in the script (which all begin with the **next** keyword) check for the existence of one of the telltale strings ("User," "---," or "The") that let us know we can throw the line away. If this is the case, we skip to the start of the loop and begin working on the next line from the command output. Otherwise, each word in the line is placed in the **%current_user** hash as a key because it must be a username. The hash is used because it makes later searches for a particular name trivial.

```
@output = `net user`;
LINE: foreach $line(@output) {
    @words = split(/\s+/, $line);
    foreach $word(@words) {
        next LINE if $word =~ /User/;
        next LINE if $word =~ /-+/;
        next LINE if $word =~ /The/;
        $current_users{$word} = " ";
    }
}
```

Of course, there are commands for retrieving the same information with built-in Perl functions. The flexibility to use the output from any utility on the system means that even as functionality that Perl does not natively support is added to NT, you can always get information one way or another. We try to use built-in Perl functions and Win32 modules whenever possible (even going to the extreme of writing our own). When these functions and modules are not available, we can always use the more traditional command-line utilities.

File Access

In addition to command-line utilities, we often need to use files for inputting and outputting data, particularly when handling large numbers of users. The syntax for files is relatively straightforward, but we thought that running through a quick example would help.

Perl uses the angle (<>) operator to grab lines from files. After opening a file, you can use the *<FILENAME>* construct to extract lines from the file. One common use is with the **foreach** loop. In this case, each transition through the loop grabs another line from the file. In the following example, these lines are passed to the *net user* command to set the home directory path for the user.

```
open(FILE, $ARGV[0]) or die "Cannot open $ARGV[0]\n";
foreach $user(<FILE>) {
    chomp($user);
    next if(!$user);
    $out = qx(net user $user /HOMEDIR:\\\\Iago\\$user\$);
}
close(FILE);
```

You will often see the `while(<FILENAME>)  {  ...  }` loop, which keeps grabbing lines from the input until there are no more. This uses the `$_` variable, which can make for some mighty confusing code. The following example prints the lines of the file that have a string matching the second command-line argument.

```
open(FILE, $ARGV[0]) or die "Cannot open $ARGV[0]\n";
while(<FILE>) {
    print if /$ARGV[1]/;
}
close FILE;
```

What is really confusing in this example is that there are no assignment operations! Instead, the `$_` variable works in the background.

Win32 Functions

Most of the built-in functions in Perl were created with the various versions of UNIX in mind. There has been a concerted effort, however, to include as many of the important Win32 Application Programming Interface functions as possible. These exist as both built-in functions and separate modules distributed with the Win32 version of Perl or available on the Web.

Using these functions is quite simple; the following two sections discuss how to use Win32 modules and built-in Win32 functions.

Win32 Modules

The Win32 modules are a collection of *pm* (Perl Module) files and *pll* (Perl Link Libraries). The link libraries implement the native code APIs; the module files hold the Perl stub code that allows you to incorporate the module into your script. In order to use a module, you must invoke the `use` command. For example, in order to use the *FileSecurity* module, you need to include the following line at the top of your code:

```
use Win32::FileSecurity;
```

From that point on, you can use any of the *FileSecurity* functions in your code. For example, to give the Administrators group as well as the username stored in `$new_user{'USER_NAME'}` full control over the user's home directory, the following code calls the *Win32::FileSecurity::MakeMask()* function, creates a hash to hold the permissions, and then passes it into the *Win32::FileSecurity::Set()* function.

```
$dir_sec = Win32::FileSecurity::MakeMask(qw(FULL GENERIC_ALL));
$sec_hash{Administrator} = $dir_sec;
$sec_hash{$new_user{'USER_NAME'}} = $dir_sec;
Win32::FileSecurity::Set($new_user{'USER_HOME_DIR'}, \%sec_hash);
```

As an additional note, notice the use of the `\%sec_hash` variable. This variable passes the security hash into the function as a reference. This is the same as using the `&` dereferencing operator in C or C++. We will see this construct in many of the functions to be called. If you are given a reference to an object the reference would appear as a scalar. One example might be: `$ref`. This could, in fact, be any type of object—all that the `$ref` holds is a scalar reference. To refer to the underlying object, we would prefix the appropriate symbol. For a hash, list, scalar, and function object, the respective usage would be: `%$ref`, `@$ref`, `$$ref`, `&$ref`. It is important to note that even a reference to a scalar value requires dereferencing.

A full list of the modules included with the current version of Perl, as well as descriptions of their use, can be found in *perl\docs\Perl-Win32\win32mod.html*.

Built-in Functions

As time goes on, however, more and more of the Win32 API functions are being incorporated into the Win32 Perl distribution. This means that you no longer need to load up separate modules to access these functions. Many of the functions duplicate the Win32 module functions, such as the *Win32::Registry* and *Win32::EventLog*. Whenever possible, our preference is to use these built-in functions. We have found them to be somewhat more stable than their module-based counterparts. As mentioned before, the Win32 and just-released 5.004 releases of Perl do not handle the Win32 API functions similarly, and until the two distributions converge, the use of built-in functions is limited to the ActiveState Win32 distribution. The following is a list of the current built-in functions. Before you start using a module, make sure the functionality is not already there in the Win32 build. Built-in functions are prefixed by *Win32::* without any additional module reference.

```
Win32::LoadLibrary($LibraryName)
Win32::FreeLibrary($hinstance)
Win32::GetProcAddress($hinstance, $procedurename)
Win32::RegisterServer($LibraryName)
Win32::UnregisterServer($LibraryName)
```

```
Win32::RegCloseKey($hkey)
Win32::RegConnectRegistry($machine, $hkey, $handle)
Win32::RegCreateKey($hkey, $subkey, $handle)
Win32::RegCreateKeyEx($hkey, $subkey, $reserved, $class, $options,
                      $sam, $security, $handle, $disposition)
Win32::RegDeleteKey($hkey, $subkey)
Win32::RegDeleteValue($hkey, $valname)
Win32::RegEnumKey($hkey, $idx, $subkeyname)
Win32::RegEnumKeyEx($hkey, $idx, $subkeyname, $reserved, $class, $time)
Win32::RegEnumValue($hkey, $i, $name, $reserved, $type, $value)
Win32::RegFlushKey($hkey)
Win32::RegGetKeySecurity($hkey, $security_info, $security_descriptor)
Win32::RegLoadKey($hkey, $subkey, $filename)
Win32::RegOpenKey($hkey, $subkey, $handle)
Win32::RegOpenKeyEx($hkey, $subkey, $reserved, $sam, $handle)
Win32::RegQueryInfoKey($hkey, $class, $numsubkeys, $maxsubkey,
                       $maxclass, $values, $maxvalname, $maxvaldata,
                       $secdesclen, $lastwritetime)
Win32::RegQueryValue($hkey, $valuename, $data)
Win32::RegQueryValueEx($hkey, $valuename, $reserved, $type, $data)
Win32::RegReplaceKey($hkey, $subkey, $newfile, $oldfile)
Win32::RegRestoreKey($hkey, $filename [, $flags])
Win32::RegSaveKey($hkey, $filename)
Win32::RegSetKeySecurity($hkey, $security_info, $security_descriptor)
Win32::RegSetValue($hkey, $subKey, $type, $data)
Win32::RegSetValueEx($hkey, $valname, $reserved, $type, $data)
Win32::RegUnloadKey($hkey, $subkey)
Win32::OpenEventLog($handle, $server, $source)
Win32::OpenBackupEventLog($handle, $server, $file)
Win32::BackupEventLog($handle, $filename)
Win32::ClearEventLog($handle, $filename)
Win32::CloseEventLog($handle)
Win32::GetNumberOfEventLogRecords($handle, $number)
Win32::ReadEventLog($handle, $flags, $rec, $evtHeader, $SourceName,
                    $ComputerName, $sid, $data, $strings)
Win32::WriteEventLog($server, $source, $eventType, $category, $eventID,
$reserved, $data, $message1, ...)
Win32::GetLastError()
Win32::PerlVersion()
Win32::LoginName()
Win32::NodeName()
Win32::DomainName()
Win32::FsType()
Win32::GetCwd()
Win32::SetCwd($String)
Win32::GetOSVersion()
Win32::FormatMessage($errorCode)
Win32::Spawn($cmdName, $args, $PID)
Win32::LookupAccountName($system, $account, $domain, $sid, $sidtype)
Win32::LookupAccountSID($system, $sid, $account, $domain, $sidtype)
Win32::InitiateSystemShutdown($machineName, $message, $timeOut,
                              $forceClose, $reboot)
Win32::AbortSystemShutdown($machineName)
Win32::GetTickCount()
```

```
Win32::IsWinNT()
Win32::IsWin95()
Win32::GetArchName()
Win32::GetChipName()
Win32::ExpandEnvironmentStrings($String)
Win32::GetShortPathName($longPathName)
Win32::GetNextAvailDrive()
Win32::MsgBox($Message [, $Buttons [, $Title]])
```

When you load a module with the **use** function, global constants that many of the Win32 functions require are automatically loaded into your script's namespace. This is not the case with the built-in functions. To load many of the variables you will need, include the following line at the beginning of your script:

```
require "NT.ph";
```

The *NT.ph* file is a Perl header file that describes all the structures necessary for a script to run the built-in functions. When accessing these constants, you use the subroutine indicator (&) because these are implemented as substatements in the *NT.ph* file. For example, using the registry function *Win32::RegOpenKeyEx* requires the use of several constants, depending on what root key you want to access and what permissions you wish to use to access it. The following call uses some of the built-in constants declared in the *NT.ph* file:

```
Win32::RegOpenKeyEx(&HKEY_CURRENT_USER,
                    'Environment\Logon\Map',
                    &NULL,
                    &KEY_ALL_ACCESS,
                    $handle) or die "unable to access registry";
```

HKEY_CURRENT_USER, NULL, and KEY_ALL_ACCESS all provide values appropriate for the API function calls. Remember to include the *NT.ph* file in your code if you are using the built-in functions.

The UserAdmin Module

We have stuck closely to the modules and functions that come with the standard Perl distribution, but in some areas the existing functions lack support for the full range of administrative options. We have taken the *Win32::NetAdmin* module that comes with the Perl distribution, and we have altered or added functions that were necessary for the examples in the book. We have named the new module *Win32::UserAdmin*, in reference to this book. You can find the module in the following places:

> *http:\\www.vne.com\ora\useradmin*
> *http:\\www.jesus.cam.ac.uk\~tdr20\ora\useradmin.html*

The additions and changes to the module fall under three broad areas: user functions, group functions, and share functions. The *Win32::UserAdmin* module works identically to the *Win32::NetAdmin* module, except for the new functions that have been changed or added. The following is intended as a quick rundown of each function, but it is not meant to be an exhaustive reference. Refer to the *readme.txt* file included with the *UserAdmin* module distribution for the latest information.

User Function Additions

The *Win32::UserAdmin* module changes to the *NetAdmin* module primarily concern supporting the different amounts of user information that can be gathered from NT. The original *UserCreate*, *UserGetAttributes,* and *UserSetAttributes* functions dealt with only the lowest level of user information (level 1), which included the following;

Level 1:
```
USER_NAME, USER_PASSWORD, USER_PASSWORD_AGE, USER_PRIV, USER_HOME_DIR,
USER_COMMENT, USER_FLAGS, USER_SCRIPT_PATH
```

Of course, this does not allow you to set many user attributes, such as workstations, full names, or logon hours. With this in mind, we have created new versions of these functions.

Win32::UserAdmin::UserGetAttributes()
```
Win32::UserAdmin::UserGetAttributes($server, $username, $level,
\%userInfo)
```

The *UserGetAttributes* function takes the name of the server, the username you are interested in, the level of detail you want, and a reference to a hash, which is filled with the details of user $username upon return of the function. The level can be an integer between 1 and 3. The keys to the hash for the level 1 structure are the items in the previous listing. Levels 2 and 3 add the following information:

Level 2: all of level 1, plus:
```
USER_AUTH_FLAGS, USER_FULL_NAME, USER_USR_COMMENT, USER_PARMS, USER_
WORKSTATIONS, USER_LAST_LOGON, USER_LOAST_LOGOFF, USER_ACCT_EXPIRES,
USER_MAX_STORAGE, USER_UNITS_PER_WEEK, USER_LOGON_HOURS, USER_BAD_PW_
COUNT, USER_NUM_LOGONS, USER_LOGON_SERVER, USER_COUNTRY_CODE, USER_
CODE_PAGE
```

Level 3: all of level 1 and 2, plus:
```
USER_USER_ID, USER_PRIMARY_GROUP_ID, USER_PROFILE, USER_HOME_DIR_
DRIVE, USER_PASSWORD_EXPIRED
```

Win32::UserAdmin::UserSetAttributes()
```
Win32::UserAdmin::UserSetAttributes($server, $username, $level,
\%userInfo)
```

The *UserSetAttributes* function is identical to the *UserGetAttributes* function except that instead of filling the userInfo hash with the details of the user, it takes the information already in the hash and attempts to change the already existing user's details.

Win32::UserAdmin::UserCreate()

```
Win32::UserAdmin::UserCreate($server, $level, \%userInfo)
```

The *UserCreate* function takes a hash filled with information appropriate to the $level argument and attempts to create a user with those settings.

Group Functions

In addition to the altered user functions, the *UserAdmin* module also adds two functions that act on groups. These can be used to get group membership information for a single user or to get all the groups on a machine.

Win32::UserAdmin::UserGetGroups()

```
Win32::UserAdmin::UserGetGroups($server, $username, \@groupArray)
```

The *UserGetGroups* function takes a server, username, and array reference and fills the array with a list of global groups to which the user belongs on that machine. If the server is the Primary Domain Controller, it will return the domain-wide global groups. If no server is provided, then the local machine will be assumed.

Win32::UserAdmin::UserGetLocalGroups()

```
Win32::UserAdmin::UserGetLocalGroups($server, $username, \@groupArray)
```

The *UserGetLocalGroups* is identical to the *UserGetGroups* function except that it returns the *local* groups to which a user belongs. This function will return *all* the local groups a user is a member of, even if the user is no longer a member of a global group that is in the local group.

Win32::UserAdmin::GetGroups()

```
Win32::UserAdmin::GetGroups($server, \@groupArray)
```

The *GetGroups* function takes a machine name and returns all the groups on that machine.

Share Functions

Finally, although not directly user related, accessing share information is important to setting up user home directories, application shares, and more. We created the following function as a utility for getting share information because there seemed to be a problem with the standard *Win32::NetResource* module.

Win32::UserAdmin::NetShareGetInfo()

```
Win32::UserAdmin::NetShareGetInfo($server, $sharename, \%shareInfo)
```

The *NetShareGetInfo* function takes a server and share name and fills the provided hash with information about the share itself. The keys provided are as follows:

SHARE_NET_NAME	SHARE_MAX_USERS
SHARE_TYPE	SHARE_CURRENT_USERS
SHARE_REMARK	SHARE_PATH
SHARE_PERMISSIONS	SHARE_PASSWORD

More Information

For more information on the *Win32::UserAdmin* module, refer to the *readme.txt* file included with the distribution. This file includes the most up-to-date information on the module and its functions. As the Perl builds become more stable, these functions may be superceded by built-in functions. In these cases, we will point you to the right places.

The next chapter begins our look at user administration in earnest by exploring how NT represents the user and how to create one. From there, we expand to group information and wider user management strategies, finally detailing the more difficult control and auditing aspects of the administrative realm.

2

Creating Users

It is all very well having a system configured, organized, and optimized, but the system's *raison d'être* is to give real people access to the resources you have so carefully put together. Real people are represented in any networking environment as users of one kind or another. They all have a basic set of attributes that are acted on by a set of rules. The rules are determined by who they are and the status they hold within both the system and the organization the system serves. Users breathe life into the system, and as administrators we often have a love-hate relationship with them; they are anathema, necessity, and occasionally inspiration.

Strategies for Creating Users

Before you jump straight into the act of user creation, take some time to organize your ideas about your overall system policy for items such as usernames and password controls. In addition, the different levels of resource access and customization will, in many ways, be affected by how you set up an account initially. Deciding on and creating a user policy before you begin will save you headaches later on when you have to explain why a user can not do *this* or have access to *that*.

Once the process of user creation begins, you will want to get users up and running on the system as quickly as possible. This means that automating the process of bulk user creation and knowing where to find all the account settings are important. This chapter steps through the many different ways of creating users in Windows NT and examines the relative merits and pitfalls of each. Ultimately, the way you go about setting up users on your system entirely depends on your environment; however, having all the options in front of you makes the job a little easier.

Username Creation

Think again if you consider the issue of username creation merely routine. As an administrator, you should first reflect on the following :

- The policy for username creation

- The process of username automation

- The creation of accounts

The following is a selection of username creation policies and their usefulness:

- **No fixed policy**. As an account is created the username is generated by the administrator, who then relies on the system to warn of any clash between that name and any account that already exists with the same name. This approach can meet the needs of only a small user environment with limited user turnaround. It in no way lends itself to automation.

- **Part names**, e.g., Bill_G, Tim_R, Rob_F, Rob_H. Although there is a uniformity about deriving the username from the user's name, the approach has several obvious drawbacks. The first one is uniqueness. What if there is another Bill_ G? This could be worked around by using the next letter in the surname, such as Bill_Ga, but the problem still exists. It is just not unique and will therefore always be prone to the possibility of conflict. The second drawback is that it is not automation-friendly. The system you implement will have to be unnecessarily complicated to deal with all the possibilities of clashing names.

- **Full names**, e.g., ashley_meggitt, john_darlington. The obvious advantage of using full names is that they are extremely readable and lend themselves well to automation. However, they are not unique; therefore, a clash could occur. If you then include an initial or two (e.g., justin_j_meggitt), the likelihood of two usernames being the same is extremely rare. This type of username policy is certainly well used.

- **User initials and an incremental number**, e.g., ajm39, tdr20. This username is unique, so there will never be a clash and thus you will never need to break the username generation method you have adopted. The initials element can easily be made up from the user's full name, assuming that you have it. The number associated with the next occurrence of that set of initials is then incremented, and the username becomes unique. A drawback to this type of username is its readability, especially in the world of electronic mail. It is easier to remember a name such as john_darlington than it is to remember the user identifier jd106. With the plethora of modern mail clients, however, creating nicknames for users is extremely easy and resolves this problem.

- **User initials, user type number, and an incremental number,** e.g., ajm139, tdr120, jd2106. One of the advantages of being able to add numbers to the username or identifier is that the numbers can convey information. In this case, the addition of a single-digit number before the unique user number gives the administrator instant information about the type of user he or she is dealing with.

For instance, in a university environment the categories of users shown in Table 2-1 may be used.

Table 2-1. User Categories

Number	Type
1	Computer staff
2	Administration
3	Undergraduate
4	Postgraduate
5	Lecturer

Therefore, the username bfm316 can be broken down as follows:

- bfm—user's initials
- 3—Undergraduate
- 16—Unique number, the 16th occurrence of the initials bfm

These categories are most useful if they reflect groups created within the system. Even though the group indexing information can be gathered from other sources, having a way to spot the general class of user immediately by username alone can be quite useful. For example, if you have a problem with the system while scanning a log file manually, you could easily spot user activity that resided outside the permissions of a particular account. Although the example may seem contrived, the purpose here is to demonstrate how you as an administrator can be inventive with such data types.

Passwords

Without exception, every user account on a network should have a password, even though the operating system allows you to forgo this security. It is probably fair to say that every user account, be it in an office or even in the home environment, should be password protected. Passwords exist to make both the user account and the operating system inaccessible to prying eyes and the occasional malicious tendency.

Choosing a password is not as easy as it seems. The ideal criteria for creating a password are to make it memorable, yet uncrackable. Although the two are not mutually exclusive, a memorable password is likely to be more susceptible to cracking. On the other hand, if the password is utterly incomprehensible, the user is far more likely to write it down and thus undermine the purpose of having a password. Using easy-to-remember passwords or writing them down is extremely common, especially in a multisystem environment where the user is expected to remember a number of different passwords. There are two main ways in which the would-be "cracker"* gets hold of the password:

- Using a password that reflects your interests, your family, or some work-related aspect like the name of the building you work in, gives the "cracker" a good chance at a correct guess. It may seem a bit far-fetched, but breaking into an account is the first and arguably the key step to the hacker's clandestine activities. From breaking one password the intruder may well be able to use earlier acquired knowledge of the operating system or system tools to cause untold damage.

- A more systematic approach to obtaining passwords is to use a password cracker. This is a program that acts directly on the file or database that holds the encrypted passwords. The programs vary in the way they work, but because modern machines are so powerful, the software can try names, dictionary words, and other words from publications in a surprisingly short time. With a systematic algorithm for looking at uppercase and lowercase words, words spelled backward, and words with numbers added to or inserted into them, many passwords you might have thought were secure can be broken in minutes.

Using a password cracker should not remain the sole preserve of the intruder. It should also be a tool in the armory of the administrator, who should run it occasionally to see how vulnerable the system is. Forcing users into changing their passwords regularly is a common way of trying to keep potential intruders off the system. This approach, though, can lead to insecurity in its own right. From experience, being forced to change a password every month on a system that is used only two or three times a month soon forces a user into adopting an easy-to-remember incremental policy. Having broken the policy, a cracker could have regular, and to a degree, protected access to the system as administrators might become complacent, assuming that every month the system would be made secure.

---

*There is an unfortunate tendency these days to use the term "hacker" when referring to individuals who break into systems, malicious or no. In fact, "hacker" originally meant a breed of inventive, off-the-cuff programmer who knew the ins and outs of the system. While this is certainly conducive to knowing *how* to break into a system, it in no way means that he or she will. You can be a hacker, without breaking into systems.

What is a secure password?

A good password is made up of a combination of uppercase and lowercase characters, numbers, and special characters and should be at least six characters long. For instance, *Cv2xG*6* can be considered a secure if not readable[*] password. *Pink-Floyd* can be considered a gift.

An effective way to make a password both secure and readable is to combine parts of two or more words, for instance, *EraS66wiCk,* which is a combination of Erasmus Darwin, Adam Sedgwick, and the year England won the world cup.

Generating passwords

It is utterly impossible for an administrator to generate hundreds of passwords without using some kind of automatic process. Many shareware or freeware programs are available to create a password file based on given criteria. The sample Perl script for creating users found in Chapter 4, *Managing Users Through Scripts,* incorporates code to do just that.

NOTE	When you set the criteria for automatic password generation, avoid the following characters as they are far too similar to each other and cause a degree of ambiguity that outfoxes many users: I (character), O o (character upper and lower), 1 (number one), l (character), and 0 (number zero).

When should a password be changed?

You should always change passwords in these circumstances:

- When a user leaves. If any accounts relating to that user are to be kept open for any reason, then the passwords must be changed.

- When an administrator leaves. All administrative passwords must be changed plus any personal accounts about which the administrator had knowledge.

- Any time you suspect that an intrusion has occurred through an account. Never be lax about this; always err on the side of caution.

- Where any user has allowed his or her password to be known by another user.

- Regularly for administrative accounts as a precaution, just in case.

As a general rule, the more power an account has over the system, the more often the password should be changed. This means that any password that has

---

[*]A friend used to use *oooh*d'lalee%DonkEyeArs.*

been cracked becomes useless at the next round of password updates. However, NT allows you to set only a single password expiration policy for the entire system, so you need to decide on an expiration rate that is both frequent enough to ensure security and consistent enough to maintain the system's usefulness for its users.

Home Directories

A home directory is the place where users can store their personal files and where they expect those files to be completely secure from other users. This directory can be assigned to a single user for his or her sole use or to a number of users who wish to share data. Some consideration should be given to how these directories are organized. Consider the situation where all users' home directories are under the single directory *users*. If an administrator wishes to make a specific backup of, say, all the lecturer's home directories, he or she would have to manually select them in some way. If all the lecturers had home directories, under the collective subdirectory *users\lecturers*, however, then carrying out the backup on that specific directory is much simpler.

The home directory is also the place to which the command prompt drops the user when invoked. It is also the default working directory for those applications that have none defined.

Creating a User with the User Manager for Domains

The User Manager for Domains (UMD) is the primary tool for a number of management activities, such as creating and managing both users and groups, setting audit policies, and defining user rights. In this section we concentrate on how the UMD is applied to user creation.

Launching the Application

To launch User Manager for Domains from a server, select **Programs→Administrative tools→User Manager for Domains** from the Start menu. Alternatively, you can launch the application from the Start menu's Run option by typing `usrmgr`.

Looking at the Interface

The window that appears is split into two; the top pane is marked **Username**, reflecting its contents, the bottom pane is marked **Group**. For our purpose, let us concentrate for the moment on the upper pane. The contents of the top pane supplies you with the descriptive part of the user account. These accounts can be arranged either by username or by full name, with every user account having an entry. This can make for a scrolling nightmare, but as you might expect, pressing the first letter of the username jumps you to the start of that alphabetical set. We assume that you are familiar with the general editing options and selection techniques available throughout NT.

Built-in User Accounts.

When a Primary Domain Controller (PDC), member server, or workstation is set up, each automatically creates two built-in accounts, Administrator and Guest.

The Administrator Account

The administrator account allows you to perform domain management, but perhaps the first use you should make of it is to create a working administrator account for yourself. The administrator account cannot be deleted or disabled; it is designed to be a permanent feature of the system, thus stopping you from locking yourself out. It does not stop you from forgetting the password. Although the account cannot be removed, it can be renamed; for security reasons, renaming is highly recommended.

The Guest Account

Like most guest accounts, this built-in one allows a user who does not have an account on the domain, trusted domains, or local networked computer access to the system. The guest account does not require a password and is disabled by default. Again, as with other network operating systems, a guest account on a member NT server or workstation can log on to that machine by default (local logon) but do very little else. On a PDC, the guest account has no other predefined rights than those given to the everyone group. So far this is all quite normal; however, there is a curious twist to the guest account that is best explained with an example.

Let us assume that the guest account on the PDC is enabled and that no password is set. Also assume that the guest account has permission to log on from the network (set under **Account** in the User Manager for Domains).

A user logs on locally to a workstation as Rob_Hopwood with a password vfat32. He then does some work and, at one point, tries to access a domain resource. Even though he has not logged on to the domain, as long as the guest account on the PDC can access the necessary resource, so can he. His request is accepted. He has made no explicit domain logon, yet he automatically acquires guest account privileges.

Be very careful with the guest account. We suggest you simply leave it disabled and, if necessary, implement another policy for your guests. As a general rule, all accounts should reflect the status of the individual user. You should never create general accounts such as backup or service, to which you then provide access for several users. These accounts are very difficult to control and end up as an administrative nightmare.

Before creating an account

Before creating your accounts make sure you have already established the groups with which you intend to control users. Do not be fooled into thinking that you'll come back to add a user into a group you intend to create later. First, you may well forget; and second, if you do this to tens or hundreds of users, you will find adding them in later is a time-consuming and tedious chore.

Look also at the password settings under the menu option **Account**. Make sure that these settings are correct. The settings under the **Account** menu option are global; therefore, any changes made will eventually affect all users. We say "eventually" because not all the settings take immediate effect on existing accounts. For instance, if a user account has a password length of five characters and the minimum password length is changed to six, the user is not obliged to change the password. Once the user decides to change the password under his or her own volition, then the user is forced to abide by the new rule.

Creating the User

From the main menu, select **User→New** User. This brings up a dialog box that, as it stands, is all you need to create a user, leaving the rest of the user's properties to be set to the defaults shown in Table 2-2.

Table 2-2. User Property Defaults

Groups	Domain User
Profile	Profile stored in *winnt\profiles*
Hours	Can log on 24 hours a day, 7 days a week
Logon to	Is not restricted to a number of machines
Account	Account never expires and is global

Filling in the first five entries is quite straightforward.

Username

Enter a unique username into the **Username** box, meeting some kind of naming policy (see "Username Creation" earlier in this chapter). Certain characters cannot be used in the username:

    "/ \ [ ] : ; | = , + * ? < >

The username can be a combination of uppercase and lowercase characters, up to 20 characters long. Although spaces are accepted, they are best avoided because any subsequent command-line arguments using the name will have to be contained in quotes. You cannot have a username simply made up of blanks or of full stops/periods; NT will not allow it.

Full name

Making an entry here is optional, but we recommend that you use it. We also recommend that you think clearly about a naming convention. Something simple would do, such as surname followed by either the user's first name or initials. One good reason for doing so is that User Manger for Domains can show the user list in two sort orders, by username or by full name. This sort order can be selected from the main menu option **View**. It is also important to enter information here—inevitably you will want to know the identity of a user for one reason or another. If you do not implement any other means of storing user information, then here is the place to do it.

Description

Description is simply a text entry to describe what sort of account this is; it can be left blank. Again, we suggest that you use it, particularly if this is the only place you intend to store user information. Typical information is the department or job title of the individual.

Password and confirm password

The Password and Confirm Password entry box may or may not require filling in, depending on the Accounts policy you have established. Assuming a sensible policy of password requirement, enter the password and its confirmation into the appropriate boxes. The maximum number of characters accepted is 14; the minimum number is determined by the Account policy.

Following the five entry boxes are five check boxes, one of which is greyed out.

Table 2-3. Account Control Options

Check Box	Description
User Must Change Password on Next Logon	This option simply forces the user to change password on next logon. For new accounts this is quite sensible and is, in fact, the default.
User Cannot Change Password	This option prevents the user from changing the password, a useful option if the account is shared. The default is unchecked. This must be the case if User Must Change Password on Next Logon is checked as they are mutually exclusive.

Table 2-3. Account Control Options (continued)

Check Box	Description
Password Never Expires	This option overrides the maximum password age set in the Account policy. Microsoft suggests that it is useful to use this option for service accounts such as replication, print managing, or backup, but we recommend you never have these types of accounts on the system. The default is unchecked.
Account Disabled	By checking this box, the user's account becomes temporarily disabled. The account is not removed. This is useful for template accounts and, in our opinion, the guest account. The default is unchecked.
Account Locked out	This option can be used only when there has been a lock out. To remove the lock on the account, deselect this check box. The default for this is as a greyed-out option.

Finally, arranged along the bottom of this window are six large buttons: **Groups**, **Profile**, **Hours**, **Logon-to**, **Accounts**, and **Dialin**. These buttons give access to the properties of the new account and provide the key to achieving flexible management of the users.

Password filtering in Service Pack 3

In addition to the default password constraints provided by Windows NT 4.0, Service Pack 3 offers more password filtering options through the use of a password filter dynamic link library named *passfilt.dll*, which is automatically installed in the *%systemroot%\system32* directory.

To enable the password filtering, you need to make sure that the following registry settings have been created:[*]

```
HKEY_LOCAL_MACHINE\SYSTEM\CurrentControlSet\Control\Lsa
Value: Notification Packages
Type: REG_MULTI_SZ
Data: Passfilt.dll
```

This password filter mandates that user passwords must be at least six characters long, with characters from at least three of the following groups:

- Uppercase letters
- Lowercase letters
- Numbers
- Any other valid password character [.,;:*%&!]

---

[*]For more information on changing Registry settings, and the registry in general, see Chapter 6.

In addition, passwords may not contain your username or any part of your full name.

User Properties

You can now specify the following properties for each user:

Groups

This option allows you to place a user in one or more groups. All domain users by default are put into the Domain Users group, which is then set as the primary group.[*]

The Domain Users group is, by default, a member of the local users group on the PDC, as well as a member of the local groups of member servers and Windows NT workstations. As such, it is worth considering removing the domain users group from the local users group, especially if there are resources on workstations to which you do not want every domain user to have access.

Profiles

In addition to letting you set the profile location here, this option also allows you to point the logon program to a logon script for that user as well as define a user's home directory. Let's start, however, with the profile path. If you decide to leave this option blank, then NT uses the default location of *\\servername\winnt\profiles*. If you plan to store your profiles elsewhere, then enter the details here, making sure that the directory for the profiles actually exists. The User Manager for Domains will not create it for you (see Chapter 7, *Controlling the User*, for a full discussion of profiles).

The logon script option simply supplies the logon program with the location of a logon script to be associated with a particular user. The default logon script path is *\%systemroot%\winnt\system32\repl\import\script*, and by placing the logon scripts here you need to enter the scripts name in only the **Logon Script Name** box. The default script path can be changed in the Server Manager application and is discussed in the next chapter. If you have a number of scripts for different groups and you wish to keep them apart, you can create your own subdirectories under the scripts path, in which case you must enter the relative path in the entry box, e.g., *\development\connect.bat*.

Finally, you can assign a user a home directory. This can be either a local one or a centralized one. The local path option allows you to specify a directory local to the workstation to which the user is to logon. For instance, you can

---

[*]A primary group is required for Macintosh clients and users running POSIX-compliant applications. Because POSIX applications and the Mac OS allow users to be members of only one group, Windows NT uses the primary group setting when providing user services.

assign the *tmp* directory of any workstation to be the home directory of a domain user by simply entering the path *C:\tmp* for the local path. This does assume that each workstation already has a *tmp* directory positioned at the root level. To create a centralized home directory, simply use the **Connect** option, supplying a drive letter from the appropriate drop-down menu and a directory path using the universal naming convention (UNC). For example, the directory may look like the following: *iago\users\students\tdr20*.

User Manager for Domains creates this directory automatically once the new user's details have been established.

NOTE   Wherever **username** is used in a path statement you can replace it
              with the predefined user environment variable **%username%**. When
              dealing with large sets of users it is extremely useful to be able to edit
              paths *en masse* in this way:

                     \\iago\users\%username%

Hours

The graphical chart available under this option gives you absolute flexibility to allow or disallow logon to the domain. If a user is connected to the server and the logon hours are exceeded, then the user becomes subject to the *forcibly disconnect* rule set by the account policy.

Logon To

This option allows the administrator to determine to which workstation the user can log on. You will see that **Users May Log On To All Workstations** is the default, and this allows the user to log on to any workstation in the domain or in any trusted domain. A second radio button, **User May Log On To These Workstations**, allows the administrator to set the names of up to eight workstations to which he or she wishes to restrict the user. Simply add the workstation name with no prefixes of any kind. When a user tries to log on to a workstation not listed, the logon program displays an "account restriction" message.

Account

This option gives you the chance to set the type of account you wish a user to have as well as a date on which the account expires. Setting this is pretty obvious: Either give the account a date, or select the option Never, indicating that the account is never to expire.

The Account Type option has two settings that need a bit of explanation as they are not immediately clear.[*] **Global Account** is the default and registers

---

[*]Well, they certainly were not clear to us when we first looked at them.

that the account is a standard domain account. The user can be seen in the **Add Users and Groups** dialog box of any trusting domain. The **Local Account** option signifies that this account is, according to Microsoft, "a user account provided in a domain for a user whose regular account is not in a trusted domain." This is best explained by the following scenario.

Consider a situation where no local accounts exist:

- Any user not in an Access Control List (ACL) is denied access to the resource with which the ACL is associated.

- The only way a user can be added to an ACL is if he or she has a global domain account or a global domain account in a trusted domain.

In this scenario, there is no method of granting a user access to a domain resource if he or she does not already have an account in that domain or in a trusted domain.

Now consider the situation where there are two domains, Shylock and Antonio. These domains do not trust each other.* As the situation stands, a user in the domain Shylock cannot access any resources in the domain Antonio. There are two ways in which this can be rectified:

- Set up a trust relationship between the two domains.

- Create a local account in the domain Antonio. This local account can be configured just like a global account, with permissions being granted or denied.

One major difference between local and global accounts is that a user with a local account cannot interactively log on to the domain. This simply means that a user with a local domain account cannot sit down at a workstation in that domain and log on. Let's look at an example:

- The user Hopwood has a global domain account in the domain Shylock.

- The user Hopwood is granted a local account in the domain Antonio.

- Hopwood wants to access a drive share in the domain Antonio.

As a local domain account does not give the user the right to log on to that domain from one of its workstations, Hopwood must first log on to a valid domain to gain access to the network as a whole. In this case, he logs on to Shylock. Having done this, he can now use Network Neighborhood from the workstation he is logged onto to find the PDC for the domain Antonio. Having selected Antonio's PDC, he is now asked for details of a valid account. At the prompting he enters the username and password of the local domain account he has been given for the domain Antonio. The resources

---

*This is, of course, not surprising.

available to that account are now seen, and any one of them can be used. He equally could have used a mapping if the resource had been a drive share.

If the domain Antonio was then to set up a trust relationship with another domain, Portia, Hopwood's local account would not appear in the **New User and Groups** dialog box of Portia. The local account is, as it says, local to domain Antonio but can be accessed only from outside that domain.

Dialin

The final option to mention is **Dialin**. Here the administrator can grant the user dial-in access to the server. Table 2-4 charts the meanings of the options.

Table 2-4. Dialin Options

Button	Meaning
No Call Back	Selecting this disables the call back feature.
Set By Caller	Here call back is enabled, and the system prompts the user is to supply the number to call back to. It then disconnects and then makes the call back. Note: Remote Access Server must be running.
Preset To	This option also enables the call back feature using a preset number to call back to.

Creating a User with the net user Command

For those of you familiar with the command line, NT offers a number of useful utilities including the `net user` command. This command has a number of purposes, but in this section we are interested only in its ability to create new users. The command can be used either at the command line or as part of a script (see later). Its syntax and parameters are as follows:

```
net user username {password | *} /ADD [options] [/DOMAIN]
```

We should mention here that all the parameters of the `net user` command are subject to the same constraints that are imposed on their GUI equivalents. For instance, the password can be no more than 14 characters and can be no less than the minimum password length set in the User Manager for Domains **Accounts** option. The following explains the parameters of the `net user` command:

- The *username* following the `net user` command specifies, as it suggests, the new user's name.

- Following this is the *password* parameter, and you can either enter a password or *. If * is entered into the password field, then on creation of the account NT requests a password from the command line. The password is not displayed as you type it in. If the password does not comply with the parameters forced on it by the accounts policy, then NT displays an error message and the account is not created.

```
net user R_Hopwood Vfat32 /ADD /expires:october,01,1999 /times:Monday-
Thursday,8-17;Friday,10-17
```

In the first case, a user named J. Darlington is added with the username J_ Darlington, comment Archaeologist, home directory *\\iago\users\J_Darlington,* and profile path *\\iago\profiles\J_Darlington.* The * indicates that on creation, the administrator is queried for a password. In the second case, a user account named R_Hopwood is created with password Vfat32 and default home and profile directories (*\\%servername%\%systemroot%\profiles*). This example also shows the use of the expiration date option (october,01,1999) and allowed logon times (Monday-Thursday,8-17;Friday,10-17). The logon hours in this case are 8 a.m. until 5 p.m., Monday through Thursday, and 10 a.m. to 5 p.m. on Fridays.

Adding Users in Bulk

Up to now, we have looked at the creation of users as primarily a one-off occurrence. You may find, however, that this is generally the exception rather than the rule. In many situations, users arrive en masse in the tens, hundreds, or even thousands. For example, at the beginning of each academic year, a university may have to add several hundred freshmen to its rolls, or companies with training cycles may hire many new employees at the same time and move them through training together. In both of these situations, a long list of new users, all of which need to be on the system by yesterday, will most likely end up on the administrator's desk.

Out of the box, Windows NT does not provide the administrator with a very satisfactory choice of tools for bulk user administration. In fact, except for the **Copy** command in the User Manager for Domains, there is no built-in tool for adding several users at once, especially not from any electronic source such as a text comma-separated values (CSV) file. Even though the UMD is an easy-to-use and powerful tool for adding individual users, opening half a dozen dialog boxes, tabbing between fields, and trying to remember where every option is set for a hundred or so users is not our idea of fun. Even with the copy feature of the UMD, you would still be required to copy an existing user and fill in several fields for every new user you needed to add. So, what options does an administrator have?

If you have forked out the money for it, the Windows NT Server Resource Kit from Microsoft has a command-line tool called *addusers.exe* that takes comma-separated variable files of users and groups and creates new user accounts. As we have mentioned before, if you are in a position where NT is going to play an important role in your organization, the resource kits from Microsoft provide not only information but also valuable tools for the administrator. The *addusers.exe* tool is a good example. If you need it at all, then you need it badly.

Ultimately, the addition of many users at one time is typical of a more general class of issue that system administrators must face. No matter how advanced the underlying system or how easy to use its interface is, the system developers will never be able to include a tool for every job you have. This fact has been understood in UNIX system administration for many years, and it has spurred the creation of many development tools that allow administrators the freedom to develop their own utilities to solve very specific problems. The advent of the Graphical User Interface (GUI) has in many ways divorced users from the use of such tools. Although Windows NT undoubtedly depends in many ways its graphical nature, there also exists subliminally an entire set of command-line utilities that allow administrators greater freedom to create their own solutions to system issues.

Template Users and the Copy Command in the UMD

If you manage a small site with a low turnover of users, or if you handle those one-off user administration chores, you may find that the last two solutions we cover here are overkill. In this case, the template user/copy route in the UMD may be the best alternative for adding as many as 10 users. The UMD allows you to create a new user based on an already existing user's settings. You can then fill in the relevant user details such as name, description, and password.

There are essentially three steps to creating users using the copy command in the UMD:

1. Create a template user from which all your new users will be copied.

2. Select the template user in the UMD, and perform the copy command.

3. Fill in the particulars for the new user.

Microsoft's use of groups (see Chapter 3, *Windows NT Groups and Security*) organizes users for the purpose of generating access control lists, which typically enact either/or situations of granting or denying access to resources. For such items as logon hours and account expiration, each user is provided with an independent set of properties that the administrator can set. These are in no way related to groups as defined by Microsoft and used in Windows NT, and they are not normally organized as such.

Creating template users in the UMD is in a way like creating groups that control the initial setting of user properties. Just as the Sales and Development groups in an organization might have different permissions on the system for file or printer access, they might also need to have different logon hours or account expiration dates. Instead of setting each user's properties individually, you can create template users that are then copied when you add users to the system.

There are essentially two ways to go about setting up template users for the copy command:

- You can use an existing user who has the same settings as those with which you want to set up your new users.

- You can create a dummy user for each type of new user and fill out its properties as needed.

The second option is by far the more convenient because it means you don't have to search for a user that fits the bill each time; if you do find one, if you ever needed to customize the original account, you would need to find another user to use as a template the next time new accounts are added. For this reason, creating a new template account for each basic class of account you might create is much simpler.

Typically, these template users correspond to an actual Windows NT global group that you have set up in tandem. Both of these together are then used to control blocks of users as a single entity. As an example of creating a new template account, you might want to set up a separate type of user for any new sales staff you need to add regularly (because Sales seems like a high-traffic department). You could create a new account with the following information:

```
Username: sales_t
Full Name: Sales Template User
Description Template User for Sales Account Creation
Password: ******
Confirm Password: ******
User Must Change Password at Next Logon: NO
User Cannot Change Password: YES
Password Never Expires: YES
Account Disabled: YES
```

You could then fill out the normal information described in the previous section on the UMD for **Groups, Profile, Hours, Logon To, Account,** and **Dialin** dialog boxes. Remember, you can fill out information such as **User Profile Path, Logon Script Name,** and **Home Directory Path** using environment variables such as %username% (discussed in Chapter 4). This makes sense when creating template users in which these elements need to be customized for each user.

One important point to make is the setting for the last item on the **User Properties** dialog box: **Account Disabled: YES.** Remember that using dummy accounts for any reason can be considered a security risk. Any account that is inherently dormant has the potential for being hijacked, and nobody would be the wiser. This can occur for two main reasons; first, a disabled account is assumed to be safe by the administrators and the tendency is to simply forget about it. Second, the account is never used and so there is no regular user to notice any erroneous changes made to the account.

WARNING   Make sure you have disabled any template accounts that exist entirely for user creation. In addition, watch them for any sign of attempt-
ed use. Even if someone can't get in, the fact that he or she is even
trying would give up the game.

Once you have your template user set up, you can simply select that user in the
UMD, press the F8 key (for mouse lovers, select **User** from the menu, then
Copy...). The typical user preferences dialog box then pops up with the **Username, Full Name, Password, and Confirm Password** entries ready to be filled in.
The **Description** field is copied from the template user and can be changed, if
necessary. All the options that are available from the buttons along the bottom of
the dialog box are filled in from the template user's account. If you copy an
existing user, the copy command replaces any occurrence of the original username with the user variable **%username%**. Because template account names are
usually created in parallel to an existing group, you want to make sure you don't
use the same names for both the group and template accounts (e.g., template
user: sales_t, group name: sales) because this could cause problems later.

Using the template/copy route for adding users is perhaps the best method for adding
users either if you don't have many to add at one time or if the list of users you have
is not in electronic form. You might find, however, that the two methods about to be
discussed provide you with a more powerful and automated way of adding users.
Each method for adding users, however, also has its drawbacks, so getting the best
setup for your system requires taking a look at each program.

The addusers.exe Command

The *addusers.exe* utility that comes with the Windows NT Server Resource Kit
allows the administrator to add several users at one time to the system from
existing text CSV files; this approach can be much more convenient than the
template user/copy routine used in the UMD. If you receive your list of new users
in electronic format, producing a file that the *addusers* command can then use to
create the new accounts is straightforward.

In fact, the *addusers* command is more than just a user creation tool. In addition,
it allows you to collect current user information and delete users from the system.
Because we are primarily concerned with the creation aspects of user administration, we will leave issues concerning maintenance of the *addusers* command until
Chapter 4.

In fact, the *addusers* command does not allow you to specify many of the settings
for accounts in advance as you would using the template/copy procedure in the

UMD. You will eventually find yourself returning to the graphical tools to tweak each user's settings. In the next section on writing your own script, we arrive at a method that provides the automated functionality of the *addusers* script, together with the convenience of the template/copy command.

The addusers command-line options

To create users using the *addusers* command, you simply need a comma-delimited file that holds information about the new users and the global and local groups you want to create. The command line to issue the command is:

```
addusers [\\computername] /c filename [/s:x]
```

The optional /s:x is used to designate a delimiter other than a comma, where *x* is the delimiter to be used. The computername option is useful if you do your work from a workstation and another computer is the primary domain controller. This way, you could execute the command and have it add the users remotely. The /c option signifies that you want to create users, and filename specifies the CSV file to use.

The addusers file format

The most difficult part about the *addusers* command is setting up the file that holds the new user information. The file format designates three areas: Users, Global, and Local. These sections are used to provide information about the new users, global groups, and local groups, respectively, and are designated in the file by the section name in square brackets (e.g., [Users], [Global], [Local]). Within the user section, each line after the heading should contain user information separated by commas (or whatever delimiter you wish to use; just remember the /s:x switch). The user information the *addusers* command accepts includes: username, full name, password, home drive, home path, profile path, and script name. As an example, you might have several lines in the new user's file as follows:

```
[Users]
kab12, Kristin A. Brannon, wQnT5sX8, H:, \\iago\users\kab12,\
\\iago\profiles\kab12, sales.cmd,
dls21, Donald L. Schilson, iHr9e5d4, H:, \\iago\users\dls21,\
\\iago\profiles\dls21, development.cmd,
```

The first line of the example shows a user, Kristin A. Brannon, being added to the system with username **kab12**, password **xQnT5sX8**, home drive *H:*, home directory *iago\users\kab12*, profile path *iago\profiles\kab12*, and logon script *sales.cmd*.

Once you have generated a line for each user, you need to provide group membership information for each of these users. In the case of adding users to a server, you will most likely use the Global section only because groups are relevant to the entire domain, not to the server itself. The group section of the file takes the group name, a comment for the group, and a list of any users that belong to that group. For example, in the case of the two previous accounts that exist in the [Users] section, we would need to add each to their respective group:

```
[Global]
development,,dls21,
sales,,kab12,
```

If you are adding users and creating new groups that do not already exist, you can fill out the comment information. Perhaps the most crucial element of the file to note is the delimiter at the end of each line. Don't forget to include this when creating your file.

Maintaining User Information Through the UMD

Subverting the GUI is often seen as an administrator's duty, and to some extent, we can agree with that. Do not casually dismiss the GUI without first finding out what it can and cannot do for you. Once you have established your groups, created users, and allocated users into these groups, the hard work of maintaining the user base begins.

Windows NT from the GUI prospective does not offer very much in the way of user management. The only control you have over the user is through the User Manager for Domains, and even then it allows you to change only user properties. For very simple changes, the UMD is the fastest way to carry them out. There are two ways in which you can manipulate user properties: as a single user or as a set/group of users.

Managing a single user

On an individual basis, changing user properties is extremely easy. Select the user in question from the UMD, and bring up his or her properties by selecting **Properties** under the main menu option **User**. The only difference between the interface that confronts you and the one described earlier in this chapter is that the username is greyed out and cannot be changed. Having selected the user, make changes to the appropriate property, or set of properties, bearing in mind that all the options are subject to the rules that apply to user creation.

Managing multiple users

Being able to carry out actions on a large user set in one hit is a feature that successful operating systems aim to achieve. A GUI, such as NT, has its work cut out trying to achieve this and is constrained by the natural rigidity of such an interface. This means it can offer only a limited service in the area of mass user management. The following describes how NT allows you to select users en masse and what global changes you can make.

There are two ways in which you can select the users whose properties you wish to modify. The first is to pick from the list of users that the UMD presents. The user list windows allow the usual methods of selection, so to pick out individuals, select the usernames from the list while holding down the CTRL key. You can select all users by highlighting the first username, then holding down the SHIFT key and pressing the END key.

The second method allows you to select an entire group in one fell swoop. From the main menu option **User**, select the item **Select Users**. A list box containing groups is presented with the options for either selecting or deselecting them. You can highlight only one group at a time, but once you make the selection the group box stays open. This allows you to select another group while the first group of users stays selected. In this way, you can collect a number of groups.

Alternatively, you can select all the users, as described earlier in the chapter, and then use the Select User option to deselect the various groups of users you want removed.

NOTE   If you are not careful about the way you select and deselect, you may well find you have either excluded or included users you never meant to exclude or include. Remember that users can be in more than one group, so selecting a group and giving it special rights may well contain some users who also belong to a group to which you had no intention of giving those rights. Remember it this way: Select adds users to a list for change, deselect removes them. Think about it.

Having picked your users from the list, you now need to set about changing the desired properties. Select the property option (see "Managing a single user"), and the first thing you will notice is that the interface is slightly different. Now that you are dealing with a number of users, certain properties cannot be changed en masse. These are the username, the user's full name, and the password. This makes absolute sense, as the username must be unique, having the same full name would make the field pointless, and all having the same password would be a massive security risk.

General points about changing properties

The following are points to keep in mind when you are changing properties:

- The properties available for this mass selection are the same as they are for an individual user, the difference being that any changes made to these properties affect every user selected.

- Any field in an option that is the same for all selected users has its contents displayed. This includes paths, radio buttons, click boxes, and list boxes. If they are not the same, then depending on the field type, they are left blank, unchecked, or showing only the common elements. For instance, if the profile path for all selected users is the same, then the profile path field is filled in something like this:

      servername\profiles\%username%

  If the usernames are not the same, then the field is left blank.

  Note that the environment variable **%username%** is used to reflect all the different user names.

- The username displayed for each option has now been replaced by a list of selected users.

- Any option that has not been affected by the editing session is left as it was. For instance, if two users are selected, and if one has a global account but the other has a local account, then the radio buttons indicating this are both unchecked. Providing neither is checked during the edit, then the user account types stay as they are, even though you may have changed their account expires date.

Group-specific points. Keep the following in mind when you edit groups:

- The list box titled **All Are Members Of** contains only those groups that are common to all the selected users.

- Any changes to the **All Are Members Of** affects only the groups listed. Those groups specific to the individual user are not erased; they are simply ignored.

Profile-specific points. When you work with profiles, remember:

- Changing the profile path does just that and nothing else. Once changed, any profile information associated with a user is made redundant. When the user next logs on, a new profile is established from the default user profile. The old profile directory is not removed and will sit around until you do something about it.

- Likewise, changing the home directory path causes NT to create a new home directory at the new specified location. The contents of the old directory are not moved; you have to do this manually.

Logon hours-specific point. The following point relates to logon hours:

- Providing the logon hours for the selected users are the same, then you can edit the graphical chart as normal. If there are some differences, then NT checks that it is OK to reset everyone to full access before allowing you to make any edits.

Grouping Users

This chapter has covered the basic material on user creation and management using NT's built-in tools. In the next chapter, we continue along this vein by presenting the default tools available for creating and managing groups, in addition to some basic information on how you might want to use groups to organize users on your system.

As you can imagine, it won't take long for us to get away from the default tools and begin using more command-line scripts to get jobs done. By the end of Chapter 3, we provide examples of how Perl can be used to automate tasks, and we devote almost the entirety of Chapter 4 to these scripts. These scripts, though, depend on the use of the tools already available, so we have still more ground to cover before we bring out the big guns.

3

Windows NT Groups and Security

One of the primary concerns administrators have with a multiuser network operating system such as NT is its underlying security. Central administration and information exchange are certainly enhanced by using client/server architectures, but the potential sensitivity of information makes security of the operating and file system paramount.

One of the original aims of Windows NT was to develop a system that provided U.S. Government C2-level security. Therefore, NT provides the following:

Secure Logon Facility
> Users must provide a password in addition to a unique logon before they are allowed any access to the system.

Discretionary Access Control
> Owners of resources are able to grant and deny access to owned resources, and they can have the operating system enforce those rules.

Auditing
> Windows NT has the ability to track security events such as creation, access, or deletion of resources and assign the actions to specific users.

Memory Protection
> It is impossible for users to access data structures created by other users in NT.

The NT Executive[*] deals with system resources as objects.[†] NT Executive abstracts the underlying implementation of, say, a process or file and allows other compo-

---

[*] The Windows NT Executive is the portion of the operating system that runs in kernel, or protected, mode on a system. This includes the actual operating system kernel and hardware abstraction layer (HAL), on which the rest of the executive components are layered, such as the virtual memory manager, the object manager, I/O and file systems, interprocess communication, and portions of the security system.

[†] This terminology can be confusing at times. Windows NT objects are not object-oriented in the programming sense of the word, with inheritance, polymorphism, and reusability implied. Instead, an *object* in NT refers to the abstraction or encapsulation of system resources such as files, serial ports, etc. You cannot, for example, inherit the attributes of a serial port object and extend it to suit your needs.

nents of the system to deal with handles to these objects instead of the underlying code or data that actually maintains the resource. One of the advantages to this approach is that NT could use a unified security manager to deal with a wide variety of system resources in a coherent manner. The information that each resource holds is stored in a *security descriptor* and contains information such as the owner of the object and a list of users and groups with their respective access levels to that object (see Figure 3-1).

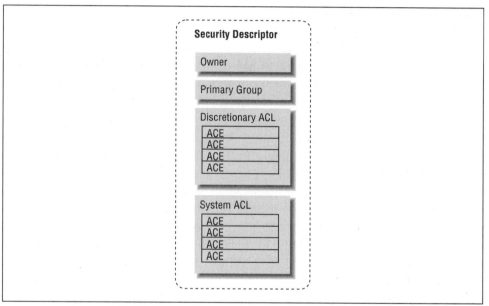

Figure 3-1. The structure of a Windows NT Security Descriptor

Access Control Lists

Access rights to objects are granted or denied through a component of a security descriptor known as an *access control list* (ACL). The ACL lists users and groups that are either specifically denied or granted access to an object. Each user or group entry in the ACL is called an *access control entry,* or ACE, and either grants or denies access to the object. When a user (or a program running under a user's control) attempts to access a kernel or user object, the ACL for that object is checked. For a user to be granted access to an object, two conditions must exist.

- The user, or any group to which the user belongs, must be granted access in the ACL.

- The user, or any group to which the user belongs, must not be specifically denied access in the ACL.

The security manager descends through the ACL, looking for ACEs that match a security token each user has. This token is given to the user at logon and corresponds to the user ID, as well as to any groups to which the user belongs. The security manager scans the ACL from top to bottom and stops on either of two conditions:

- An ACE granting the permission the user is asking for matches the user's token.

- An ACE denying the user permission to use the object is reached.

If the security manager reaches the bottom of the ACL without matching an ACE to the user's token, then the user is implicitly denied access. In the case of a user having multiple matching entries in an ACL (for example, from membership in different groups), the security manager skips any entries that do not meet the permission requirements. Because ACEs that deny users access to an object are traditionally placed at the top of an ACL, the ACEs override any other permissions a user might have.

Figure 3-2 shows a typical ACL for a file that a user might try to access. If user rjh39 tries to get read access to the file, then the security manager runs through the ACL, stopping when it reaches the read permission match (see pointer **a** in Figure 3-2). If rjh39 is then ready to save the file, the security manager then looks for write (or *change* in NT terminology) permission in the ACL (see pointer **b** in Figure 3-2). In the case of user srw1001, the security manager stops on the *access denied* entry, even though srw1001 might have read permission lower down in the ACL (see pointer **c** in Figure 3-2) through membership in the sales group.

It is not a requirement, however, for all objects to have an ACL. Objects must be first *given* ACLs in order for any security check to take place. If an object does not have an ACL associated with it, then the object is considered to have open access—and it is globally available. Finding an object without an associated ACL in Windows NT is rare, and it obviously is not recommended.

File Permissions and the ACL

One of the first places administrators begin to think about controlling access to resources is within the file system. The centralization of information in a client/server environment means that drives have the potential to hold everything from the number of toilet rolls purchased over the last year to the secret plans for the company's next stealth bomber. These resources will, of course, need differing levels of control; the Windows NT file and security systems allow this.

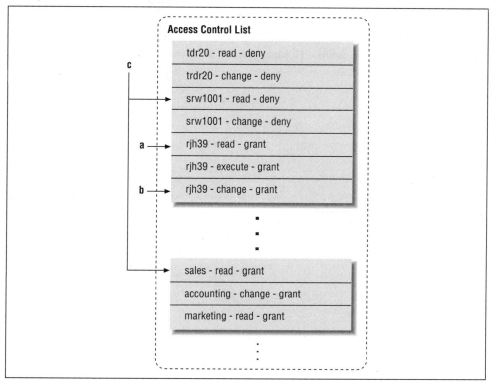

Figure 3-2. An example ACL

WARNING File-system security under Windows NT is done jointly by both the security manager and the NT File System (NTFS). This means that in order to have the C-2 government level security, you must also be using NTFS on any drives you wish to make secure. It will not work with DOS/Windows 95 FAT filesystems or OS/2 HPFS. Additionally, physical security is important, because tools are now available for reading NTFS partitions from DOS (which, of course, would not first check for permission). Dual boot machines, or even the ability to boot from a floppy or CD-ROM, render your system susceptible to attack this way.

Security on NTFS files systems can be set in several ways in Windows NT, both graphically and through the command line. Using *Explorer*, you can interactively view and set permissions on NTFS files and directories. By right-clicking on a file or directory you wish to modify, you can select the **Properties...** option from the pop-up menu. This produces a dialog box from which a **Security** tab is available.

The security features presented for the file system are identical[*] to those provided by all NT resources and reveal the object-oriented nature of the underlying NT security model. Because all objects expose identical security descriptors, they can be controlled through identical interfaces. The three options typically provided are **Permissions, Auditing,** and **Ownership.** The **Permissions** option is the one that allows the owner or administrator to graphically edit the ACL for a resource by selecting users or groups and choosing appropriate permissions such as read, write, or print.

In addition to the graphical editing of file and directory ACLs, the *cacls* command-line utility allows an administrator to set permissions for file-system entries. The *cacls* command takes a filename, or wildcard combination of files, and alters or replaces the ACLs for those files with a list of username-permission combinations. The syntax for the command is as follows:

```
cacls filename [options]
```

filename is the file or files *cacls* is to act on, and the options are these:

/t

Indicates that the command should look in subdirectories for matching files as well as the current directory.

/e

Denotes that the ACL for the files should be edited, not replaced. If you do not use this option, you will implicitly deny access to everyone not given permission with the command because the original ACL is wiped.

/c

Indicates that the program should continue with the remaining files if any files in the filename parameter throw access denied errors.

/g *user*:perm

Is used to grant the user certain access rights, where perm can be **r** for read access, **c** for change access, and **f** for full control.

/r *user* [...]

Is used to revoke a specified user's rights. Note that this option makes sense only when using the /e option because not using the /e option automatically revokes everyone's rights since the ACL is replaced.

---

[*]Or should we say *almost* identical. The only differences are typically the resource-specific kinds of access you can allow and deny or the events you can audit. For example, the printer security dialog has items such as print and manage documents, while the file permissions include traditional selections like read and write.

/p *user*:*perm* [...]

> replaces an already existing user's access rights with **r** (read), **c** (change), **f** (full control), or **n** (none).

/d *user* [...]

> is used to deny access to the user. Note that the **/g,** **/r,** **/p,** and **/d** options all take more than one user as an argument, and the user argument can take group names as well as usernames.

WARNING	It is important to remember that using the *cacls* command without the **/e** option *replaces* the ACL. This means that any permissions already set in the ACL will be lost. You know when you have issued the *cacls* command without the **/e** option because it will verify that you want to make the changes.

If, for example, you wanted to make your Perl *scripts* directory writable by your webmaster's group, you could issue the following command:

```
D:\perl5> cacls scripts /e /g webmasters:f
processed dir: D:\perl5\scripts
```

If you also wanted to allow them full access to the files in the *scripts* subdirectory, you could issue the command with the **/t** option:

```
D:\perl5> cacls scripts /t /e /g webmasters:f
processed dir: D:\perl5\scripts
processed file: D:\perl5\scripts\addtogrp.pl
processed file: D:\perl5\scripts\logon.pl
processed file: D:\perl5\scripts\addusers.pl
processed file: D:\perl5\scripts\passage.pl
processed file: D:\perl5\scripts\foobar.pl
```

ACLs Beyond the File System

Using the *cacls* command is a powerful way to control access to files from the command line. Files, however, are only one set of resources that a network will need to control. Printing, backup, drivers, processes—all of these resources can be controlled through their security descriptor's ACL. Even though all these resources have graphical means of altering their permissions, auditing, and ownership, outside the file system, there is no consistent command-line technique for editing these ACLs. To many minds, the lack of a full set of command-line utilities shackles NT to its Windows GUI ancestry and does not allow it the full freedom of the UNIX-like systems to which it aspires.

There is, in fact, a way to provide resource control from the command line, as we shall see later, but developing such a system depends on using groups to encapsulate these permission settings. The next section presents Windows NT groups, how they are created, and how you can use them to organize your system. As you will see, our philosophy is highly dependent on the use of groups to organize users and simplify administrative tasks.

Local Groups and Global Groups

Before we look at how to create groups with the UMD, we should first look at the two types of groups that NT allows us to create. Distinguishing their differences and their interaction is important.

Definition of a Global Group

A global group is a group made up solely of domain users. Its function is to supply a container of users that can be seen and moved effortlessly around in the Windows NT networking environment. The global group gives flexibility to domain administrators as they attempt to allocate local resources to differing sets of both local domain users and users from any trusted domains.

An administrator should be aware of several points when dealing with global groups; they are as follows:

- Global groups can be created only on a primary domain controller.

- These groups can contain only domain users who are registered in the domain where the group was created. No local users, local groups, trusted domain users, or other global/domain groups can be contained in a global group.

- Global groups can receive rights and permissions from administrators in other domains provided that a trust relationship has been established.

- Any NT workstation joining a domain automatically has two global groups inserted into two local groups. They are as follows :

  — Global group Domain Users is placed into local group Users.

  — Global group Domain Admins is placed into local group Administrators.

Definition of a Local Group

A local group is a group that can be made up of local users, domain users, trusted domain users, domain global groups, and trusted domain global groups. It is one of the mechanisms by which a domain administrator can control both the access to and management of a resource.

Note the following points:

- Local groups can be created on any server, member server, or workstation.

- Local groups can contain all types of user and global groups. They cannot contain local groups.

- These groups cannot be seen by trusted domains.

- These groups can receive rights and permissions only in the local (single) domain.

ACL Control Through Groups

All the books on NT that we have come across say that the only ACLs you can directly modify from the command line are file ACLs. This, in the strictest sense of the word, is true. With a bit of thought, though, it is possible to arrange the way you work to achieve control over nearly all the ACLs from the command line. The method hinges on the versatility of local groups to contain a wide range of user and group entities—as well as the fact that object ACLs can contain groups as ACEs. We call the groups that provide access to a resource's ACL *Resource Groups*. Resource Groups work by shifting the ACEs from an ACL into an appropriate local group, then assigning that local group the permissions that would have been afforded the users. The local group or groups, depending on the permissions you wish to allocate to the users, are made the only entries in the resource's ACL. Once in the ACL, the permissions you want associated with a set of users are then allocated to the local group in which they are contained. Because group membership now confers access to the resources for which that group has permission, we can now use the command-line utility `net group` to effectively add users to the ACL of a resource. It is not only the command line that benefits from using resource groups; you also give effective control of a resource's ACL to the UMD, which then allows for a single point of resource administration.

To achieve such a high degree of control the administrator has to be prepared to create a set of resource groups for each new resource. Let's step through a series of examples to clarify things a bit. First, we need to look at the way a local group can be set up to act as a "gateway" to a resource.

A local group used to manage a resource

Figure 3-3 is made up of three basic components:

- A local group called Resource A Users that the administrator has created specifically to contain users who have permission to use Resource A

- The ACL of the resource that allows actual access to the resource along with defined permissions

- The resource itself whose access is controlled by its ACL

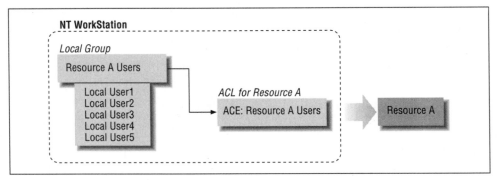

Figure 3-3. Resource groups

The local group Resource A Users is populated with users who have access to Resource A. This group is then entered into the ACL of Resource A as an ACE, and appropriate permissions are applied. We could just have easily entered the users individually into the ACL of Resource A, but remember we are demonstrating the fundamental action of creating a resource group. If Resource A were a file-system object, such as a directory share, as it stands there is arguably no advantage to using a local group to manage this resource. If Resource A were a printer, however, then by creating a local group we have created the ability to provide users with permission to access the printer without necessarily resorting to the printer's GUI property page. We could issue a `net group` command from the command line instead and add them to the appropriate group. This command-line printer access control was not possible before.

Global and local group interaction

This example takes us one step further by showing how a global group can be used to give access to a resource for a group of domain users. It also demonstrates the control you have over the resource in terms of granting or denying access to the resource without having to directly edit the ACL of the resource. Figure 3-4 shows how this example works.

Again, let's split up the figure as follows:

- A global group called Special Users is created by the domain administrator on a PDC. This contains a number of privileged domain users that the administrator wants to have access to Resource A.

- A local group called Resource A Users that is created by the local administrator to act as a resource group. This group is located on a domain workstation.

- The ACL for Resource A.

- The resource itself whose access is controlled by its ACL.

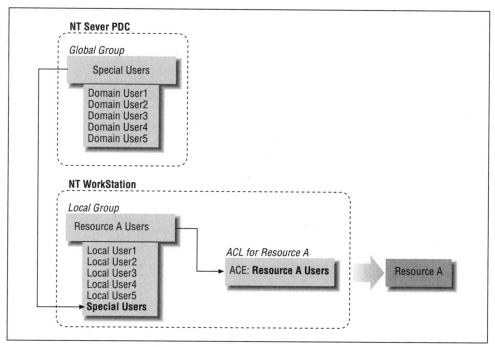

Figure 3-4. The relationship between groups over a domain

As with the local group example, the only entry in the ACL of *Resource A* is the local group Resource A Users. However, you can now see that along with a list of local users in the local group Resource A Users is an entry for the global group Special Users. By simply adding this global group into the local group (remember from earlier discussions that this allowed) the administrator has given everyone in the global group access to Resource A. Let's now have a look a working example.

A resource group

The scenario for this example is as follows:

We have a printer we wish to share, and we want to set up two categories of users: print-only capability for a number of nonadministrative users, and full control for all domain administrators.

Figure 3-5 shows how we go about resolving this situation.

Again, the first thing we must do is split up the diagram into its component parts:

- There is a list of global groups on the PDC of which three have access to the specified printer. They are Postgraduates, Undergraduates, and Domain Admins.

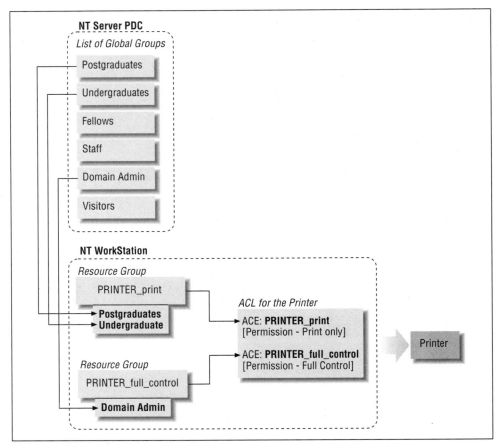

Figure 3-5. Using resource groups to control resources

- On the workstation to which the printer in question is connected, two local groups act as resource groups. They are PRINTER_print and PRINTER_full_control, respectively.

- There is the ACL for the printer.

- And there is the printer itself.

We can see from the list of global groups that Postgraduates and Undergraduates both have entries in the resource PRINTER_print, while another global group, Domain Admins, has an entry in the other resource group, PRINTER_full_control. The ACL for the printer contains two ACEs representing the two resource groups, each with different permissions. The PRINTER_print entry is given only print privileges; the PRINTER_full_control ACE is give full control over the printer. This solution allows us to add, remove, or modify groups of users effectively from both the command line and the UMD. It gives us the flexibility to grant access to a distant resource by simply adding a domain user to a global group or by adding a global group to a resource group. In fact, if a global group has entries in a large number of resource ACLs, then simply adding a domain user to this group immediately grants access to all these resources without the need to edit all the individual ACLs.

The advantages of using resource groups are that they do the following:

- Stop repeated editing of the ACL to set up users or global groups who want the same permissions.

- Add functionality to the UMD. Encapsulating the ACLs of resources in a resource group or groups gives effective control of the ACLs through the UMD. This supplies a single point of administration.

- Give the command line the capability to grant or deny user access to a resource other than the file system.

- Give a clearer view of the ACL audit trail. By reducing the ACEs to the resource groups, then any modifications to the ACL are clearly illegal.

Disadvantages of using resource groups are as follows:

- Local groups cannot be placed in resource groups (remember, no local groups inside local groups).

- It requires some time to set up.

- If the type of permissions you wish to grant vary widely, then you need to create a fair number of resource groups. Remember, however, that permissions granted through the ACL are accumulative. If you create a resource group to supply read-only access and another one to supply write access, then if a user is placed in both, that user has both rights to the resource. There is no need to create a read/write resource group.

User rights and user rights groups

User rights are basically a set of rules by which NT controls the actions a user can perform on a given machine. The list of actions is predetermined by NT, and new actions cannot be added.[*] NT supplies a number of built-in local groups whose purpose is to act as what we like to call *user rights* groups. These groups have predefined roles and are given particular user rights out of the box to match these roles. The following is a description of each of these groups:

Administrators[†]

This group has full control over the computer. It is the only group to be granted all user rights by default. If this group is on a domain controller, then

---

[*]Later versions of NT may well allow additions to the user rights list.

[†]Local groups on both NT Servers and Workstations.

the global group Domain Admins is an automatic member of the group and cannot be removed.

Account Operators

Members of this group can use the User Manager for Domains to create user and group accounts, as well as to modify or delete these accounts from the domain. Account operators can log on to domain servers, shut them down, and use server manager to add workstations to the domain.

Backup Operators*

Members of this group can back up and restore files from the PDC and BDCs, log on locally to the domain controllers, and shut them down.

Print Operators

Here, operators can create, delete and manage print shares on the domain controllers. Like Backup Operators, they can log on locally and shut the system down.

Server Operators

Members of this group have the same user rights as the Backup and Print Operators. In addition, they can create, delete, and manage network shares, format a server's hard disk, lock and unlock the server, and change the system time.

Replicator*

This group should contain only a single domain user account to log on replication services. It has no other function and should not contain any normal user accounts.

Users*

Members of this group cannot log on locally at machines running NT server. They have no entries in the user rights list and, as such, have no permissions. It is a basic group for the administrator to use. By default, it contains the Domain Users group, which can be removed. On a workstation, members of this local group can keep local profiles, lock the workstation, and create, delete, and modify local groups. They can also access the server over the network.

Guest*

This group is intended for the transient user and is disabled by default. Members of this group can access only the server over the network and have no rights on the domain server. By default, this group contains the Domain Guest group and the local guest account. These can be removed.

All the above groups are local groups for a domain controller and, with the exception of the Replicator group, can contain users and global groups. Although the

---

*Local groups on both NT Servers and Workstations.

user rights for these groups are predefined by NT, it does not mean that they cannot be changed. If you find that none of these groups matches your needs, it would better to simply create a new one and give it the rights you require. It is probably best to stick to using local groups as user rights groups, simply because they can contain both users and global groups and so are more flexible. You can, however, grant user rights to global groups if you choose.

The actions governed by the user right rules are described in Table 3-1; the scope of their rules is as follows:

- User rights assigned on a PDC apply to that PDC and all other BDCs in the domain.

- User rights assigned on a workstation apply to that workstation only. The same goes for a member server.

Table 3-1. User Rights

User rights	Comments
Access this computer from network	Gives a user the right to connect to this computer over the network.
Add workstations to domain	Allows a user to add a workstation running NT to the domain. This allows the workstation to see domain users and global groups.
Back up files and directories	Gives a user the right to back up files and directories, superseding any existing rights on those files or directories.
Change the system time	Allows the user to change the system clock.
Force shutdown from a remote system	Is not implemented yet (Version 5?).
Load and unload device drivers	Gives the user the right to load and unload device drivers.
Log on locally	Allows a user to log on to the machine locally.
Manage auditing and security log	Allows the user to use the Security tab in the Properties dialog box to set audit tracking for files, directories, and other objects.
Restore files and directories	Like Back up, this right supersedes file and directory rights in order to allow a user to carry out a file and directory restore.
Shut down the system	Gives the user at the computer the right to shut down that computer.
Take ownership of files or other objects	Allows a user to take over the ownership of files, directories, or other objects.
Bypass traverse checking (advanced right)	Allows the user to traverse through a directory tree even if he or she has no permission to do so.
Log on as a service (advanced right)	Allows a user to register a process as a service with the system

The last two user rights entries in the table are advanced rights and are included here as they have a more general role to play in user and group management. Other advanced rights are really useful only to programmers wishing to write applications for NT machines; therefore, they are not covered by this book.

Granting user rights to groups

Granting user rights to a group is a straightforward procedure, but it can be done only through the UMD. From the UMD's main menu, select **Policies** then **User Rights**. You are presented with a dialog box that contains a drop-down menu for selecting the user right you are interested in, and a windowpane where groups or users with that user right are displayed. To add a new group to the user right list, select the **Add** option and pick your group from the list presented to you. Go through the user rights, adding your group to all the lists to which you want rights.

Creating Groups with the User Manager for Domains

The idea here is to give you a simple guide through the steps required to create a group using the UMD. We do not intend to give you a lesson in point and click, so we assume that you will click the appropriate OK, Cancel, and Add buttons where necessary.

Steps for creating a global group

- Select from the UMD's main menu the option **New** and then **New Global Group**. A simple dialog box appears.

- Enter the name and description of the new group in the appropriate data entry boxes.

- Select the users required from the **Not Members** pane, and add them to the group. Beware that there is not a user already placed in the **Member** pane. If, when you invoked the New Global Group dialog box, a domain user was highlighted, then this user will appear in the **Member** pane. The same, in this case, does not go for local users or groups, as only domain users can be added to a global group. Remember, only domain users from the local domain can be added to a domain group.

Steps for creating a local group

From discussion earlier in this chapter, you will remember that local groups can contain all types of users as well as global groups. For this reason, the addition of a user or group object to the group is much more wide-sweeping. The consequence of this is that the add function must not only be able to find local users, domain users, and global groups, but also be able to search out domain users and groups from other trusted domains. For this reason, a number of dialog boxes are required to allow for all options.

- From the UMD's main menu, select the option **New** and then **New Local Group**.

- Fill in the name and description as before.

- Now select the **Add** button; a second dialog box is generated.

- From here, select the users you wish to add to the group. You will notice a drop-down selection box at the top of the window. This allows you to select the domain from which you wish to add domain users and groups. A search option is also available, allowing for the search for a specified user or group in either one or all the trusted domains.

Creating a group by copying

Another way to create a group is to make a copy of one that already exists. This has the sole advantage of copying all the users from the existing group to the new one. The only task you need to do is to give it a name because everything else is copied. Making a copy, however, does not give the users of the copied group the same rights and permissions associated with the original group. These need to be allocated separately.

The sequence of steps for copying a group is as follows:

- From the group pane of the UMD, highlight the group you wish to be copied.

- Select from the UMD's main menu the option **New** and then **Copy** (press F8 for a shortcut).

- Depending on whether you are copying a local or global group, an associated dialog box appears. Notice that it already has a list of selected users.

You have now created a new group and can go about manipulating the contents as you will.

We should also mention here how to remove a group. This could not be easier; simply select the group from the UMD main group pane that you want to remove. Now press the DELETE key or select the **Delete** option under **Users** from the UMD's main menu; the group is removed (once you have assured NT you really mean to do it).

Creating groups with the net group command

NT supplies a number of useful utilities that, when used in conjunction with a scripting language such as Perl, offer a powerful and flexible way for the administrator to manage the system. The NET command is one such utility. It has a number of functions, but in this book we expand only on those directly related to managing users and groups.

The **net group** command offers the administrator the following functions:

- Show the global groups that exist on the server

- Show the users contained within a particular global group

- Allow for the creation of new global groups

- Allow for the removal of existing global groups

- Allow for the addition of users to a particular global group

- Allow for the removal of users from a particular global group

For the moment, we will not talk about the first two bullet points, except to say they supply the basic information required to manage users. Refer to *Chapter 4, Managing Users Through Scripts,* for a detailed discussion on how to make good use of them.

We start by looking at how to create a single global group. The syntax for this is as follows:

```
net group groupname /ADD /COMMENT:"text"
```

The net group is the command, the groupname is the name you wish to give the new global group, the /ADD tells the command it is a new group to be added, and the /COMMENT supplies the description of the group. Here is an example:

```
D:\>net group "All Students" /ADD /COMMENT:"Postgraduate and\
Undergraduate students"
```

Note that the group name is enclosed by quotation marks. A group name can be either a single word, in which case the quotation marks are not necessary, or two or more words enclosed by quotation marks. A group name can be up to 20 characters long.

Removing a group is quite straightforward: Just replace /ADD with /DELETE and drop the comment.

As mentioned, the **net group** command deals only with global groups. To administer local groups, the **group** part of the command needs to be replaced with **localgroup.** The syntax of the command is the same, with all details now referring to local groups.

What about the users?

It may have struck you that in the earlier section on the **net group** command, we did not make any mention of users. Obviously, having created a group we need to add users or, depending on the group type, other groups. We also need to assign user rights to some of those groups.

The `net group` command has an option for adding users. The following is the syntax:

```
net group groupname username /ADD
```

The only point to notice is the addition of the username. If there is more than one user to add, then include them on the command line, leaving a space between them.

```
D:\>net group "All Students" ajm39 tdr20 sjl11 /ADD
```

This is all well and good, but adding a large number of users to the group or to several groups is a bit laborious, to say the least.

A more efficient way is to have a batch or Perl script that supports command-line parameters of, say, a text filename, containing a list of users, followed by multiple group names. Read on.

Creating a Script for Adding Users to Groups

Using the `net group` command to control system resources is a perfect way to begin using scripts to automate tasks. The following example is a brief look at how adding users to groups can be automated in Perl. The *addtogrp.pl* script takes the following command-line syntax:

```
addtogrp [/v] [/q] [/d domain] [/c] filename group [ group ... ]
```

where *filename* is a text file of usernames (one to a line) and *group* is a list of groups to which you wish to add them. The /v option is used to print out what the script is doing in verbose mode, while the /q option turns off all output together. The /d option is used to specify the domain in which you wish to work. The /c option is used to automatically create any groups that do not already exist. The script does several checks while adding the users to groups, including asking if you wish to create any groups listed on the command line that do not already exist. In addition, it checks for the existence of users in a group before trying to place them in that group. As with the traditional `net group` command, you cannot use groups for the entries to be added to the global groups. It would be a simple matter to create a `net localgroup` version of this script for adding lists of users or groups to local groups on a system by replacing the `net group` command call with a `net localgroup` command.

One possible use of the script might be the following, where you add a list of users to a new local resource group:

```
D:\> addtogrp /v plotusers.txt PLOTTER_print
```

Example 3-1. Listing of the addtogrp.pl Script

```perl
use Win32::UserAdmin;
$domain = '';

# First, we pull off the name of the file to load from the command line,
# and load the usernames into an array

$filename = shift @ARGV;

$not_quiet = true;
$verbose = false;

if($filename eq "/v") {
    $verbose = true;
    $filename = shift @ARGV;
} elsif ($filename eq "/q") {
    $not_quiet = false;
    $filename = shift @ARGV;
}

if($filename eq "/d") {
    $domain = shift @ARGV;
    $filename = shift @ARGV;
}
Win32::UserAdmin::GetDomainController('', $domain, $server);

if($filename eq "/c") {
    $create_auto = true;
    $filename = shift @ARGV;
}

open(USERLIST, $filename) || die "unable to load $filename\n";
@ARGV || die "no group names provided\n";

print "Retrieving usernames from $filename...\n" if $not_quiet;
while (defined($username = <USERLIST>)) {
    chomp($username);
    $usernames{$username} = " ";
    print "$username\n" if $verbose;
}

# In order to check for the existence of the groups to which we are adding
# a user, we first need to load the current groups on the system. In order to
# facilitatesearching the list we will place the names as indexes into a
#     hash table.

print "Retrieving group names from system...\n" if $not_quiet;

Win32::UserAdmin::GetGroups($server, \@groups);
foreach $group(@groups) {
    $system_groups{$group} = " ";
    print "$group\n" if $verbose;
}
```

Example 3-1. Listing of the addtogrp.pl Script (continued)

```
foreach $group(@ARGV) {
    if (!$system_groups{$group}) {
        if($create_auto) {
            print "Creating $group_type $group...\n" if $not_quiet;
            Win32::UserAdmin::GroupCreate($server, $group, 'generated by
addtogrp script')
                || die "unable to create group";
        } else {
            print "Create the group $group [y/n]? : ";
            if (<STDIN> =~ /^y/i) {
                print "Enter COMMENT details : ";
                $comment = <STDIN>;
                print "Creating $group...\n" if $not_quiet;
                Win32::UserAdmin::GroupCreate($server, $group, $comment)
                    || die "unable to create $group";
            }
        }
        print "Adding users to $group...\n" if $verbose;
        @user_array = keys %usernames;
        Win32::UserAdmin::GroupAddUsers($server, $group, \@user_array);
    } else {
        # we need to load the usernames from a group into
        # a hash to make sure we are not repeating users
        print "$group exists\n" if $not_quiet;
        print "Retrieving users from $group..." if $not_quiet;
        %usertemp = %usernames;
        Win32::UserAdmin::GroupGetMembers($server, $group, \@groupusers);
        foreach $groupuser(@groupusers) {
            print "\n$groupuser";
            if(exists $usertemp{$groupuser}) {
                delete $usertemp{$groupuser};
                print " - match" if $verbose;
            }
        }
        print "\n" if $not_quiet;

        print "Adding users to $group...\n" if $not_quiet;
        @user_array = keys %usertemp;
        Win32::UserAdmin::GroupAddUsers($server, $group, \@user_array);
    }
}
```

Moving on to User Management

This chapter and the previous one have focused on the basic building blocks of administration under Windows NT (and, for that matter, any NOS)—users and groups. Because of its GUI background, NT is rich in graphical tools but shy on the command-line side of user administration. By understanding how users, groups, and security permissions interact, it is possible to create a rich command-line environment from which to manage a Windows NT system. In the next few chapters we will expand on some of the simple administrative tasks shown here and provide more examples of how to control the Windows NT environment for users.

4

Managing Users Through Scripts

As an administrator of any sizable network, you probably feel that there is enough work for more than your fair share of hours in the day. Answering user queries, fixing broken hardware, and generally trying to order the chaos that is your world are a never-ending job. The most frustrating element of the job is its repetitiveness, continually doing the same thing over and over again, telling yourself, "There *has* to be a better way" or "I could have done this better." Well, your time has come.

In the previous chapter, we showed you an example of how you could use Perl to create a script to add users in a file to a list of groups. Certainly it is not the end-all-be-all of Perl scripts, but an example of how you can extend the functionality of NT with your own programs. This flexibility extends throughout the gamut of NT administration, and Perl will be used often in the rest of the book to automate tasks or create solutions.

Up to this point, our main focus has been to present the basic elements of users and groups, and introduce the programs NT provides for administering them. This chapter presents several examples of how to use a mixture of Perl and NT command-line utilities to automate administrative tasks. In Chapter 6, *NT Internals and Managing Users*, we will look at more NT and Perl internals that allow us to skip command-line utilities altogether.

A Quick Example

One example of using Perl to automate a task is the creation of user shares that can be mapped to a user's home drive when the user is logged on. If you have inherited a system, it is highly possible that it may not be set up the way you would like. For example, many administrators share only the root user directory and map the H: drive to this, meaning that whenever users go to the H: drive, they see not only their own directories, but everyone else's. For a 10-user system this is acceptable, but for 100 it gets pretty annoying. A better solution is to set each user's home drive to his or her directory. This involves two steps:

1. Create shares of all the user directories.

2. Map the home directory of each user.

If your user's home directories are created under the username itself, then creating a Perl script to perform item 1 is simple. Example 4-1 shows a Perl script that takes all the subdirectories of a given directory and shares them as the name of the directory with an added $ to hide them from browsing.

Example 4-1. A Perl Script to Share User Directories

```
$dir = $ARGV[0];
opendir (DIR, "$dir");
@files = readdir DIR;
closedir DIR;
foreach $file(@files) {
    next if ($file eq '.' || $file eq '..');
    $fullname = "$dir\\$file";
    if (-d $fullname) {
        print "Sharing $fullname\n";
        $out = qx(net share $file\$=$fullname);
        print $out;
    }
}
```

The next step in sharing the user directories is to change the home directory to the new share. This process can be somewhat convoluted due to the way NT's utilities work. If you use the UMD to set a user's home path, you cannot use the `%user-name%` environment variable with the $ after it. This means changing each user's home path one at a time. On the other hand, the command-line `net user` command does not have the ability to designate which drive letter to map the home directory. The home drive is automatically mapped to `Z:.` In the case of our example here, we assume that the home drive letter has already been assigned in the UMD. If this is the case, *changing* the home drive using `net user` retains this drive letter for the mapping and changes only the target share. Therefore, we could use another script, shown in Example 4-2, to load the users we wish to change from a text file and alter their home drive.

Example 4-2. A Perl Script to Change a User's Home Directory

```
open(FILE, $ARGV[0]) or die "Cannot open $ARGV[0]\n";
foreach $user(<FILE>) {
    chop($user);
    next if(!$user);
    $out = qx(net user $user /HOMEDIR:\\\\Iago\\$user\$);
```

Example 4-2. A Perl Script to Change a User's Home Directory (continued)

```
}
close(FILE);
```

One thing to remember is that share names are promoted to the top of the hierarchy. That is, when you browse a machine over the network, all shares appear as if they were at the root. Even if you are sharing *D:\users* and the new directories are under *users*, you still use *\\servername\sharename*, where *sharename* is the username itself with the $ appended to the end. For example, the directories *D:\users\tom*, *D:\users\dick*, *D:\users\harry* on the server *iago* would map to *\\iago\tom$*, *\\iago\dick$*, *\\iago\harry$*.

Logon Scripts

Windows NT provides the administrator with a variety of mechanisms for massaging the users' environment; on the whole, the tools do their job well. Needless to say, any predefined tool has its limitations, and so it is with the NT tools. You never can tell what an administrator may need to do to satisfy the baying pack of the user hounds. (Well, it feels like that sometimes.) Logon scripts offer a high degree of flexibility as they are both easy to create and simple to modify. They can be batch files or executables (*.bat*, *.exe*, or *.cmd*) and are designed to run automatically when a user logs on. NT allows the administrator to assign a logon script to a single user, a group of users, or indeed all users (more on this later).

Logon scripts can help manage the following:

* Network integration; for example, with Novell or LAN Manager
* General network connections
* Automatic application launching
* Circulation of information; for example, through message of the day

Where the Logon Scripts Go

When a user logs on, NT looks for a logon script under the following path:

```
%systemroot%\system32\repl\import\scripts
```

%systemroot% is usually *winnt*, although it can be anything that the person installing the system wanted to call it. This directory is shared as *NETLOGON* by the domain controller to all workstations logging on in the domain.

Why here? When a user logs on to a domain, the logon script is run from the server performing the authentication. When a domain has more than one domain controller, then any one of those servers can authenticate the user's logon and thus allow the logon script to be executed. To ensure that the logon script on all the servers is kept up to date, the replication service needs to be run. This service uses the path shown above as well as a partner directory *%systemroot%\system32\repl\export\scripts*. You can, in fact, change the path of the logon script using the Server Manager (one of the suite of server management tools). Having started the application up, select the machine you are interested in by double-clicking on its entry in the main window. This brings up its property box. Select the **Replication** option, and then simply edit the **Logon script path** field.

NOTE   Replication between domain controllers is often the source of many problems with logon in domains with more than one controller. If you are having problems getting your logon scripts to run, make sure your replication is set up correctly. Authentication can occur on any domain controller, so logon scripts must be replicated properly to them all.

From the discussion in Chapter 2, *Creating Users*, you will remember that you can set the logon script path of each user in the **Profiles** option of the UMD. By placing your logon script in the default directory, you simply need to enter its name in the **Logon Script** field and NT will find it. You can create subdirectories under the default directory and place the logon scripts there, as long as you include the relative path along with the script name.

What Can You Put in a Logon Script?

A logon script is typically a batch file and can contain all the commands and utilities from the command line. It can also make use of the special logon script variables, as shown in Table 4-1.

Table 4-1. Logon Script Variables

Variable	Description
%HOMEDRIVE%	The drive letter associated with the user's home directory
%HOMEPATH%	The full path of the user's home directory
%HOMESHARE%	The share name containing the user's home directory
%OS%	The operating system of the workstation from which the user is logging on
%PROCESSOR_ARCHITECTURE%	The processor type of the workstation

Table 4-1. Logon Script Variables (continued)

Variable	Description
%PROCESSOR_LEVEL%	The processor level of the workstation
%USERDOMAIN%	The domain containing the user's account
%USERNAME%	The user's name

Logon scripts can also call other batch files as well as executables. The following is an example of a logon script that contains some commands as well as a call to a Perl script. Its purpose is to synchronize the workstation's time with that of the server, establish the type of home directory associated with a user, and then display one or more messages depending on the groups to which the user belongs.

```
Rem LOGON.BAT
@echo off
```

The `subst` command is used to substitute, or remap, drive letters. Because the `subst` command will throw an error if you attempt to map a drive letter that has already been set, the following line is required to remove any existing substitution. The next line then sets the proper time with the *iago* server.

```
subst H: /d > nul
net time \\iago /set /yes >nul
```

When we create a user we generally designate the drive letter H: to represent his or her home directory. The user's home directory is then mapped from the file server to the workstation on logon. We occasionally use a directory on a local workstation in individual instances. To stay consistent, we map the local home directory, which is something like *C:\users\jjm1000*, to H: by using the `subst` command. First we check to see if the user has a local home directory or one mounted from a server. Using the special logon variable `%HOMEDRIVE%` we can find this out in the following way:

```
rem checks to see if it is a network drive - H: is our designated home
rem drive letter

if "%homedrive%"=="H:" goto groups

rem must be local directory so use the subst command to map it as a drive

subst H: %homedrive%%homepath%

rem Call the perl script passing the parameter %USERNAME%

:groups
perl logon.pl %username%
rem End of logon.bat
```

The following is the Perl script called from *logon.bat*. It takes the username as its parameter and finds all the groups to which the user belongs. It then uses the name of each group to print the contents of a text file of the same name. The idea is to display a series of messages of the day relating to each group. You could just as easily carry out some other action of user management using the groups as your filtering/selection method.

```perl
# the GetUserGroups function is used to retrieve the
# groups to which a specific user belongs
sub GetUserGroups {

    # pull off the username from the function argument list
    my $username = shift @_;
    my $groupsection = 0;

    # the map function is used to gather all of the group names
    # from the 'net user' command associated with the user
    # $username. The grep function is used to
    # isolate the lines of output from the 'net user' call
    # that contain the groupnames themselves. These lines are
    # then passed onto the map command. The regular expression
    # used in the map command splits the line into
    # group names based on the fact that each group name begins
    # with the asterisk (*).
    map /\*(\S.{1,19}?)\s\s+/g, grep {
        if (/^Logon hours/) {
            $groupsection = 1;
            0;
        } else {
            $groupsection = 0 if /^The command/;
            $groupsection;
        }
    } qx(net user $username);
}

$user = shift @ARGV;

foreach $group(GetUserGroups($user)) {
    $group = $group."\.txt";
    open(MESSAGE,"$group");
    while (<MESSAGE>) {
        print;
    }
}
```

Writing Your Own User Creation Script

In Chapter 2, we covered the tools Microsoft has provided for adding user accounts in bulk. Even though each of these utilities is useful, you may find that creating your own tools for adding users to the system allows you much more freedom and control over the entire process. In this section, we look at the use of Perl as a customized scripting tool that facilitates user creation. Our requirements are as follows:

- The automatic generation of a username based on the full name of the user, a number that designates the user's group, and a sequence number to ensure that the username is unique

- The generation of a random password for each user

- The configuration of the account properties based on a template user account

- The output of a comma-separated value (CSV) file to provide users with their account details

When the script is complete, the only information the administrator will need to provide is the user's full name, comments, the template group, and any additional groups to which the user should belong.

Generation of Usernames

As you recall from Chapter 2, username generation really depends on what you think is best for your site, as a combination of readability versus guarantee of uniqueness. In this user creation script example, we use the initials, group number, and sequence number designation for our username. Of course, to be able to create a sequence number list, we will need to load a list of the current users on the system to which we can compare our new users. The script does this by issuing the `net user` command, which lists all the users on the system. One caveat: There is nothing in this script that attempts to detect duplicate user entries. Because of the way the script works, it will simply create a new user with the same initials, but increment the postfix index by one.

Generation of Passwords

In addition to the generation of usernames, the user creation script also needs to create unique passwords for each user. The administrator then provides the password to users so they can log on for the first time. For this script, we have created an array with all possible numbers and characters we wish to use in the password, while avoiding ambiguous letters and numbers (l1O0o). Eight of these characters are then randomly selected for each password itself.

Collection of Template User Account Information

The `net user /add` command does not have the equivalent of the UMD **Copy...** command, used when creating new users in the graphical interface tool. For this reason, all the template user information must be pulled out of the database in order for it to be used for creating the new users. When you invoke the `net user username` command, it prints out information about that user, including the information we need. The script executes this command to get information such as account expiration date, group membership and profile, home directory, and script paths. This script does not set rules such as logon hours and permitted work-stations,* although this information is available from the `net user` command. It is not always the case that the command-line utility provides identical functionality to the UMD. For example, dialin permissions cannot be defined from the command line, so they must be set in the UMD to force users to change their password on next logon. Other elements, such as which drive is mapped to the user's home directory, can be solved in their logon scripts as shown earlier.

Generating the template user for our home-grown script is the same as creating a template user for the UMD with one additional piece of information. Because of the requirement to generate usernames with an index indicating which department they are from, the template account needs to store the number for that group. We have used the user comment field (which does not appear in the UMD) to store the string: `Index: n,` where n is the number to be appended to any users created with that template. To add this information to the template account, you need to issue the following command:

```
net user username /USERCOMMENT:"Index n"
```

This command places the index string in the user account database, which can be extracted later by the script.

Creation of the Output File

Because we have generated random passwords, the script needs to generate an output log that holds the full name of the user, the username, and the password. This file can then be passed into your favorite word processor to be mail merged with a form you send out to your users. Remember to do something immediately with this file! The script changes the permissions on the file so that it is readable only by the user running the script. This file would provide a would-be intruder with not one, but a multitude of keys.

WARNING   This script generates a file with not only the unique username for
           each account, but also an initial password. This file is a *very* large se-
           curity risk. Use the file immediately so that you can remove it from
           the system. Additionally, follow the regular precautions of forcing us-
           ers to change their passwords on first logon and disabling accounts
           that haven't been used for a specified period of time.

---

*With a 24-hour computer lab and many workstations, neither of these settings really makes sense; however, if you need to add these elements, you can use the extraction of group information from the user database as an example. Note, however, that the output of the `net user` command does not always match the input you might require, so some reformatting is needed. This is especially true of the logon hours allowed information.

The Input File

To input user information, this script uses a file similar to that used by the *addusers* command; however, because templates are used to provide all the initial information for each account, there is no need to include the same amount of information. The file is constructed by placing one user per line, with the first line holding the template username to use for the users that follow. Multiple templates can be used by separating the new template from the previous user list by a blank line. For example, you could add two people to sales and two to development as follows:

```
template_sales
Kristin A. Brannon; Midwest Division; Sales;
Steve J. Howard; East Coast Division

development
Steve Waterhouse; Speech Recognition Division
Donald L. Schilson; Database Division
```

This script accepts delimiters that are either commas or semicolons. The information for each user consists simply of his or her full name and any comments about the user. The rest of the information needed is gathered from the template accounts that head each section.

The bulk user Perl script

The code for the *addusers.pl* script begins with the normal initialization chores associated with Perl scripts. In this case, we need to load the *UserAdmin* and *FileSecurity* modules that will be used in the script. In addition, at this time we can grab the command-line information about whether to run the script in verbose mode and the input filename.

```
# addusers.pl script used to create bulk users
use Win32::UserAdmin;
use Win32::FileSecurity;

$verbose = false;
$arg = shift @ARGV;
if($arg eq '/v') {
    $verbose = true;
    $arg = shift @ARGV;
}
$userfile = shift @ARGV;
```

The first serious block of code in the script is used to generate the random seed for the password generator. The script then proceeds to fill the $passchar scalar with the characters we want to use for the passwords, skipping those that are considered ambiguous.

```
# srand is used to seed the randomization routine
# for creating user passwords. The series of 'for'
```

```
# loops then propagates an array with possible
# password characters.
srand( time() ^ ($$ + ($$ << 15)) );
$char_index = 0;
for($num = 50; $num < 58; $num++){$passchar[$char_index++] = chr($num);}
for($num = 65; $num < 73; $num++){$passchar[$char_index++] = chr($num);}
for($num = 74; $num < 79; $num++){$passchar[$char_index++] = chr($num);}
for($num = 80; $num < 91; $num++){$passchar[$char_index++] = chr($num);}
for($num = 97; $num < 108; $num++){$passchar[$char_index++] = chr($num);}
for($num = 109; $num < 111; $num++){$passchar[$char_index++] =
    chr($num);}
for($num = 112; $num < 123; $num++){$passchar[$char_index++] =
    chr($num);}
```

We still have to take care of one more housekeeping item before we can start loading in new users. When we get to the point of creating new usernames, we need to compare them with existing names to determine whether the suffix index needs to be incremented to ensure that the new name does not match any existing names. Using the *Win32::UserAdmin::GroupGetMembers* method, we can grab an array filled with all the users in the Domain Users group (which should be everyone we need to compare against[*]). We store these usernames in a hash variable called `%current_users` as the key to a blank value. By storing the username as a key in a hash variable, we do not have to search an array for a match. Instead, we simply see if the username returns an undefined value when used as a key in the hash variable, which would indicate that the username did not exist.

```
# need to get the list of current users
# this will also include the names of the
# computers in the domain, but we can ignore these
Win32::UserAdmin::GroupGetMembers('','Domain Users',\@users)
    || die "Unable to list current users";

# place the current usernames in a hash instead
# of an array for easier lookup.
print "Current Users:\n" if $verbose;
foreach $user(@users) {
    $current_users{$user} = " ";
    print "$user\n" if $verbose;
}
print "\n" if $verbose;
```

We are now ready to begin reading in users from the input file provided. In addition, the script needs to open up the output log file to which we will be writing the final usernames and passwords. Once these files are open, the script begins to read from the new user file one line at a time. Because we know that the first line must hold the name of a template account that will be used in the creation of the users that follow in the file, we can split out this template name from the first line.

---

[*]In addition, this command returns the names of the workstations registered in the domain. We will not require these.

```
open(NEWUSERS, $userfile) or die "cannot open user file $!\n";
open LOGFILE, '>>.\out.log' or die "cannot open log file $!\n";
TEMPLATE: while($line = <NEWUSERS>) {
    ($template, @template_config) = split(/\s*[,;\n]\s*/,$line);
    chomp($template);
    if($current_users{$template}) {
```

The last line of the above block checks the existence of the template in the $current_users hash variable. If the account exists in the user database, then we can proceed to gather that user's information from the user database using the *Win32::UserAdmin::UserGetAttributes* method. In this case, because we will be setting information such as the profile path for the new user, we need to use the largest user structure available, which is indicated by the third argument as 3. This user information is loaded into the hash reference \%temp_info. Finally, should the template user read in from the file not exist in the user database, then the script exits. One point to notice: The template index number (which is used in the generation of usernames later on) is stored in the user comments field as Index: *n*.

```
Win32::UserAdmin::UserGetAttributes('', $template, 3, \%temp_info)
        || die "Unable to get template information\n";

$_ = $temp_info{'USER_USR_COMMENT'};
(/Index:\s+(\d+)/);
$template_index = $1;
} else {
    die "Template User $template does not Exist";
}
```

Once the script has collected the information we need from the template user, it can now read in each line of the new user's file, which holds the full name and comments for an individual. The script first checks each line to see whether it is blank. If so, it assumes it has reached the end of that block of users and returns to the previous block to gather the information for the next template account. The last two lines in this block remove any trailing newline character and split the full name and comment sections into their relevant variables.

```
while($line = <NEWUSERS>) {
    foreach $key(keys %temp_info) {
        $new_user{$key} = $temp_info{$key};
    }
    next TEMPLATE if $line eq "\n";
    chop($line);
    ($fullname, $comment) = split(/\s*[,;]\s*/,$line);
```

Once we have the full name of the user and the template group to which he or she belongs, we can begin to generate the unique username. A temporary name is generated using the first letter from each name in the $fullname variable and the index number for the template being used to generate the new account. Then, a suffix number is appended to the temporary name and checked against the list of current users generated at the beginning of the script. If the new name matches with a key already in existence, the suffix index is incremented by one, and the current user list checked again. This process is repeated until a unique username is found. Because this script increments until it finds a unique name, it always generates a new account, even if the full name and template index match exactly.[*]

```
$new_user{'USER_FULL_NAME'} = $fullname;
$new_user{'USER_COMMENT'} = $comment;

@names = split(/\s+/,$fullname);
$username = ""; $initials = "";
foreach (@names) {
    /(\w)./;
    $initials .= "\L$1";
}
$tempname = $initials . $template_index;
$index = 1;
while($current_users{($username = $tempname . $index++)}){}
$new_user{'USER_NAME'} = $username;
```

The generation of a password for each user is a relatively simple affair. Using the character array created at the beginning of the script, eight random numbers are generated between 0 and the length of the array. These values are then indexed into the array to access one character in the password. This routine ensures that each user has a unique password and that the passwords cannot be guessed from the username.

```
$password = "";
for($num = 0; $num < 8; $num++) {
    $password .= $passchar[rand($char_index)];
}
$new_user{'USER_PASSWORD'} = $password;
```

One important element to creating each user involves altering the home directory, profile, and script names should any of these elements be based on the username itself. The following block in the script takes each of these paths, looks for an occurrence of the template username in them, and then replaces it with the username of the account being created. This code replaces only one occurrence of the template username, so it would need to be altered if you use the username more than once. If you use a directory scheme where the user's home directory is in a group subdirectory off the users directory (i.e., \users\sales\username), make sure that the template username is not the same as the main group to which an individual belongs; otherwise, the script might alter the wrong name. If the template username is the last element in any path (after any possible matching group name), then the greedy nature of Perl's string matching replaces the last

---

[*]This can be considered a feature or a bug, take your pick.

template username occurring in the string. In the end it is better to make sure the template username is different from any Windows NT group name to which it might be related. Also, remember that share names are promoted to the root level when browsing,. This means we must get the absolute path information from the template user share using the *Win32::UserAdmin::NetShareGetInfo* method. Using the path information this passes back, the absolute directory can be created, as well as the proper shares.

```
$_ = $temp_info{'USER_PROFILE'};
s/(.*)$template(.*)/$1$username$2/;
$new_user{'USER_PROFILE'} = $_;
`mkdir $new_user{'USER_PROFILE'}`;

$_ = $temp_info{'USER_SCRIPT_PATH'};
s/(.*)$template(.*)/$1$username$2/;
$new_user{'USER_SCRIPT_PATH'} = $_;

# we need to make the home directory and share it
# first, get server and share name from template user
$_ = $temp_info{'USER_HOME_DIR'};
/(\\\\.*)\\(.*)/;
$home_server = $1;
$template_share = $2;
Win32::UserAdmin::NetShareGetInfo($home_server,
                                  \$template_share, %share_info);

foreach $key(keys %share_info) {
    print $share_info{$key},"\n" if $verbose;
}

$_ = $share_info{'SHARE_PATH'};
s/(.*)$template(.*)/$1$username$2/;
$homedir_absolute_path = $_;

$_ = $temp_info{'USER_HOME_DIR'};
s/(.*)$template(.*)/$1$username$2/;
$new_user{'USER_HOME_DIR'} = $_;
$netname = $username.$2;


print "home dir path: $homedir_absolute_path\n" if $verbose;
`mkdir $homedir_absolute_path`;
`net share $netname=$homedir_absolute_path`;
```

Now we can finally start adding the user. The next few lines print out the user information being created if the script is in verbose mode, then create the user using the user information hash altered from the template user.

```
foreach $key(keys %temp_info) {
    print "$key:\t\t$temp_info{$key}\t\t$new_user{$key}\n"
        if $verbose;
}
```

```
if(Win32::UserAdmin::UserCreate('', 3, \%new_user)
   || die "user creation failed") {
```

Once the user has been created, additional chores still need to be done. We need to set the permissions on the home directory using the *Win32::FileSecurity* module. The script then adds the user to all the groups of which the template user is a member. Finally, the username is added to the `%current_users` hash variable, and the full name, username, and password are passed to the logfile. The script continues by returning to the top of the block and reading another user from the input file.

```
$dir_sec = Win32::FileSecurity::MakeMask(qw(FULL
                                            GENERIC_ALL));
$hash{Administrator} = $dir_sec;
$hash{$username} = $dir_sec;
Win32::FileSecurity::Set($homedir_absolute_path, \%hash);

Win32::UserAdmin::UserGetGroups('', $new_user{"USER_NAME"},
                                \@groups);
foreach $group(@groups) {
Win32::UserAdmin::GroupAddUsers('', $group,
  $new_user{"USER_NAME"});
}

$current_users{$new_user{"USER_NAME"}} = " ";
print LOGFILE $new_user{"USER_FULL_NAME"}, ", ",
  $new_user{"USER_NAME"}, ", ",
  $new_user{"USER_PASSWORD"}, "\n";
} else {
    print LOGFILE "Unable to create user ",
      $new_user{"USER_NAME"}, " for ",
      $new_user{"USER_FULL_NAME"}, "\n";
    }
  }
}

close NEWUSERS;
close LOGFILE;
```

Ultimately, the security issues involved with creating hundreds of users at a time can be quite enormous. More than likely, each user needs a letter with his or her username and initial password printed out and sent, and some accounts will never be used at all. For these reasons, if at all possible, once you have created bulk accounts, it is a good idea to leave them disabled. The account can be enabled once you either have handed the username and password information to the new users in person or get a call from them after they have received their account information through the mail. This approach reduces the chance that enabled, but unused, accounts could lie dormant for someone to hijack.

In addition to controlling the enabling of accounts, it is also a good idea to track when the accounts were last active and disable them after a certain amount of time if there has been no user activity. We will discuss these and other maintenance issues in the next chapter.

Deciding on a User Creation Method

Ultimately, you need to decide on which method you wish to use for creating users on your system. This, of course, is highly dependent on your situation, and no one method is guaranteed to provide the fastest way of getting things done every time. As far as flexibility goes, using the UMD always provides you with the most options for setting up users; if there are only a few users, copying an existing template user and updating the relevant fields is the fastest way to go. If the number of users you are adding runs into double digits, you need to employ one of the later methods. If you do not need the complexity of a customized script, then by all means use the *addusers* utility. Later on, when we discuss deleting users, this utility could come in useful. If you haven't purchased the Resource Kit or if you have specific requirements for user creation (such as username generation), you will find using your own scripts for this kind of activity very useful because they provide the ultimate flexibility and ease (not necessarily *while* you write the scripts).

Checking File Security

As we will see in later chapters, keeping track of user activities can be a full-time job. With limited resources and the seemingly innate need for users to mess about with a system, making sure that everything is as it should be can sometimes seem like finding a needle in a haystack when you aren't sure if the needle is even there. For example, how could you find all the files and directories to which a user had access? The user's access is, of course, localized in the ACL for every file and directory; checking this means scanning every file and record, obviously not something to be done by hand.

Keeping track of user access to files includes three elements:

- You should define all the file permissions on your servers before adding users and give permissions only to groups so that any activity in the ACL under an individual username can easily be spotted.

- You should audit changes to permissions for all important files, as well as any changes to group membership. Later on, we will show you how to set up a system to watch for events and provide warnings to an administrator when events such as file access modifications do occur.

- Finally, when you do think that someone has done something suspicious, you need a way to find out what permissions they have to files on the system. The following script is used just for that.

There are several steps to finding the permissions that a user has in a directory tree:

1. Collect all groups a user is in; if a group has permission to access a file, then the user inherits that permission.

2. Because global groups can be included in local groups, and because this membership could confer file access, list all local groups a user is a member of *through* a global group.

3. Compare file ACLs with the groups to which a user has membership.

Example 4-3. Collecting User Permissions for a Directory Tree

```
# this will scan a disk/directory, and look for all of the files to which a user
# has access in that tree. It finishes by dumping the information into a file
# called out.log

use Win32::UserAdmin;
use Win32::FileSecurity;

# The GetUserGroups function takes  a username and returns all of the
# local and global groups to which that user belongs.

sub GetUserGroups {
    # move the first two arguments into their respective variables
    my $server = shift @_;
    my $username = shift @_;

    # get the local and global groups for the user
    Win32::UserAdmin::UserGetLocalGroups($server, $username, \@localgroups);
    Win32::UserAdmin::UserGetGroups($server, $username, \@globalgroups);

    # assign the local and global groups to a list, which is
    # used as the return from the function call
    @groups = (@globalgroups, @localgroups);
}

# The RecurseDir function is where all the work is done. It takes a
# directory and hash of user and group names, recurses down through
# the directory, checking for the existence of any of the $usergroups
# entries in a file's ACL. If the file has an entry, it is added to the
# %list hash, which is returned at the end.

sub RecurseDir {

    # grab the directory and username arguments
    my ($dir,$usergroups) = @_;
    my ($file,$fullname);
```

Example 4-3. Collecting User Permissions for a Directory Tree (continued)

```perl
my %list = ();

# open the directory, and read all of the files in it
# into the @files list
opendir (DIR, "$dir");
my @files = readdir DIR;
closedir DIR;

# go through each file in the directory
foreach $file (@files) {

    # don't act on . and ..
    next if ($file eq '.' || $file eq '..');

    # generate the full path name
    $fullname = "$dir/$file";

    if (-d $fullname) { # if the file is a directory

        # get the file security attributes for the directory
        Win32::FileSecurity::Get($fullname, \%ACL);

        # go through each of the
        foreach $ACE(keys %ACL) {
            # check to see if the username, or one of the groups
            # the user belongs to is in the ACL (also "Everyone")
            if(exists $usergroups{$ACE} or $ACE eq "Everyone") {
                # get the rights
                Win32::FileSecurity::EnumerateRights($ACL{$ACE},
                    \@rights);

                # add the rights to the output list
                $list{$fullname} = join("\t", @rights);

                # since this is a directory, recurse down through it
                my %list2 = &RecurseDir($fullname,$usergroups);

                # add the lists returned from the recursive calls
                # to the output list
                foreach $key(keys %list2) {
                    $list{$key} = $list2{$key};
                }
            }
        }
    } elsif (-f $fullname) { # otherwise, if file is only a file
        # get security attributes for file
        Win32::FileSecurity::Get($fullname, \%ACL);

        # check each ACE for match with user's groups
        foreach $ACE(keys %ACL) {
            if(exists $usergroups{$ACE} or $ACE eq "Everyone") {
                # when there is a match, place the rights onto
```

Example 4-3. Collecting User Permissions for a Directory Tree (continued)

```
                    # the output list
                    Win32::FileSecurity::EnumerateRights($ACL{$ACE},
                        \@rights);
                    $list{$fullname} = join("\t", @rights);
                }
            }
        }
    }
    return( %list);
}

# get username from command line

$user = $ARGV[0];
print "Finding ACL entries for $user in $ARGV[1]\n";
Win32::UserAdmin::GetDomainController('','',$server);

# first, we need to find out all the groups to which the user belongs
# and put them in a hash table. We also place the username in the table

@usergroups = GetUserGroups($server, $user);
foreach $usergroup(@usergroups) {
    $usergroups{$usergroup} = " ";
}
$usergroups{$user} = " ";

# finally, we open an output file and set the &RecurseDir function
# running, outputting the results into the out.log file.

open(OUT, ">out.log") or die "Cannot open output";
%files = RecurseDir($ARGV[1],\@usergroups);
foreach $file(keys %files) {
    print OUT $file,"\t",$files{$file},"\n";
}
```

Removing Users

Removing users is something many administrators would rather put off till tomorrow, as it can be a painful exercise in spelunking the file system to remove all the relevant files and directories associated with an individual. Windows NT does not give you much assistance with this process, supplying only the delete user function from the UMD.

Removing a User with the UMD

To remove users with the UMD, highlight a user or users from the window showing a list of all users, then select from the main menu the option **Users**. From the drop-down menu select **Delete** (press the DELETE key for a shortcut). NT reminds you that once the user is removed you cannot simply recreate the account with the same username and expect to regain the original access rights (see Chapter 3, *Windows NT Groups and Security*). Once you have assured the system that you really mean to delete the user, the user is removed and its entry in the user list of the UMD disappears. Unfortunately the UMD does not remove the user's home or profile directories; this task is left for you to tidy up manually.

Removing a User with a Script

Once again, producing and using your own scripts give you the chance to do what the GUI does not; in this case, we use a script to remove the user's home and profile directories, plus the user identifier. The following code makes use of the *UserAdmin* module to both collect user information and delete the users from the Registry. The directory removal is carried out using a simple call to the `rmdir` command. Note that this utility is answerable to the same security requirements as any NT program, so you will need permission to delete the directories. On account creation, the UMD creates an associated home directory. This home directory has only one ACE and that is the user, so if you need to delete that user's home directory you need to add yourself to the ACL with the appropriate permissions. The syntax for calling the *rmusers.pl* script is as follows:

```
remusers [/v] [/q] [/r] filename
```

where *filename* is a text file containing usernames per line, the /v option puts it in verbose mode, the /q disables all output, and the /r option signifies auto-remove mode.

Example 4-4. Removing Users from the System

```
# This function returns the paths for the profile and home directories
use Win32::UserAdmin;

sub GetProfileHome {
    my $server = shift @_;
    my $username = shift @_;
    my $directories = 0;
    Win32::UserAdmin::UserGetAttributes($server, $username, 3,
        \%user_info);
    @paths = ($user_info{'USER_HOME_DIR'}, $user_info{'USER_PROFILE'});
}

# Get the filename and flags from the command line

$filename = shift @ARGV;

$not_quiet = 1;

if($filename eq "/v") {
    $verbose = 1;
    $filename = shift @ARGV;
```

Example 4-4. Removing Users from the System (continued)

```perl
} elsif ($filename eq "/q") {
    $not_quiet = 0;
    $filename = shift @ARGV;
}

if($filename eq "/r") {
    $auto_remove = 1;
    $filename = shift @ARGV;
}

# get the default server name. If you wish to make this script
# multidomain capable, you can add the domain name you wish to work
# on as the second argument. ...('',$domain, (OUT)$server)
Win32::UserAdmin::GetDomainController('','', $server);

# Open the file containing the usernames and load them into an array
open(USERLIST, $filename) || die "unable to load $filename\n";

print "Retrieving usernames from $filename...\n" if $not_quiet;
while ($username = <USERLIST>) {
    chomp($username);
    @users = (@users,$username);
    print "$username\n" if $verbose;
}

# For each user in the array we call the GetProfileHome function and
# remove their profile and home directories. Finally we delete the
# user from the registry.

REMOVE: foreach $username(@users) {
    if (!$auto_remove) {
        print "Remove the user - $username? [Yy/Nn] : ";
        if (<STDIN> =~/^y/i) {
            foreach $path(GetProfileHome($server, $username)) {
                qx(rmdir /s /q $path);
                print "removing $path\n" if $verbose;
            }

            Win32::UserAdmin::UserDelete($server, $username);
            print "removing $username - manual \n" if $verbose;

        } else {
            next REMOVE;
        }
    } else {
        foreach $path(GetProfileHome($server, $username)) {
            qx(rmdir /s /q $path);
            print "removing $path\n" if $verbose;
        }
        Win32::UserAdmin::UserDelete($server, $username);
        print "removing $username - auto \n" if $verbose;
    }
}
```

Expanding the Scope of User Management

So far we have focused on user management within the context of a single domain, but now it is time to give some thought to the idea of user management over multiple domains. The following chapter is aimed at opening up the scope of user management, expanding the role to encompass a range of interdomain scenarios. We must deal with the concept of trust relationships and learn how these relationships can be used to implement suitable domain models.

5

In this chapter:
* *Domain Overview*
* *Domain Models*

Managing
Domain Users

What have domains got to do with it? The answer is simple: users. It is sometimes easy to lose track of the purpose of a network, the reason why you work so hard to build a stable and efficient system. We have to remember that, like many businesses, at the end of the day we are here to supply a service to one set of users or another.

Domains are NT's idea of a management unit. They are the building blocks by which we can create a global community, supply it with resources, and control it through centralized management. To achieve this, we need to understand how these blocks can be put together and how the arrangements bring to the fore differing benefits or impose unnecessary constraints. If you do not match your management requirements to the most efficient domain model, you are making your job as an administrator that much harder. This particularly applies to large organizations where inefficient management techniques are greatly amplified. Domain models are influenced by a mass of parameters such as geographical location, hardware limitations, security issues, and the ever-present political machinations of management. For these reasons, and many more of your own, you should consider your domain model carefully. It will be hard to backtrack if you do not get it right.

Domain Overview

A *domain*, at its most fundamental level, is how NT defines a collection of computers that are controlled through a central server. These computers share both a common security policy and a common user accounts database. A domain is analogous to a club. You have to join to use its facilities, you are obliged to abide by its rules, and you must work with its regulations. Once a user has been granted a domain account, he or she can use any workstation in the domain to log on and can use any resources in that domain to which he or she has been granted access. Each domain is completely independent of any other and has no knowledge of other NT domains unless explicitly informed. For independent NT domains to both recognize and cooperate with each other, a trust relationship must be established.

Trust Relationships

Before we can discuss the various domain models at our disposal, we need to look at the mechanism and method of creating trust relationships. A *trust relationship* is a link between two domains, allowing each domain to recognize the other and, depending on the trust configuration, trust its authentication abilities. This means that a domain user who has been authenticated on one domain (the trusted domain) is accepted by the second domain (the trusting domain) and has access to whatever resources are made available to that domain's users without the need for further authentication. The trust relationship can also create a single management unit, thus enabling administrators from one domain to manage users from another. There are two states in which you can employ a trust relationship: one-way trusts and two-way trusts (see Figure 5-1).

One-way trust relationship

As its name implies, this relationship is one way: One domain trusts another domain's users and allows those users to access its resources. The trust, however, is not reciprocated. This means that a domain (the trusting one) trusts the domain controller of a second domain (the trusted one) to have authenticated all user accounts of those who are to have access to its resources. For example, suppose we have two domains, *Iago* and *Othello*, and we want users in *Othello* to have access to the resources in *Iago*. To do this, we create a one-way trust relationship between them, where *Iago* is the trusting domain and *Othello* is the trusted domain. Users in the *Othello* domain can now have access to the resources in *Iago*. With this relationship, however, the reverse is not possible. If we want to give users in *Iago's* domain access to resources in *Othello,* then we must establish a two-way trust relationship.

Two-way trust relationship

A two-way trust relationship is actually two one-way trusts: a mutual trusting relationship between two domains. Each domain trusts the other, as described previously. Now all global groups and domain accounts can be used by either domain to give access to their respective resources. Not only this, combining the domains to create a single center of user management is now possible. To do this, the Domain Admin group from each domain must be placed in the local *Administration* group of the other trusted domain. Now any administrator from either domain can create, delete, and modify any user on either of the domains.

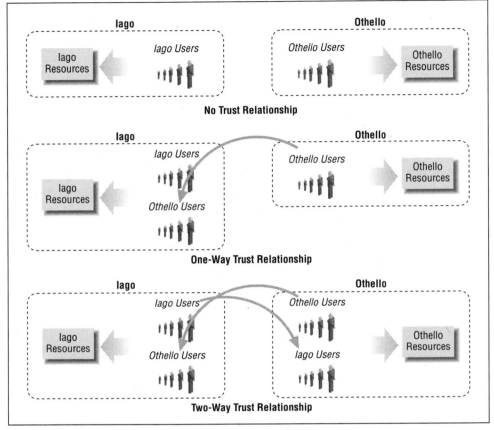

Figure 5-1. Trust relationships

Creating trust relationships

Creating a trust relationship is a two-stage affair and is achieved through an option available from the UMD. Let's assume we want to set up a one-way trust relationship between the domains *Jesus-Accounts* and *Jesus-Library*.* The respective primary domain controllers (PDC's) are called *Cantons* and *Oberon,* and we want *Jesus-Library* to trust *Jesus-Accounts.*

From the main menu of the UMD on *Cantons* we select **Policies→Trust Relationships**. We are presented with two options; we can add a domain either to the

---

*We should mention right now that our examples are real-world reflections of the situation we have here at Jesus College, Cambridge. It is common convention to distinguish colleges from each other on the network by using a prefix to domain names with either the college name or an abbreviation of it. We, therefore, use the name Jesus as a representation of our college; this should not be interpreted as a blasphemous act.

Trusting Domains list or to the **Trusted Domains** list. As we are to be trusted by the *Jesus-Library* domain, we add *Jesus-Library* to the trusting domain list. On adding this domain to the list, we are asked for the name of the trusting domain and an associated password. This is the trust password, used in the next stage of relationship creation.

Having done this, the administrator of the *Jesus-Library* domain must now set *Oberon* up to trust the *Jesus-Accounts* domain. To do this, the administrator adds the domain *Jesus-Accounts* to the trusted domain list. He or she must supply the trusted domain name and the trust password that we created earlier. We have now established a one-way trust relationship. To turn this into a two-way trust relationship, we simply need to carry out the mechanism described here but reverse the domain names.

Creating trust relationships is simple to do, but do not let that fool you. Trust relationships are the key to successful resource sharing and user management within your organization. Initially, nothing much seems to have been achieved, but the following discussion on domain models highlights the importance of such relationships.

Domain Models

To demonstrate how the following domain models operate, we intend to supply a description of their operation and then apply the model to our own environment. To do this, we need to describe the situation at our site.

We have a localized site with all college buildings within reach of our fiber backbone; thus, we have no remote sites to worry about. All accommodation, studies, seminar rooms, and offices are connected back to a central switch through remote hubs. The switch is located in our computer center. We have 1000 users and 150 workstations, give or take one or two. Every year, approximately 200 new students arrive and 200 graduate. The college has natural zones of information that can be divided into *Accounts, Personnel, Student, Library,* and *Computer Administration.* All secretarial staff and college administrative staff have individual workstations; students use either those workstations available in the computer center or those from their own rooms.

We needed to take into account these criteria when selecting a domain model:

- There needs to be some form of centralized management, preferably both user and resource.

- *Accounts, Personnel,* and the *Student* zones need to have additional localized administrators.

- The *Accounts* and *Personnel* zones must be administratively isolated from the *Student* and *Library* zones to secure sensitive resources.

Now that we have the details, let's describe the different models and then apply the criteria to them in turn to see which model best suits our needs.

The Single Domain

The single domain is perhaps, from an administrator's point of view, the preferable model to use. All users and workstations are registered within the domain; it is quick to set up and, for a moderate-sized establishment, easy to manage. There are no complicated trusted relationships, and its global view of the situation offers the following benefits with respect to user management:

Centralized account management
> This is a great benefit in terms of user administration time. All users are contained within a single domain; therefore, direct manipulation of their accounts is quick and straightforward. Centralization can be achieved either through the GUI or through scripts, such as the Perl scripts demonstrated in earlier chapters.

Centralized resource management
> Like all users, workstations are also registered in the single domain. This allows the administrator the freedom to manage all resources associated with both the workstations and servers of the domain, granting or denying users access to them centrally. Again, there is no complication in first having to determine the type of trust relationship you would need to establish with other domains, then having to negotiate which resources are available from those domains and what their current permission state is.

A number of limitations are associated with this model; they are as follows:

Geographical
> Like many other network operating systems, NT does a lot of talking from machine to machine. These perpetual broadcasts cost bandwidth, and a WAN connection can get overloaded with the chatter. You must also consider the load placed on a WAN by the need for user authentication, profile administration, and remote resource access. There is also the overall reliability question. The single-domain model does not allow any degree of autonomy for a remote site.

Institutional structure
> Often it is simply the case that different organizational departments see, or indeed have, no need to share resources with other departments. Users within these departments have tightly defined roles and goals and there is no boundary overlap.* The single-domain model does not allow for this.

---

*Politics also play a major role here; *c'est la vie.*

Account database

According to Microsoft, the recommended size of the Security Access Manager (SAM) database is 40MB. This translates to approximately 26,000 users and associated workstations, so if you accept the 40MB limit as gospel, and if you have more than 26,000 users, then you should consider a different model. The SAM is loaded in RAM, so the larger the SAM, the more memory you need to service it. The size of the SAM also has a bearing on the speed at which the servers boot as well as the time taken for users to log on. Microsoft supplies a formula for calculating SAM sizes:

1. Allow 1KB for every user account.

2. Allow 0.5KB for every workstation/server account.

3. Allow 4KB for every group account.

4. Multiply the total of 1, 2, and 3 by .001024 to calculate the SAM size in MBs.

It is difficult to suggest a practical size for the SAM except to say you should carry out your own tests on the system on which you intend to implement NT. No two cases are the same.

Security

The single-domain model does not physically separate users. All users are contained within the domain and, therefore, if allowed, can access all resources within that domain. Although NT supplies plenty of security features, it is often best to isolate, as much as possible, certain resources such as the accounting database or personnel files.

Applying the single-domain model

We can apply this model to most of our criteria laid out at the beginning of the section in the following ways:

- We need to accommodate the five information zones identified earlier within a single domain. To do this, we use the group capabilities of NT, creating a minimum of five domain groups[*] of the appropriate names and permissions. Users are then sorted into these groups.

- To control access to resources, we need to establish a comprehensive permissions policy and apply it rigorously to all users and groups within the domain. For instance, we can make use of the ability of local groups to contain global groups to fine-tune access to individual resources (see Chapter 3, *Windows NT Groups and Security*, for details) through tight control of its ACL.

---

[*]In reality, you are likely to have many more than this to take into account all the subcategories of the differing information zones, not to mention local groups to handle resource access.

- We need to give some administration rights to the localized help, which includes students, so we establish a number of new administration groups whose scope does not go beyond their administrative boundaries.

What are the overheads and possible problems with doing the above? The large varied collection of groups makes for quite an administrative overhead. You need to keep careful track of the relationships between the global groups, the users, and the local groups, being aware of the permissions you allocate to these groups, their intended role, and the users contained within them. A misplaced user could cost you dearly in the security stakes.

No segregation of specific resources from the user base as a whole occurs. Having a valid account on a domain gives the user a chance to probe your system for any lapse of security. The wider the user base is on a domain, the more likely you are to have security breaches. In sharing a single domain for all users and resources, you are obliged to create a more complex security model. The more complex the model, the more likely you are to miss something. By removing users from the vicinity of sensitive resources—that is, to another domain—you lessen the natural curiosity of the average user and thus the security risk. You also establish another line of defense: the need for a valid account.

Creating management groups that have different scopes yet the same administration capabilities is not possible. NT is not flexible enough to segregate these responsibilities within a domain. Being able to create group administrators, such as those found in Novell, whose management scope is limited to a set of defined groups, would be extremely useful in our situation.

Conclusion. We cannot use this model as it is not nearly secure enough. The close proximity of sensitive resources to possible hostile users and the inability to tightly define the scope of administration groups are the main factors in this decision.

Single Master Domain

This model (Figure 5-2) is designed to alleviate some of the administrative overheads associated with a large single domain, as well as to accommodate departmentalization within an institution. The model proposes that a single domain is split into a one *master* domain and one or more *resource* domains. The creation of these domains allows some administration duties to be devolved to local administrators working within their own domains.

The model shares a lot in common with the single-domain model in that it still offers centralized user administration and, if domain relationships are established correctly, resource management. The real differences lie in the movement of the resources from the central domain and the passing of workstation accounts to the local domain controllers. To achieve this, we need to use the trust relationship

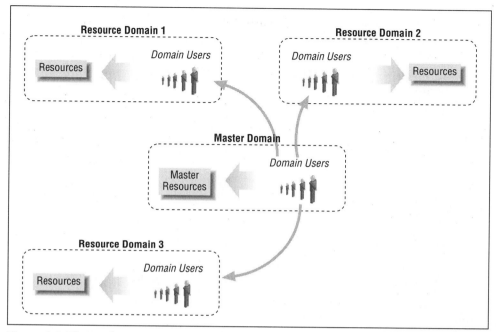

Figure 5-2. The single master-domain model

mechanism and apply it in one direction only. All the resource domains trust the central master domain.

What is a master and resource domain? A *master domain* is the domain that all other domains trust. This domain handles all user authentication and can, if allowed, allocate some or all the resources from itself and all other domains. A *resource domain* is one that contains resources associated with a localized institutional unit. These resources can be shared with not only those users belonging to that unit's groups, but all users within the master domain. It recognizes domain users and global groups through the trust relationship that has been established with the central domain.

The following is a list of the benefits of the single master-domain model:

Centralized user management

All users are administrated from the master domain. Again, it is easy to both create and manage users en masse, without encountering the barriers that are imposed on the administrator when dealing with users located on separate domains.

Localized resources and resource management

A department or institutional unit can have a local resource domain manager whose role is to administer access to the resources. This gives a degree of autonomy to the domain, allowing the administrator to grant or deny access to the resources using global groups and/or domain accounts. It is also possible for the local administrator to grant the central administrator the rights to carry out the allocations on his or her behalf. If this is done for all resource domains, then resource allocation becomes completely centrally managed.

Security

The model allows for the relocation of resources to other domains. Having users and resources in different domains greatly increases the security of the resource: The resources are seen by the master domain as points of presentation only. These are contained shares and do not constitute a whole machine/ domain; thus, breaching the share does not breach the machine. For example, we may present users with a particular view of a database through a shortcut to a database application located on a share. It may be that we have other database information that we do not want them to see, so we have removed the files to another nonshared directory. The users have no way of knowing those files exist, let alone getting their hands on them; the only aspect of the database they see is that exposed by the share.

Reduced SAM

Now that there are a number of localized domains, workstation accounts can be split off from the central SAM and stored in the local one. This, at its maximum, decreases the size of the central SAM by a third and can reduce both server boot time and workstation logon time.

Institutional structure

The model now reflects the organization of an institution, splitting the resources along more natural department or divisional lines.

This model does have limitations, documented as follows:

User base

This model is still likely to be limited by the user base; as with the single-domain model, all domain users must be registered in a central SAM. Again, you should give some thought to RAM requirements and what is considered an acceptable logon time for a user.

Management overhead

Overall management overhead is increased simply by having more domains. Each domain needs individual configuration, administration, and maintenance.

Localized resource management

Microsoft suggests that the single master-domain model offers localized resource management, which it does. It is somewhat inflexible, though, and in order to maintain security, local administrators must use domain accounts only when allocating resources and not global groups. Why? Well, the answer lies in the administrative scope of the local administrator. He or she is limited to the global groups and domain user accounts from the master domain. If the local administrator allows a particular global group to have access to a resource, he or she assumes that the users within this group have been verified by the master domain administrator. Now that a global group has been given permissions to a resource on a local domain, the master domain administrator can arbitrarily place any domain user into the group, giving him or her access to a resource that the local administrator never intended users to have. The only way a local administrator can guarantee that he or she has control over local resource allocation is to explicitly place user domain accounts into either dedicated local groups associated with the resource or the resource's ACL.

Security

The previous point highlights a security problem with the model. This is reflected here, in that it is still not possible to create separate administrative groups to handle differing sets of users. Their scopes cannot be controlled well enough to allow for group administration. Also, with regard to earlier discussions, any users promoted to administrators have access to all global groups and therefore any resources for which these global groups have permissions.

Geographical

Although resource domains supply some autonomy and thus a degree of geographic independence, authentication and the mechanism of profile management still require connection to the master domain. This model needs good connectivity, and WANs can still suffer from the bandwidth problem, as mentioned in the single-domain model discussion.

Applying the single master-domain model

Let's again attempt to apply this model to the criteria laid out at the beginning of this section.

We can split the five college information zones into separate resource domains, *Accounts, Personnel, Library, Student*, and *Administration;* the master domain is *Administration*. We create the one-way trust relationship between the Administration domain and the rest so that all resource domains trust the *Administration* domain to authenticate users. Having done this, we create our global groups to supply units for user management.

The central allocation of resources is now subject to their availability from the resource domains. This is controlled by a local administrator that we place in each of the resource domains. In our example, the sensitive resources associated with

Accounts and *Personnel* need to be partitioned off and access limited. This is now achieved.

Although we now have resource domain administrators, we still need a set of administrators on the master domain that deal with users that belong to each information zone. To do this, we need to give the resource domain managers the ability to manage users on the master domain.

Overhead and problems with this model. The main problem we have with this model is the security aspect. As we make use of student assistance to administer the student part of the network, we need a more rigorous security model in operation. As we cannot separate the management responsibilities of users within the master domain, we leave ourselves open to the possibility of the misuse of the privileges.[*]

The problem of large numbers of groups still persists and, in fact, is more likely to be worse if we accept the use of global groups as a method of resource allocation. We need to divide the users into smaller units to make it easier for resource domain managers to know which users they are managing. The smaller the unit, the tighter the administrator's control on the resource.

Conclusion. If it weren't for NT's inability to grade the privileges of domain administrators, then we could make use of this model.

Multiple Master Domains

The multiple master-domain model (Figure 5-3) is simply a collection of single master-domain units with each master domain establishing a two-way trust relationship with the others. Resource domains are connected as for the single master-domain model; for users in all domains to have possible access to all resources, a one-way trust relationship must be established between each resource domain and each master domain. By creating a full trust relationship between the master domains, administrators from these domains can manage all domain users regardless of the domain in which they are registered. This model is especially good for a large company that has sites located in geographically removed areas.

The strengths of this model are much the same as for the single master-domain plus that it allows for geographically divided sites. Institutions can simply divide themselves up along geographical lines and devolve user and resource management. This reduces WAN traffic as authentication and profile traffic are kept within each individual master domain. If associated resource domains supply most of the resources required by the users located at each master domain, then this type of traffic is also reduced.

---

[*]This is not to say we do not trust such help, but it is simply better not to put any student in a position of such responsibility, for his or her own good and the peace of mind of the College management.

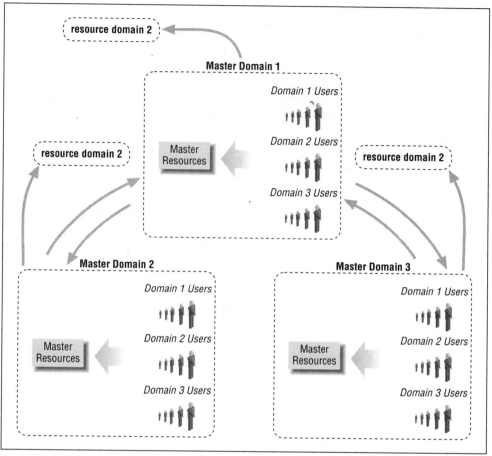

Figure 5-3. The multiple master-domain model

The problems with applying this model to our situation

We could create five master domains to reflect our five information zones, but we do not have the extensive user or resource requirements for which the model is designed. Our site is not geographically divided, so we have no need for a WAN and therefore no need to worry about overloading it. Also, to truly reflect the model we would have to make unnecessary equipment purchases to create contrived resource domains. Our management overheads would also increase for no functional gain, and the security issue we had with the single-domain model still exists. Although there are now five separate master domains, the full trust relationship established between them still allows any administrator to manipulate domain users or global groups within any domain.

Independent Domains with Trust Relationships

As its name indicates, this model is designed to accommodate a collection of independent domains whose connectivity to other domains is formed on an *ad hoc* basis through trust relationships. This is really a catch-all model with no specific rules. If you cannot easily use those predefined models, then you need to sit down and design your own. This is what we have had to do to accommodate all the criteria laid down at the start of this section (Figure 5-4).

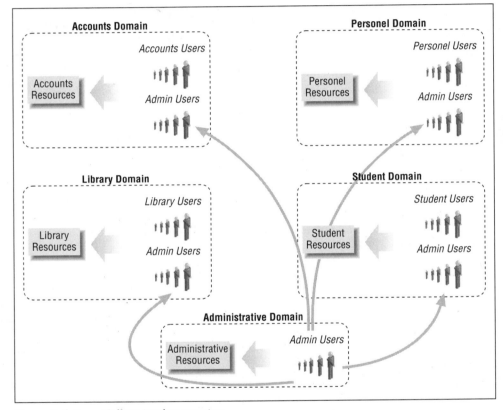

Figure 5-4. Jesus College implementation

The crux of the problem is to segregate the resources belonging to the *Accounts* and *Personnel* information zones, supply those areas with their own administration, and yet keep some form of centralized control. The following lists components of our domain setup:

- Five single domains are created, *Accounts, Library, Personnel, Student,* and *Administration.* Each domain has its own set of users, resources, and administrators.

- The domains *Account, Library, Personnel,* and *Student* all establish a one-way trusted relationship with the domain *Administration.* They all trust *Administration* and have the *Domain Admin* group of *Administration* added to their local administrative group.

- The only registered users on the *Administration* domain are those that need to have full administrative rights for all domains. These people could be termed "Super Administrators."

So what does this configuration actually do for us?

- Splitting the information zones into five individual domains physically separates the resources. Doing this gives us the level of detachment insisted on by the college management. There is no common pool of institution-wide domain users; therefore, the risk of a security breach of any specific domain is reduced. This meets the second of our criteria.

- All domains can now have administrators whose scope is limited to their own domains. As each domain is now, to all intents and purposes, isolated from the others, we can set up a local administrator without fear of his or her having management capabilities on the other domains. This meets the third of our criteria.

- The central trusted domain *Administration* has user management capabilities on all other domains. This is achieved through the *User Manager for Domains.* It allows the administrator to switch domains and presents him or her with a list of users and groups from the newly selected domain. These accounts can be manipulated in the usual way.

- Central administrators can also set up and remove directory shares from all the trusting domains. This can be achieved through the *Server Manager.* Again, it allows an administrator to switch domains and then create, remove or change permissions on any directory shares. You do not have this control over resources such as printers, but then that is the same for all the models.

- Central administrators can create trust relationships dynamically from one trusting domain to another. This can be achieved through the *User Manager for Domains.* Once more, you use it to switch domains and then set up the appropriate level of trust you need between the domains. For instance, we can share the CD drive on a server called *Oberon* in the domain *Jesus-Library* with users in the domain *Jesus-Accounts.* This can be achieved from a workstation in the domain *Jesus-Admin,* as long as the workstation is running UMD. We select the domains *Jesus-Library* and *Jesus-Accounts* in turn, establishing a one-way trust relationship between them. *Oberon* is set to trust the *Jesus-Accounts* PDC called *Cantons.* Having done this, we then run Server Manager, switch to the domain *Jesus-Library,* select *Oberon,* and create a new share of the CD. You can do all this without leaving your desk. The trusting relationship can also be terminated in the reverse manner. This point and the previous two meet the first of our criteria.

Managing Users and Resources Through Trust Relationships

We mentioned a number of administrative tasks you can perform as an administrator of a domain that takes part in a trusted relationship. We would like to reiterate some of those and mention a few more. It is important to spot the administrative tasks that are of importance to you and make sure that you have a way to carry them out in a multidomain environment. Let's run through a number of primary tasks that an administrator would expect to be able to do:

User creation, deletion, and modification

To carry this out you, must be an administrator of a trusted domain and have the global group Domain Admin as a member of the trusting domain's local group Administrator. Having established this, you can now use the UMD to switch domains (as explained earlier) and administer all the users and groups in the trusting domains. Obviously, any domain that trusts another in this way can be managed centrally. Other functions of the UMD can be carried out over domains; they are as follows:

- Audit policies
- User rights
- Trust relationships

For details on audit policies, refer to Chapter 8, *Auditing and Windows NT;* for details on user rights, refer to Chapter 3. Trust relationships are described earlier in this chapter.

Mass user management

The same drawback occurs for multiple-domain user management as it does for a single domain, and that is that the UMD is very limited in its capabilities to deal with mass users. (See Chapter 2, *Creating Users;* Chapter 3, *Windows NT Groups and Security;* and Chapter 4, *Managing Users Through Scripts*). As we hope earlier chapters have shown you, one way to deal with this limitation is to use Perl to create customized scripts. It is possible to implement these scripts across multiple domains, but unfortunately the current Perl modules have a few bugs that need ironing out. The Win32 build of Perl is under constant revision, so you will more than likely find that the current version has fixed many of these problems.

Creating and removing shares

Share management can be done centrally through the administration tool Server Manager. We ought to look at the Server Manager to show you how to go about using its resource management facilities. Launch Server Manager, say from Start Menu→Programs→Administrative Tools (Common), and select the option **Computer** from the Server Manager's main menu. Under this option you will find all the primary functions of the tool. By selecting **Shared Directories** you will see which shares are available from the current domain. Here you can also create new shares, remove redundant ones, and change properties of those that already exist. If you have a printer configured for sharing, Server Manager will also show it as a directory share and you can manipulate it in the same way that you can manipulate any standard directory share. Unlike directories, though, if a printer is not already configured for sharing by the local administrator, then you cannot create the share for it. To see resources on another domain over which you have administrative rights, choose **Select Domains** from the main menu option **Computers**. You will be presented with a list of domains that trust your domain; simply select the one you are interested in and you will see all the relevant information for that domain.

Under the Hood

Now that you have seen how to manage users at an individual level, en masse, and over a number of domain models, it is time to look at some of the under-the-hood mechanics that make up a user. By "under-the-hood" we mean the Registry and, in specific, those parts of it that represent the user and his or her environment. The following chapter charts a passage through the Registry, introducing you to many of its concepts and highlighting those that have specific relevance to users and their management. We will also extend the use of command-line utilities in our Perl scripts and look at the Win32 Registry and Perl internals that allow an administrator to hack the raw iron of NT.

6

In this chapter:
- *The Registry*
- *The Registry Editor*
- *The Registry and Perl*
- *Getting a Grip*

NT Internals and Managing Users

In discussing user administration issues so far, we have focused primarily on the tools available either within Windows NT or as freeware. Understanding these tools is an important element of an administrator's repertoire; however, there are times when using tools is not enough. Understanding the underlying system is imperative to getting the job done and automating mundane tasks. Within Windows NT, essentially two areas are important for understanding users within the operating system. These two areas are the Windows NT Registry and the Win32 Application Programming Interface (API).

The Registry in Windows NT is the central database for all system settings and holds information about hardware, software, and (most importantly for us) users. Almost all modifications to a Windows NT system filter down to being a modification of the Registry. Understanding the Registry, what information is stored in it, and how it can be used and modified is important to understanding how the graphical user tools work and how you can go beyond these with your own customized tools.

Of course, to use any of this information about the Registry we are required to use the Perl versions of the Win32 application programming interface. The previous chapter discussed the Win32 version of Perl and some of the Win32 functions that use the native application programming interface for Windows. This chapter focuses on the organization of the Registry and where you are likely to find the configuration information you seek. Additionally, the Registry functions in Perl are discussed, as well as scripts that can be used to interact with the Registry from the command line.

The Registry

Whereas almost all the settings for a UNIX machine are stored in text files scattered throughout the system, Windows NT puts its settings within a database known as the Registry. And, just as all the UNIX configuration files make sense once you get to know them, understanding and using the Registry are just as simple, once you understand how it works.

Registry Structure

The Registry is organized in a tree structure much like the directory/file organization of a hard disk. Instead of directories, the Registry has *keys*, and instead of files, it has *values*. Figure 6-1 shows an overview of the Windows NT Registry and points out where keys and values occur.[*]

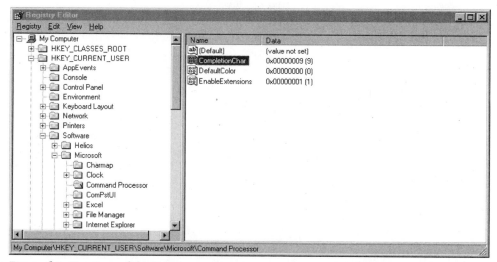

Figure 6-1. Structure of the Registry

Keys are the referential information within the Registry used to group information into related areas. For example, under the root key HKEY_LOCAL_MACHINE, there are five keys: HARDWARE, SAM, SECURITY, SOFTWARE, and SYSTEM. Each of these keys groups values and additional keys under it into specific areas. Just like directories, a key can hold both values and more keys, or a key can exist without holding any values or additional keys at all.

---

[*]For those used to the UNIX tab-completion character, notice the setting of the value CompletionChar to 0x00000009, which sets the tab character to the same function on the command line.

Even though the presence of a key can convey information, it cannot hold any more information than its name. Any additional information must be stored in a value. Values in the Registry hold information under a name and are designated to contain specific data types. Table 6-1 presents the different types of Registry values available.

Table 6-1. Registry Value Types

Value Type	Description
REG_BINARY	Unlimited binary information as a stream of numbers
REG_DWORD	A 32-bit number
REG_DWORD_LITTLE_ENDIAN	The same as REG_DWORD, but the most significant byte is in the high-order word (this is the format used, for example, on Intel processors)
REG_DWORD_BIG_ENDIAN	The same as REG_DWORD, but the most significant byte is in the low-order word [a]
REG_SZ	A null-terminated string
REG_RESOURCE_LIST	Information for Windows NT device drivers
REG_MULTI_SZ	A list of null-terminated strings with two null characters as the list terminator
REG_NONE	No defined value type
REG_LINK	A Unicode symbolic link
REG_EXPAND_SZ	A string with unexpanded environment variables like *%USERNAME%* to be filled in when the value is used

[a] All processors on which NT runs are either little endian (such as x86) or switchable between little and big endian (Alpha and PowerPC), so that NT always runs in the little endian mode. If for some reason you need to support big endian encoding (for some proprietary hardware drivers, for example) you can use this registry value flag.

Values can be any of the above types, but the tools provided with NT do not provide quite this much flexibility. If you are editing Registry values through *regedt32,* the registry editing tool supplied with NT, only the following subset is available: REG_BINARY, REG_DWORD, REG_EXPAND_SZ, REG_MULTI_SZ, and REG_SZ.

Hives of the Registry

The Registry in Windows NT is an amalgamation of information derived from a number of permanently stored files as well as data extracted from the system at boot time. These permanent files are called *hives* and contain data that does not require checking at startup. When an NT workstation is powered up, it creates a section of the Registry, the hardware section, that contains information that NT has put together by parsing the system. This happens every time the machine is booted and enables NT to pick up any configuration changes made to the system. User information, on the other hand, does not need to be verified at boot time as it is not required at this point, and it contains information that should not have changed since it was last saved.

The hives of the Registry are created from their namesake hive files that are stored in the directory *%systemroot%\System32\Config*. The exception to this is the hive file concerned with individual user configuration, *Ntuser.dat*, and its associated log file, *Ntuser.dat.log*, which are stored in the user's profile directory. More on this hive later.

Hives must be attached to the Registry database directly below a root key. A root key is a predefined handle giving an access point into the database. To discuss user-related areas of the Registry, we must step through the Registry hives, describing both their purpose and their user-associated content. Before doing this, we should note what root keys are available and what is their overall purpose. Their purpose dictates which hives are stored below them.

Root keys

Five Registry root keys are described here.

HKEY_LOCAL_MACHINE

> The details of how the local machine is to be configured at boot time are stored here, and the prime subkey is HARDWARE. HKEY_LOCAL_MACHINE also contains details on security, software configuration, and operating system behavior such as services and device drivers loaded at boot time. This key is a true root key containing information that is reflected by other root keys.

HKEY_CLASSES_ROOT

> The prime purpose of this key is to give backward compatibility to the much cruder Windows 3.1 registration database. It also handles information about file associations and data associated with COM objects (OLE). This key is actually mapped from HKEY_LOCAL_MACHINE\Software\Classes.

HKEY_CURRENT_CONFIG

> Changes made to the standard hardware configuration are stored here. This allows a user to create a number of hardware profiles, based on the original. Any of these profiles can be chosen at boot time. This information is a reflection of the contents of the key HKEY_LOCAL_MACHINE\System\CurrentControlSet\HardwareProfiles\Current.

HKEY_USERS

> This root key contains details of the users logged on to the local system. In reality, this contains details of only two users, the default one and the user actually logged on locally. This a true root key, supplying information reflected by HKEY_CURRENT_USER.

HKEY_CURRENT_USER

This contains the user profile of the currently logged-on user and is arguably the most important key with respect to the individual user.

Now that we have read a résumé of the root keys, we can take a more detailed look at the hives loaded below them.

Hives

The root keys are supported by hive files, as described here.

HKEY_LOCAL_MACHINE\SAM

The first point to note is the name and extensions of the hive file and other support files. The file *SAM*, with no extension, is the hive file, or if you prefer, a copy of the loaded hive, which amounts to the same thing. *SAM.log* is a log file of all changes made to the keys and values of the hive. *SAM.sav* is a copy of the hive at the end of the text mode step of the startup process. On restart, it allows NT to skip the text mode section and rerun only the graphic part.

The SAM[*] (Security Access Manager) hive's purpose is to store all security information concerned with users. This takes the form of details regarding user and group accounts for a local machine, as well as domain security if the local machine is a PDC. This information can be viewed through the User Manager or the User Manager for Domains. The data stored in this hive is in binary format, and it is not advisable to try your hand at hacking this part of the Registry.

HKEY_LOCAL_MACHINE\Security

Like SAM, the Security hive has three files associated with it, *Security, Security.log,* and *Security.sav.* The Security hive holds, as its name suggests, security information for a local machine. This information includes user rights details, password policy, and membership of local groups. Again, this data is stored in binary format and cannot be easily manipulated except through the User Manager or User Manager for Domains.

HKEY_LOCAL_MACHINE\Software

Again, the same extensions and their definitions apply here. This hive has little to do directly with users. It contains mainly information concerned with locally installed software and associations for data files with executables.

HKEY_LOCAL_MACHINE\System

This hive has the same file extensions as SAM, but it also has an additional one, the *.alt* extension. The file *System.alt* contains the Last Known Good

---

[*] Now called the Directory Services Database.

profile. It's essentially a backup of the hive and is used as the new system hive if a fatal error bedevils the original.

The System hive contains system information that NT does not have to generate at boot time. This hive contains a full complement of parameters required by services and devices to help bring up the system successfully.

HKEY_CURRENT_CONFIG

This is simply a reflection of the subkey `HKEY_LOCAL_MACHINE\System\ CurrentControlSet\HardwareProfiles\Current`. It does not have its own hive, but it uses the System one. It is still considered a Registry hive as it attached to the root of the Registry and is created from static data. Why have it? It seems that this hive was added to NT 4.0 to offer compatibility to Windows 95 programs that make use of the equivalent hive found in the 95 Registry. Again, no specific user data is found in this hive.

HKEY_USERS\.DEFAULT

This hive represents a default user and is used by NT when no users are logged in. It contains all the same keys, subkeys, and values that you find in the user-specific hive, *Ntuser.dat*. The contents of the hive can be edited to customize the general desktop environment presented to users at login.

HKEY_CURRENT_USER

Only two extensions apply to this hive, and they are *.dat* and *.dat.log*. The file *Ntuser.dat* is the hive file that contains registry settings for an individual user, and it is stored in the profile directory of each user. The additional file, *Ntuser.dat.log*, performs the same role as the other *.log* files, that is, to document any changes made to the hive. Because this hive contains so much user-specific information, it is worth a brief description of the roles of the primary subkeys.

- *AppEvents*. Here application and system events are defined. The definitions appear under the EventLabel subkey and simply supply referential information about the events. Sound schemes, for instance, appear under the subkey */Schemes* and are sets of sounds associated with a series of user actions. The key

  ```
  HKEY_CURRENT_USER\AppEvents\Schemes\Apps\.Default\
  SystemStart\.Current
  ```

  has the following value:

  ```
  <no name> REG_SZ: Windows NT Logon Sound.wav
  ```

  This is the short bit of sound you hear when you log on, and it can be easily changed to suit your temperament.

- *Console*. There are no subkeys below this key, only values. The values define the appearance and operation of the console, which includes the

NT command prompt. Typical settings are font type, window size and position, and colors. For instance, the value

```
InsertMode: REG_DWORD: 0x1
```

sets the console default to be in insert mode for line editing. Changing the value to 0 changes the edit mode to overwrite. Changing these settings is most easily done through the GUI application, Console, supplied by the control panel.

- *Control Panel.* This contains a range of subkeys that are configurable through the control panel. If you study the subkeys you will see that they mostly hold information concerned with the appearance of and access to the desktop. For instance, they contain color schemes, screen saver options, sounds, mouse details, desktop settings, and more. One such value, a trivial one but always the first to be changed, is the wallpaper setting. The key

```
HKEY_CURRENT_USER\Control Panel\Desktop
```

holds the values associated with the desktop including the wallpaper one. The following value is one of our current built-in favorites:

```
Wallpaper: REG_SZ: C:\WINNT\Coffee Bean.bmp
```

Again, most of the time it is easier to modify these settings from the control panel GUI applications. If you have loaded up a user's hive in the Registry Editor, then you can make changes to the loaded database directly through the editor. The control panel applications work only on the data held in **HKEY_CURRENT_USER**.

- *Environment.* The values under this key correspond to an individual's environment variables, with the variables *Tmp* and *Temp* automatically set up for each user. These values can be modified and new ones created through the control panel application, System. It is worth noting that you can change both user environment and system variables through the control panel. System variables are not mapped to this key; they reside under a subkey of **HKEY_LOCAL_MACHINE**:

```
HKEY_LOCAL_MACHINE\System\CurrentControlSet\
Control\Session Manager\Environment
```

These variables are used only by the command prompt and non-NT-based applications.

- *Keyboard Layout.* This key contains information concerning the current user's keyboard layout. The keyboard layouts are defined by the key

```
HKEY_LOCAL_MACHINE\System\CurrentControlSet\
Control\KeyBoard Layouts
```

For instance, the value entry for the keyboard used by one of the machines to write this book is 00000809, which means absolutely nothing until you look it up under the `HKEY_LOCAL_MACHINE` key, where you find it's the UK keyboard layout. Of course, it would have been easier to look this up using the control panel application keyboard, but well . . .

- *Network.* Microsoft documentation suggests that this key is no longer used, but you will find values stored under it. It seems it was used by NT 3.51 to hold persistent connection information that has now been moved to

  ```
  HKEY_CURRENT_USER\Software\Microsoft\WindowsNT\
  CurrentVersion\Network\Persistent Connections
  ```

  The data stored under the Network key gives information about each of the connections in use such as the type of connection, who the provider is (NT, Novell, etc.), the provider type, the username required to make the connection, and the path of the connection. It seems to be a supplement to the Persistent Connections key.

- *Printers.* The subkeys here hold basic information concerning the types of printer to which the user has a connection, which includes details such as the printer description, the name of the machine to which the printer is attached, and the spool library in use.

- *Software.* Subkeys here reflect the installed software to which the user has access. These subkeys contain software configuration information directly related to the current user. The structure of the key is based on the structure of `HKEY_LOCAL_MACHINE\Software` but is not a pointer to it.

- *UNICODE Program Groups.* This is not used at all by Windows NT 4.0.

- *Windows 3.1 Migration Status.* This subkey is also a product of an upgrade, but this time from Windows 3.1 to NT 4.0. If you have upgraded, the subkeys contain information on the success of the upgrade in converting program groups and *.ini* files to NT 4.0 format.

The Registry Editor

Windows NT 4.0 provides two tools for graphically editing the Registry: *regedit* and *regedt32.* If you have upgraded to NT 4.0 from 3.51 or earlier, you will already be familiar with *regedt32* because this program was the original program for editing the Registry provided with Windows NT. When Windows 95 was released, it came with a slightly more user-friendly Registry interface, called *regedit,* that used the newer tree controls for viewing and editing the Registry. This program is missing many of the more advanced features of the older *regedt32* program, however, and is almost entirely unusable for all but the most basic editing (we assume because users of Windows 95 are not *supposed* to know what to do with a Registry). Instead, if you are willing to forgo an admittedly slicker interface you will find the *regedt32* application a much better tool. This is, in fact, the utility we cover in the next few pages.

WARNING   Before we start on our discussion of Registry editing, we should throw in a word of caution. Any hacking of the Registry should be considered a potentially hazardous action. It is quite possible to disable your machine, cause software to stop working, or damage user information irredeemably. We suggest you back up the Registry before you make any changes, especially when testing your Perl scripts. Backing up the Registry is covered later on in this chapter.

Regedt32 is not installed by default as a shortcut on the Start menu under Windows NT 4.0. You need to run the program by selecting **Start→Run...** and then entering *regedt32* as the file to open. You can use the same command to open the application from the command line. Of course, if you are using it regularly, it is easier to add it to the list of administrative tools under **Start→Programs**. No matter how you decide to start it, *regedt32* opens with five windows, each displaying one of the predefined root keys of the Registry: `HKEY_LOCAL_MACHINE`, `HKEY_CURRENT_CONFIG`, `HKEY_CLASSES_ROOT`, `HKEY_CURRENT_USER`, and `HKEY_USERS`. From here you can carry out several actions, which can be broadly grouped into four areas:

- Save and restore portions of the Registry
- Create, edit, or delete keys and values in the Registry
- Set read/write permissions on keys and values
- Search for entries in the Registry

The first step to working with the Registry is, of course, to decide what Registry you want to work with and open it. By default, *regedt32* opens with the five root keys on the local machine. You are not, however, limited to looking at the Registry on your local machine. You can use the **Registry→Select Computer...** option to bring up a dialog box from which you can select the remote computer to which you wish to connect. When connecting to a remote computer, notice that instead of all five keys, you see only the two absolute root keys: `HKEY_LOCAL_MACHINE` and `HKEY_USERS`. You might soon find that opening several Registries at once can become congested. The application does not allow you to perform many of the traditional windows interface functions (such as drag-and-drop), so you will find that closing any Registries you are not using (**Registry→Close**) will be much cleaner and easier to follow. An additional note of warning: You cannot actually close any of the key windows individually without closing all Registry root windows for a computer. At most, you can minimize individual root windows, which sends them to the bottom of the *regedt32* parent window. If you have scroll bars, these minimized windows might disappear off the bottom and you will need to scroll down to find them. If you need to get back to the local Registry, simply use the **Registry→Open Local** menu option.

Saving and Restoring Portions of the Registry

One of the most important roles of *regedt32* in relation to user management is saving and restoring portions of the Registry. In most day-to-day Registry hacking, the keys and values you need to access have been loaded into the system by default. An individual user's Registry key is not loaded unless he or she is logged on. To edit a non-logged-on user's Registry values, you will need to load their *ntuser.dat* hive into the Registry, make the changes you require, and then save it back to disk.

In dealing with sections of the Registry, there is an important distinction to make: Are you dealing with a hive or a .standard key subtree? If you recall the earlier discussion of Registry fundamentals, you will remember that a *hive* is a subkey directly attached to one of the two principal root keys, HKEY_LOCAL_MACHINE and HKEY_USERS, and includes all subkeys and values under that key. For example, SOFTWARE, SECURITY, and SYSTEM are all hives attached to the HKEY_LOCAL_MACHINE root. Any other subkey not directly attached to one of these two root keys is simply a subtree. Because user profiles are stored in hives and loaded only at logon, to edit a specific user's settings you must be able to load and save portions of the Registry from disk.

When saving portions of the Registry (i.e., a key and all its attendant keys and values) no distinction is made about whether the key is a hive. In this case, you select the key you wish to save, choose (**Registry→Save Key...**), and provide the filename under which to store the key and all associated subkeys and values. This Save method places the Registry subtree into a binary file. If you wish to save the key in a text format, you can use the **Registry→Save Subtree As...** in the same manner as the regular Save option. In this case, the file format will be in a standardized text format, shown in Example 6-1.

Example 6-1. Textual Output of a Subkey from regedt32

```
Key Name:        SOFTWARE\Microsoft
Class Name:      <NO CLASS>
Last Write Time: 2/12/97 - 6:20 PM
Value 0
  Name:          Exchange
```

Example 6-1. Textual Output of a Subkey from regedt32 (continued)

```
    Type:           REG_SZ
    Data:           D:\Program Files\Windows NT\Windows Messaging\exchng32.exe
Value 1
    Name:           MlSet
    Type:           REG_SZ
    Data:           D:\Program Files\Windows NT\Windows Messaging\mlset32.exe

Key Name:           SOFTWARE\Microsoft\Access
Class Name:         <NO CLASS>
Last Write Time:    2/12/97 - 9:25 PM
```

Additionally, you can send textual Registry information straight to a printer using the **Registry→Print Subtree**.

Restoring subtrees saved with the Registry editor can take two forms: restoring a key or loading a hive. Hives are, by their very nature, expected to be loaded and unloaded from/to disk. Because of this, *regedt32* provides two special methods for loading and unloading hives in the Registry.

Registry→Load Hive allows you to load a presaved subtree underneath one of the two absolute root keys: **HKEY_LOCAL_MACHINE** and **HKEY_USERS**. This menu option will be available only if you have one of these two keys selected. When you load a hive, you're asked for the filename as well as the name of the key under which you wish to load the hive. If, however, a hive already exists under the name you've chosen, you will be unable to complete the command. Once you have finished working with the hive, you can issue the **Registry→Unload Hive** command to remove the selected hive from the Registry. Because Registry updates are effected immediately, no Save function is required. Unloading the hive simply removes the key and all subkeys and values.

As mentioned before, one common use for loading hives into the Registry is to edit user profiles. If you recall from earlier discussions, each user's personal Registry entries are stored in a file called *ntuser.dat* that is loaded into the Registry under **HKEY_USERS** when a user logs in and pointed to directly by **HKEY_CURRENT_USER**. Each user's personal hive is stored in the root of his or her profile directory as well as in *%systemroot%\profiles\%username%* when locally cached on the machine a user has logged into. When a user is not logged in, the only way to get to his or her Registry information is to load a copy of his or her *ntuser.dat* file as a hive. For specific jobs, there are more graphical approaches to altering a user profile, such as with the System Profile Editor covered in Chapter 7, *Controlling the User*. For full flexibility, though, editing a user's Registry information directly always provides a more complete set of options.

Creating and Editing Keys or Values in the Registry

Of course, unless you simply use the Registry editor for backup, you will most likely be interested in how to edit settings in the Registry. The **Edit** menu option provides all the functionality for editing the Registry in *regedt32*.

To add a key to the Registry, select **Edit→Add Key** and then type in the name of the key, in addition to the class of the key (typically the class is left blank, even by Microsoft). You can add a key either as information in and of itself or as the location for additional keys and/or values. There are some places you cannot add keys. For example, you will find yourself unable to add a key underneath either **HKEY_USERS** or **HKEY_LOCAL_MACHINE**. These absolute root keys accept only hives, or keys automatically generated at boot time. If for some reason you need to add a key directly to one of these two root keys, you could always create the key/value tree as a subtree somewhere else, save it, and then load it as a hive. Otherwise, you will find that, except for security reasons, you should be able to place a key below any already existing key in the Registry.

Adding a value to a key can be done using the **Edit→Add Value** option, which prompts for the name and type of value you wish to add. The values supported by *regedt32* are **REG_BINARY**, **REG_DWORD**, **REG_EXPAND_SZ**, **REG_MULTI_SZ**, and **REG_SZ**. Once the name and type of the new value are selected, you are prompted to enter the data you wish to hold in the value. For **REG_SZ** and **REG_EXPAND_SZ**, you are given a single line in which to place a string. For **REG_MULTI_SZ** you are provided with a multiline dialog box within which you can place several strings in separate lines. The **REG_BINARY** and **REG_DWORD** work in a similar manner. For **REG_DWORD**, you are provided with a single line in which to place a binary, hex, or decimal number. The **REG_BINARY** editor allows you to enter information in either binary or hex format, providing a multiline entry field with markers for the end of word and line placements. The binary format is typically used for proprietary information you would need a special program to decipher. Unless you are absolutely sure of what you are doing, you should probably not mess around too much with **REG_BINARY** values.

If you need to delete a key for any reason (if, for example, you have just *added* a key incorrectly), you will find the **Edit→Delete** option useful. This menu selection deletes the currently selected key or value after prompting you for confirmation. Unlike hives, keys that do not exist directly below either **HKEY_USERS** or **HKEY_LOCAL_MACHINE** cannot be loaded and unloaded. If you are careful and make sure you save a subtree as previously specified, you should be able to delete and reload a key as if it were a hive anywhere in the Registry hierarchy.

In addition to creating values, the **Edit** menu also has options for editing them. If you have selected a value in the data pane of one of the root key windows, you can select **Edit**, and then one of the following options: **Binary**, **String**, **DWORD**, **Multi String**. These options bring up the relevant editor for the selected value. The edit mode you choose is independent of the value type, and you can look at any value type with any of the editors. Of course, some of the edit modes may not make sense for the data type selected. Make sure that any changes you make are with the most appropriate editor.

Registry Permission

In addition to adding and editing keys and values in the Registry, *regedt32* also allows an administrator (or anyone with sufficient privileges) to set permissions on keys. The security features of the Registry act exactly like those for all other NT objects and can be viewed as a file system, where permissions can be set for directories and subdirectories. There is one significant difference, however: Registry permissions are at the key level only. You cannot set permissions for individual values using *regedt32*. Once you have selected a key in which you are interested, you can choose **Security→Permissions**, which provides you with the standard permissions dialog box for reviewing and adding the permissions of users and groups. If you wish your changes to affect all subkeys of the currently selected key, you can toggle the **Replace Permissions on Existing Subkeys** selection box. Besides either **None** or **Full Access**, you can assign varying degrees of access with the **Special Access** option. The different settings are listed in Table 6-2.

Table 6-2. Access Options for Registry Keys

Option	Resulting Permission
Query Value	Allows the selected user or group to read values in the key
Set Value	Allows the user or group to change value entries for a key
Create Subkey	Allows the user or group to create subkeys beneath the selected key
Enumerate Subkeys	Allows the user or group the right to list all subkeys beneath the currently selected key
Notify	Allows a user or group to set the auditing of notification events related to the key
Create Link	Allows a user or group to create symbolic links and nest subtrees in different keys in the Registry (it is not possible to create links using *regedt32*)
Delete	Allows the user or group to delete a key and all subkeys associated with it
Write DAC	Allows the user or group to change permissions for a key
Write Owner	Allows the user or group to change to ownership of a key
Read Control	Allows the user or group to view information about the security settings on a key

In addition to setting permissions for keys, the **Security→Owner** option allows a user to take ownership of a key or subtree in an identical fashion to that of a directory.

Searching for Entries in the Registry

One of the biggest problems with the Registry is that, although certainly better than environment variables or widely scattered configuration files, it is still a simple way of storing information. It is no smarter than any hierarchical storage scheme, and finding anything usually means knowing where to look first. The Registry is not a database from which you can easily retrieve information. It does not use any query language, but instead relies on each Registry viewer to provide its own built-in search engine. This is regrettably one area where *regedt32* falls behind its successor, *regedit*. *Regedt32* provides only the facility to search by key name (**View→Find Key**). *Regedit,* on the other hand, allows an individual to search not only by key name but also by value name and data contents. If you need to do extensive searching, you would be better off using *regedit* instead of *regedt32*. We hope that Microsoft will merge the functionality of the two in the next incarnation of NT.

The Registry and Perl

As we have seen in earlier chapters, the Win32 version of Perl includes many hooks to the Win32 API function calls. Although not exhaustive, the list of functions available does provide for the creation of tools that interact with many of the low-level system features of NT. One of those low-level features is the Registry. In the next few sections, we detail some of the built-in Registry functions of Perl and how they can be used in conjunction with information we have already shown you about the Registry in previous sections.

Opening Registry Keys

One of the first things you will want to do with Perl and the Registry is read or write keys and values. In fact, aside from a few housekeeping chores, this is all you *can* do with the Registry. To read or write to the Registry, you must first have a handle to an already open key. You might be asking yourself how you get a handle to an open key. Well, Perl provides us with a function to do just that.

Win32::RegOpenKeyEx()

```
Win32::RegOpenKeyEx($hkey, $subkey, $reserved, $sam, $handle)
```

`$hkey` is a handle to an already open key. `$subkey` specifies the subkey underneath the key specified by `$hkey`. `$reserved` is unused by the system and is typically set to &NULL, as defined in the file *NT.ph*. $sam is a combination of security attributes with which you wish to open the key. For example, if you wanted to open the key with permission to read entries, you would use &KEY_READ, or if you wanted full access, you would use &KEY_ALL_ACCESS. Table 6-3 lists all the possible security combinations. If you want a combination of access rights you can link them together using OR.

Table 6-3. Key Access Options

Key Access Options

KEY_READ*	READ_CONTROL	WRITE_DAC
KEY_WRITE*	SYNCRONIZE	STANDARD_RIGHTS_REQUIRED
KEY_EXECUTE*	GENERIC_READ	STANDARD_RIGHTS_WRITE
KEY_ALL_ACCESS*	GENERIC_WRITE	STANDARD_RIGHTS_ALL
GENERIC_EXECUTE	KEY_QUERY_VALUE	STANDARD_RIGHTS_EXECUTE
GENERIC_ALL	KEY_CREATE_SUB_KEY	STANDARD_RIGHTS_READ
KEY_SET_VALUE	DELETE	SPECIFIC_RIGHTS_ALL
KEY_NOTIFY	WRITE_OWNER	ACCESS_SYSTEM_SECURITY
KEY_CREATE_LINK	MAXIMUM_ALLOWED	KEY_ENUMERATE_SUB_KEYS

The first four security access options (marked by asterisks) are combinations of the other atomic security options required to provide the expected functionality from traditional security rights. For example, KEY_WRITE is actually the following combination of access rights:[*]

```
(&STANDARD_RIGHTS_WRITE | &KEY_SET_VALUE | &KEY_CREATE_SUB_KEY) &
(~ &SYNCRONIZE)
```

Of course, if you have been following closely, you will find that we have maneuvered ourselves into a small chicken-and-egg problem. We presented the RegOpenKeyEx() function as a way to get an initial key handle, required to work with the Registry. The first argument we have to provide is an *already* open key! Luckily, NT (and the Perl programmers) has provided us with a couple of keys that are kept open all the time, with handles we can use to bootstrap ourselves into the Registry. These handles are, among others as you might expect,

---

[*]Access masks work by assigning each flag a number whose binary equivalent has a specific meaning. As a contrived example, consider file access, where you might want read, write, and execute access. READ might be decimal 1, which would be 0001 in binary. WRITE might be decimal 2, which would be 0010 in binary, and EXECUTE would be 4 in decimal, or 0100 in binary. Using the OR command, you could string together all the flags (READ | WRITE | EXECUTE), which would produce in binary 0111 or 7 in decimal. Or, if you wanted only read and execute permission (READ | EXECUTE), the resulting number would be binary 0101 or decimal 5. By reading off each bit in the resulting figure, the set of permissions can be determined using a single number.

the root keys that each have their own window in *regedt32*. The list of keys with handles available to use is as follows:

```
HKEY_CLASSES_ROOT
HKEY_CURRENT_USER
HKEY_LOCAL_MACHINE
HKEY_USERS
HKEY_PERFORMANCE_DATA
HKEY_PERFORMANCE_TEXT
HKEY_PERFORMACE_NLSTEXT
```

NOTE   Many of the Win32 constants (those that are typically in all upper-case, such as **HKEY_USERS**) are provided as subroutines in the file *NT.ph,* which must be included in any script with the **require** keyword. To use these functions, an ampersand should be prefixed to the function name (**&HKEY_USERS**).

The argument **$handle** is a return value that holds the handle to the key indicated by combination of the **$hkey** and **$subkey** variables. For example, if you wanted to open the **HKEY_LOCAL_MACHINE\SYSTEM\CurrentControlSet** key, the following Perl code would do that:

```
require "NT.ph";
$hkey = &HKEY_LOCAL_MACHINE;
$subkey = 'SYSTEM\CurrentControlSet';
$sam = $KEY_ALL_ACCESS;
Win32::RegOpenKeyEx($hkey, $subkey, &NULL, $sam, $handle);
```

If the function succeeded, the variable **$handle** would provide the necessary link to the open Registry key needed by the function to read and write from and to the Registry. Once you are finished with a key, just as with a file, you should issue the close command:

```
Win32::RegCloseKey($handle);
```

Reading Registry Keys and Values

Once you have a handle to an open key, you may want to start reading the contents of that key. As with all matters Registry-related, reading keys and values is similar to looking through directories and files. You must treat the keys and values differently.

To see what subkeys are available in the current key, you must use the *Win32::RegEnumKeyEx()* routine. By calling this function repeatedly, you can move through the various subkey entries. The definition for the function is as follows.

Win32::RegEnumKeyEx()

```
Win32::RegEnumKeyEx($hkey,$index,$subkeyname,$reserved,$class,$time);
```

$hkey is the handle to an already open key. This can be one opened with the previously described open function, or it can be one of the predefined keys. $index is a running count of the keys for which you wish to find information. For example, if the key

```
HKEY_LOCAL_MACHINE\SYSTEM\CurrentControlSet
```

had four subkeys:

```
Control
Enum
Hardware Services
Profile
```

Index 0 would point to Control, index 1 to Enum, index 2 to Hardware Services, and index 3 to Profile. When the key is first called, you should start $index at zero (0) and increment one (1) each additional time it is called. $subkeyname is a return value that holds the name of the indexed key. $reserved is set to &NULL. $class returns the class of the key, and $time returns to the last time the key was written.

Of course, subkeys are not the only items that can exist in a key. They can also hold values. There is an additional function for enumerating the values that reside in a key and gathering information about their name, type, and data.

Win32::RegEnumValue()

```
Win32::RegEnumValue($hkey, $index, $valuename, $reserved, $type,
     $value);
```

$hkey, $index, and $reserved are identical to the arguments for enumerating keys. $valuename is a return variable that holds the name of the indexed value on function completion. $type returns the type of value (REG_DWORD, REG_SZ, etc.). $value holds the data stored in the value on completion of the routine. You should not mistake the enumeration function with the query version:

Win32::RegQueryValueEx()

```
Win32::RegQueryValueEx($hkey, $valuename, $reserved, $type, $value);
```

Note that all arguments are identical except for the fact that there is no $index argument. Instead, $valuename is not a return value, but it is used to provide the function with the name of a specific value from which you wish to obtain data. This, of course, depends on your already having the name of the value you wish to search, which is not always possible.

The following Perl example uses the enumeration functions of the Registry to search for a string provided on the command line.

```
grepreg rootkey subkeyname string
```

rootkey can be either HKEY_USERS or HKEY_LOCAL_MACHINE. You can add more keys if you feel these don't offer enough flexibility. subkeyname is the name of the subkey where you wish to begin the search. string is the string you wish to search for within the names of the keys and values in the Registry.

Example 6-2. Searching a Registry for a String

```
# grepreg.pl
# this script is used to search for a key or value name
# within the registry

# here is the typical include for all Win32 perl scripts
require "NT.ph";

# the search that is performed on the registry is recursive.
# the printmatch subroutine is the function called each time
# to begin a search on a key. It takes three arguments:
# the handle to an already open key, the subkey under that
# handle, and the string to look for.
sub printmatch {
    my $rootkey = shift @_;
    my $subkey = shift @_;
    my $string = shift @_;
    my $index = 0;
    my $handle = "";

    Win32::RegOpenKeyEx($rootkey, $subkey, &NULL, &KEY_ALL_ACCESS, $handle)
        or die "unable to open key $subkey";

    # here is where we look through all of the subkeys of our target key
    while(Win32::RegEnumKeyEx($handle, $index++, $keyname, &NULL, $class,
            $time)) {
        if($keyname =~ /.*$string.*/) {
            print "$subkey\\$keyname\n";
        }
        if($subkey eq "") {
        } else {
            $keyname = "\\$keyname";
        }

        # for each subkey, we initiate a new search starting
        # at that point
        &printmatch($rootkey, "$subkey$keyname", $string);

    }
    $index = 0;

    # here is where we look through all the values of our target key
```

Example 6-2. Searching a Registry for a String (continued)

```
    while(Win32::RegEnumValue($handle, $index++, $valuename, &NULL, $type,
            $value)) {
        if($valuename =~ /.*$string.*/) {
            print "whoopie";
            print "$subkey\n";
        }
    }

    Win32::RegCloseKey($handle);
}

$rootname = $ARGV[0];
$subkey = $ARGV[1];
$string = $ARGV[2];

if ($rootname eq 'HKEY_USERS') {
    $rootkey = &HKEY_USERS;
} elsif ($rootname eq 'HKEY_LOCAL_MACHINE') {
    $rootkey = &HKEY_LOCAL_MACHINE;
}

&printmatch($rootkey, $subkey, $string);
```

Creating and Removing Registry Keys and Values

Now that we have seen how to read Registry keys and values, we will look at how to create them. To do this we need to use three more Win32 API functions that so far have not been documented.

Win32::RegCreateKey()

```
    Win32::RegCreateKey($hkey, $subkey, $handle)
```

$hkey is, in this case, a handle for an already opened key, $subkey is the name of the new key, and $handle is the handle for the newly created key. You must have first opened a key using the previously defined function *Win32::RegOpenKeyEx()*. Once you have created the new key, you can start to add values. To do this you need to call *Win32::RegSetValue()*:

Win32::RegSetValueEx()

```
    Win32::RegSetValueEx($hkey, $valuename, $reserved, $type, $data)
```

Once again, $hkey is the handle for an open key, $valuename is a string containing the name of the new value, $reserved is not used and so can be set to &NULL, $type is the type of the new value (refer to Table 8-1 for details), and $data is whatever value you want associated with the value name. Remember to match the data with the value type.

Win32::RegDeleteKey()

```
Win32::RegDeleteKey($hkey, $subkey)
```

`$hkey` is the handle for the open key that contains the key for deletion. `$subkey` is the key you actually want deleted. Incidentally, you can remove a key even if it has values associated with it. These values are simply removed. For instance, if you wish to remove a key called `Registration` with the following path:

```
HKEY_LOCAL_MACHINE\System\Registration
```

you need to open the key `HKEY_LOCAL_MACHINE\System` and then supply the function with the handle for this open key (`$hkey`), along with the name of the key you wish to remove (`$subkey`). In this case, it is `Registration`.

The following Perl script demonstrates the use of the above functions. It allows you to create keys and values, with the value being of any value type. It also allows you to remove keys and their associated values. The syntax for invoking the Perl script is as follows:

```
ADDKV.pl rootkey subkey
```

`rootkey` must be one of the two major root keys (see earlier discussion in this chapter for details), but the `subkey` must be an existing key located below the root key. The following is a list of the switches that are used by *ADDKV.pl*, along with their values. The order is significant:

`/t`

Turns on talk (or verbose) mode

`/d`

Removes the key specified by the */k* option

`/k keyname`

Specifies the new key to create or, if the */d* switch has been used, specifies the key to remove

`/v valuename valuetype value`

Specifies the value name followed by the value type and a value

For instance, to add the key `ACCESS` to the key `HKEY_LOCAL_MACHINE\System` with a value name of `ACCESSTYPE` and a value of 1, use the following syntax:

```
ADDKV.pl HKEY_LOCAL_MACHINE System /k ACCESS /v ACCESSTYPE REG_DWORD 1
```

To remove the same key, use the following:

```
ADDKV.pl HKEY_LOCAL_MACHINE System /d /k ACCESS
```

Example 6-3. Adding Keys and Values to the Registry

```perl
#addkv.pl
#Adds a key and or value to one of the root keys
#Also removes keys and their associated values

require "NT.ph";

#A function for setting the value type
sub GetType {
   my $ptype = shift @_;

   if ($ptype eq "REG_BINARY") {
      $type = &REG_BINARY
   }elsif($ptype eq "REG_DWORD") {
      $type = &REG_DWORD
   }elsif($ptype eq "REG_EXPAND_SZ") {
      $type = &REG_EXPAND_SZ
   }elsif($ptype eq "REG_MULTI_SZ") {
      $type = &REG_MULTI_SZ
   }elsif($ptype eq "REG_SZ") {
      $type = &REG_SZ
   }
}


#Grab the root key, either HKEY_LOCAL_MACHINE or HKEY_USERS, and a
#subsequently defined subkey
$Root = shift @ARGV;
$SubKey = shift @ARGV;

#Die if the user fails to pass the appropriate rootkeys is not specified
if ($Root ne "HKEY_LOCAL_MACHINE" && $Root ne "HKEY_USERS") {
   die "\n+++ No ROOT KEY included or incorrect ROOT KEY supplied +++\n"
}

#Get the next few arguments
$Parameter = shift @ARGV;

if($Parameter eq "/t") {
   $Talk = 0;
   $Parameter = shift @ARGV
} else {
   $Talk = 1
}

if($Parameter eq "/d") {
   $Delete = 1;
   $Parameter = shift @ARGV
} else {
   $Delete = 0
}
```

Example 6-3. Adding Keys and Values to the Registry (continued)

```
#Get key and value
if($Parameter eq "/k") {
    $NewKey = shift @ARGV;
    $KVState = 1;
    if (shift @ARGV eq "/v") {
        $KVState = 2;
        $NewValueName = shift @ARGV;
        $ActualType = shift @ARGV;
        $ValueType = GetType($ActualType);
        $Value = shift @ARGV;
    }
#Get just value
}elsif($Parameter eq "/v") {
    $KVState = 3;
    $NewValueName = shift @ARGV;
    $ActualType = shift @ARGV;
    $ValueType = GetType($ActualType);
    $Value = shift @ARGV;
} else {
    die "\n +++ No KEY or VALUE supplied +++\n";
}

if ($Talk) {
    print "\nRoot Key     - $Root\n";
    print "Subkey       - $SubKey\n";
    print "NewKey       - $NewKey\n";
    print "NewValueName - $NewValueName\n";
    print "ValueType    - $ActualType\n";
    print "Value        - $Value\n";
}

#Having established the argument list, call one or other functions
#to open the key
if ($Root eq "HKEY_LOCAL_MACHINE") {
    Win32::RegOpenKeyEx(&HKEY_LOCAL_MACHINE,$SubKey,&NULL,&KEY_WRITE,$hkey)
        || die "Failed to open the key - ";
} else {
    Win32::RegOpenKeyEx(&HKEY_USERS,$SubKey,&NULL,&KEY_WRITE,$hkey)
        || die "Failed to open the key - ";
}

#Add the new key or remove it if the /d option was used
if($KVState eq 1 || $KVState eq 2) {
    if ($Delete) {
        Win32::RegDeleteKey($hkey, $NewKey);
        die "\n+++ Key $NewKey removed +++\n"
    } else {
        Win32::RegCreateKey($hkey,$NewKey,$KeyHandle)
    }
}
```

Example 6-3. Adding Keys and Values to the Registry (continued)

```
#If you need to create a value under either an existing key
#or one you have just created, do it here. The first call
#uses the newly created key handle, the second call uses the
#one specified by $subkey in the Win32::RegOpenKeyEx function
if($KVState eq 2 ) {
    Win32::RegSetValueEx($KeyHandle,$NewValueName,&NULL,$ValueType,$Value);
} elsif($KVState eq 3) {
    Win32::RegSetValueEx($hkey,$NewValueName,&NULL,$ValueType,$Value)
}

Win32::RegCloseKey($hkey);
Win32::RegCloseKey($KeyHandle);
```

Checking Up on Users Through the Registry

The previous Perl Registry examples have dealt with the general requirements of getting at and editing Registry information. Except for changing your wallpaper settings in a somewhat roundabout way, what else can Registry tools be used for in reference to users?

The flexibility of modern operating systems is a boon when you consider the plethora of tasks to which a typical computer can be put. At the same time, this flexibility imparts certain risks when computers are linked in a network environment. This is certainly true when it comes to new software and the Internet. Keeping a close rein on users in a connected environment is essential to ensure that internal systems are not being compromised or used for illegal activities. Luckily, because programs use the Registry as standard storage for configuration information, it is a simple matter to check how a user's computer is set up.

One useful area for scrutiny is email. A common problem with most email programs is the ease with which spoofing (or forging email addresses) is possible. You may have disgruntled employees wanting to get a boss into trouble or simply to play practical jokes. Either way, mail spoofing can take up a sizable chunk of time. In either case, because the installation programs for most email packages depend on user input for configuration, setting the username and email address to bogus entries is relatively easy.

Of course, this information is stored conveniently in the Registry, where it can be checked and changed, if necessary. Microsoft's Internet Mail, for example, stores user email information in the following key with a value of **Sender eMail**:

```
HKEY_CURRENT_USER\Software\Microsoft\Internet Mail and News\Mail
```

By placing the code in Example 6-4 into a Perl logon script, you can check this value for a correct entry.

Example 6-4. Checking Email Configuration

```
# check for spoofing

require "NT.ph";

# open the Internet Mail key

Win32::RegOpenKeyEx(&HKEY_CURRENT_USER,
                    'Software\Microsoft\Internet Mail and News\Mail',
                    &NULL, &KEY_ALL_ACCESS, $hkey)
    or die "email not installed";

# Check the 'Sender eMail' value
Win32::RegQueryValueEx($hkey, 'Sender eMail', &NULL, $type, $data);
$data =~ /(\w+?)(@.*)/;
if($1 ne $ENV{USERNAME}) {
    print "############## WARNING ##############\n";
    print "you may be in violation of Computing\n";
    print "Center rules in regards to email\n";
    print "spoofing. Your email address is being\n";
    print "set to your username.\n";

    #reset the email address to the company default

    $newemail = ($ENV{USERNAME}.'@domain.com');

    Win32::RegSetValueEx($hkey, 'Sender eMail', &NULL, &REG_SZ, $newemail)
        or die "Unable to change email, please seek an administrator";

}
```

By placing this code in a logon script, each time a user logs onto the system, it checks the current mail configuration to see if the settings have changed. If so, the script restores the standard company email address. This method for checking addresses depends on a copy of the Perl interpreter, in addition to the Win32 Perl libraries, residing on the local machine.

Of course, using such a technique depends on knowing the specific settings for each particular software program. If in doubt about where a program's configuration information might be stored, you can use the *grepreg.pl* script to search for the software title or publisher name in the Registry. Additionally, if the software does not support multiple users (for example, by placing configuration information in a user-independent area of the Registry), you could change configuration information dynamically on login to personalize the software.

At the end of Chapter 7, we discuss further integration of Perl and logon scripts where a Perl logon script checks Registry settings under HKEY_CURRENT_USER and performs drive mappings and script execution based on what it finds. Setting these Registry values for each user is made easier by the System Policy Editor and Template Policy files.

Getting a Grip

We've looked in some detail at user-related items of the Registry and how to access the Registry both through the GUI and from the command line. This chapter also introduced Win32 API functions supplied by Perl for interacting with the Registry. Of course, user information and customization are not stored only in the Registry. User *profiles* also hold data about what a user sees when interacting with Windows. The next chapter takes a look at user profiles, as well as more automatic ways of creating and implementing system policies through the System Policy Editor. This combination of profile and policy management allows a refinement of control over users on the system.

7

Controlling the User

Controlling users is perhaps the one thought that continually pushes its way to the forefront of an already overworked systems administrator's mind. Certainly in an environment similar to ours, where students, by their nature an inquisitive body, often pursue an unhealthy interest in the forbidden, controlling them is paramount. Machines left open, that is, without appropriate restrictions in place, soon become dysfunctional, and this generally leads to two situations: A student finds himself or herself up in front of the authorities for computer misuse, or a number of students suffer the annoyance of having a machine down over the weekend, just when the all-important essay is due, or both. Neither is acceptable.

Control should not only be considered a way to prevent misuse, it should also be considered a tool for creating both a suitable and safe working environment. For instance, users with limited computer goals can often feel intimidated by the sheer variety of options a modern system offers them. One way to allay such fears is to simplify the environment, hiding the complexity of the system behind a well-managed interface.

How does the systems administrator go about creating the appropriate environment for his or her users? NT offers us two methods, the System Policy Editor (SPE) and the User Profile. The SPE gives both direct control of the user, through the management of the user's hive, and indirect control, through the manipulation of the operating system and application software settings. The user profile offers the administrator a way to create a controlled environment, add to it dynamically, and even lock it down so that no changes can be implemented by a user. The combination of these two methods gives the administrator a heady concoction of environment restriction and fine tuning.

The System Policy Editor

The primary function of the SPE is to combine individual policies to produce a single strategy with the aim of restricting the actions of both users and machines alike. These policies are in essence a collection of Registry keys and values that are imposed on the Registry of a target machine when a user logs on. The SPE aims to supply a workable interface, an abstraction of the Registry, that allows for easy manipulation of given components of the Registry. These components are defined in files referred to as *template files.* NT supplies two sets of template files that cover what Microsoft considers the most appropriate Registry keys and values that an administrator would need to control. These template files are named *winnt.adm* and *common.adm,* and they can be found in the directory *%system-root%\winnt\inf.* The *.adm* extension associates this file type with the SPE.

NOTE   To apply a policy, the component, such as the shell or specific appli-
                cation, has the responsibility of checking the Registry and acting on
                the information it finds. This means you can impose a policy on a
                component only if the component knows that it should be checking
                for one.

A Closer Look at a Policy

An individual *policy* can be regarded as an invitation to constrain an item, action, or object. All policies have the option of being enabled or disabled, and they can contain, depending on the type of policy, a number of associated settings. These settings are referred to as *parts,* and a policy can contain many such parts of varying data types, typically Boolean, numeric, or string values. For instance, there is a policy supplied by NT that allows the administrator to force display restrictions. This policy, called *Restrict display,* has a number of parts associated with it. All these parts are Boolean values and are represented by check boxes. Each part enables or disables options available to the user with regard to display settings. One such part hides the screen saver tab, thus stopping the user from changing whatever the current setting happens to be. How you actually achieve this through the SPE is covered later in this chapter. Similar policies are grouped together to form *Categories.* Categories can contain either policies or other categories. Continuing with the discussion of the display settings, Figure 7-1 shows the hierarchy of a section of a system policy. This has a category called *Control Panel* that contains a subcategory called *Display* that contains a policy called *Restrict display* that contains five Boolean parts.

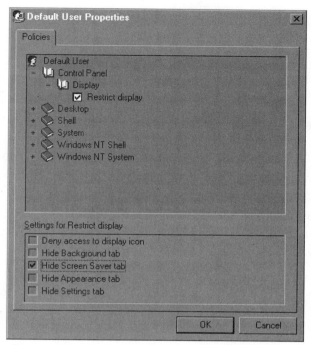

Figure 7-1. Components of the machine-specific policy

Individual categories are grouped together to form either a user- or machine-specific strategy. User-specific strategies act directly on the Registry key HKEY_CURRENT_USER; machine-specific strategies act on HKEY_LOCAL_MACHINE. To all intents and purposes then, the SPE is a Registry editor, albeit an indirect one. To illustrate this, let's look at the connection between the single policy selected in Figure 7-1 and the Registry settings of a participating user.

The policy selected through the SPE is *Restrict display,* and out of the five parts available, the part Hide Screen Saver tab has been enabled. What happens in the Registry? In this case, NT adds a new key and associated value to the Registry, one that it knows to look for when executing the policy. The added value is located under the new key System in the following section of the Registry:

```
HKEY_CURRENT_USER\Software\Microsoft\Windows\CurrentVersion\System
```

The new value name is **NoDispScrSavPage** with a value of 0x1 of type REG_DWORD. There are two states to this Registry value. Either it is set to a value 0x1, in which case the tab element of the display property is not shown, or it is set to a value of 0x0, in which case the tab element is shown.[*]

---

[*]Initially the value does not exist at all. In this case, the tab element is shown.

NOTE	Any policy put in place will continue to be effective until it is specifically revoked. Simply removing the system policy from the Primary Domain Controller has no effect as the local Registries have already been amended. You must explicitly change the system policy to undo the restrictions.

The above example demonstrates the control available to you through predefined policies. Being able to use these policies relies on the programmers' having supplied either a policy template file (*.adm*) or the details of the policies known by the software. Another way to use the SPE is to create your own template files that affect known Registry elements.

Later in this chapter we explain how to create your own template file.

Creating a System Policy

Having launched the SPE (from **Start→Programs→Administrative Tools (Common)**), you must first open a new policy, **File→New Policy**. This places two icons in the SPE window, named *Default Computer* and *Default User.*

Default Computer

This icon represents the machine-specific settings that can be used to control any machine that has not had a specific policy associated with it. When a system policy is invoked, the workstation first looks to see if a computer policy is associated with the name of the workstation itself. If not, it looks for the default policy. If one does not exist, then the machine-related part of the workstation's Registry is left untouched.

Default User

As with the default computer policies, if a user policy has been neither specifically created nor associated with a group policy, then the default user controls are evoked.

The administrator must first decide what criteria to apply to split the users and machines into appropriate control units. Machine restriction can be configured only through the default machine or specially created individual machine policies. Users, on the other hand, can be controlled through the default user, specific individual users, and groups. Doing this does beg the question of which control unit—the default, individual, or group—takes priority. The following list shows the order:

- A specific user policy takes precedence over any group policy that applies to that user.

- Any group policy that applies to a user takes precedence over the default user policy.

- A specific user policy takes precedent over the default user policy.

- If many group policies apply to a user, then the group that appears highest in the group priority list takes precedent. The group priority list is maintained through the main menu item **Option→Group Priority**.

Adding a new user, group, or machine is done through the menu option **Edit**, followed by the appropriate menu item. Having made your selection and named it accordingly, you open it by double-clicking on it. You are now presented with a series of categories that contain either other categories or actual policies. The interface is the usual Explorer type. If you open a user policy and navigate down through the option *Control Panel*, you are presented with the same details as shown in Figure 7-1. From looking at Figure 7-1, you can see there is only the single policy, *Restrict display*, that, if you highlight its name but do not select the check box, shows you the five parts associated with it. The check box alongside the policy name supports three states; these are as follows:

- A ticked check box indicates that the policy is enabled.

- An empty check box indicates that the policy is disabled.

- A greyed-out check box indicates that the policy should be left in its current state.

This last state is an interesting one. All policies are initially in this state, allowing the settings of `HKEY_CURRENT_USER` and `HKEY_LOCAL_MACHINE` to remain set to their defaults until a change is required. If you did not have this neutral state, then all Registry settings would have a policy forced on them even if one was not required or desired. You should be very careful here; do not go about clicking policies without having first considered the consequences. For instance, changing any policy that is not of a simple Boolean type without first noticing its original settings may well leave your workstation in an unusable state.[*]

Having added and configured new machines, groups, and users, you must save the settings into a system policy file. These files use the extension *.POL* and can be stored just like any other file. For a system policy to take effect, you must store the policy you wish to use in the *NETLOGON* share of the PDC. This is actually the *%systemroot%\system32\repl\import\scripts* directory. The policy file must also be called *NTCONFIG.POL*.

Adding Templates

If you want to use template files either of your own design or supplied by a third party, you need first to load them in the SPE. Doing this is quite straightforward.

---

[*]We have certainly done this a few times, and recovering from it can be very difficult.

From the main menu select **Options→Policy Template**; you will see which template files are currently in use. You can now include a new template through the Add option. Having done this, you will see new policies appear under any subsequent computer- or user-specific sections of the system policy.

Registry Editing

The SPE also gives the administrator the ability to directly view or edit a subset of both a machine's and a user's Registry entries. Selecting **File→Open Registry** displays these details through the same interface SPE uses to allow policy control. Obviously, by doing this you see only the settings that the SPE knows about from the template files. By highlighting the various individual policies you can determine the current settings for the local machine and the currently logged-on user. The SPE also allows the administrator to look at the Registry of any machine in the domain providing an active user is logged on. To do this, select **File→Connect** and enter the name of the machine you wish to investigate. For some annoying reason, there is no browse capability here. This Registry editing feature gives the administrator the chance to view the current setting of a machine's Registry before a system policy is deployed. Its usefulness lies in the fact that you can document the details of any Registry entries your system policy intends to change. Although reinstating any changes to Boolean values is not a problem, reinstating string variables is troublesome as the variable could have contained any text. If you did not make a note of it, you may find it impossible to find its original form. No changes you make to a Registry have any effect until you explicitly save them.

Downloading the Policy

Having created a system policy, the administrator must consider in which way he or she wishes the policy to be distributed, if at all, to the workstations and member servers of the domain in question. The option that dictates the type of download is itself found in the set of computer-related sections (such as the default computer) of the system policy. The download policy for the default computer is found under *Network\System\policies\update*.

Three states can be set for downloading policies:

Off (No Policy)
> If the download option is set to Off, then all local user and computer Registry settings are left untouched.

Automatic
> Policies are automatically downloaded from the *NETLOGON* share of the PDC. This is the default option for newly created system policies.

Manual

> Policies are downloaded from a specific path that specifies both the path-name and the policy file. The specified path can take the form of either a UNC path or a mapped path.

Deploying system policies through the manual download option needs a bit more explanation because what happens to the Registry during the manual setup is not immediately obvious.

Remember that we are dealing with Registry settings and as such must consider the way in which NT loads and observes these settings. Let's look at the order in which settings are loaded from the system policy and when those loaded changes come into effect. When a user logs on to a domain workstation, the following occurs:

- The computer-specific settings within the system policy are loaded into the Registry of the local machine. These settings have no effect on the machine until a new logon has occurred. Why? Because the hardware part of the logon process has occurred before the computer-specific settings from the system policy have been loaded. It takes a new logon to activate them.

- The user-specific settings from the system policy are merged with the settings from the *Ntuser.dat* file of the user logging on. These settings take immediate effect as they are loaded into the Registry before any user-specific actions occur and are therefore considered the current settings.

Bearing this in mind, we now look at an example. Suppose we have 10 machines we wish to use as library terminals and we want them all to share the same system policy. Also assume that we have other machines on the network dedicated to other purposes, so we need to make the destination clear. The following actions need to take place.

First, we need to create the policy that the 10 library workstations will use. We do this by using the SPE to edit the default computer setting that will enforce our restrictions. We save this policy to a directory that has sharing enabled, in this case *LibData*, and we call the policy file *LibWorkStations.POL*. It is worth stating here exactly what we have set in the policy. First we should mention that the library machines are set to automatically log on a user called LibUser. This user's profile is mandatory with all profile directories except the *Start Menu\programs* directory, which keeps shortcuts to two applications to which we want the users to have access. These applications are a library program and Internet Explorer. The computer-related part of the library workstations policy, default computer, consists only of the enabling of the logon banner with customized text. This is done under *Windows NT System\Logon\Logon banner*. The text threatens the usual prosecution, fining, and death if users abuse the machine. The user-related part of the policy, default user, is more interesting. You could impose dozens of individual policies on a user, but the following lists the ones we chose for this example:

Control Panel\Display\Restrict Display

> All the associated parts of this policy are selected. This disables the user's ability to use any display property tabs, as well as the **control panel** application **Display**, to change any display properties.

Shell\Restrictions\Remove Run command from Start menu

> This removes the **Run** command from the Start menu, thus stopping users from attempting to run unauthorized applications from the command line.

Shell\Restrictions\Remove folders from Settings on Start menu

> Again, as it says, this removes the control panel and printer folders from the Settings option on the Start menu. It stops users from trying to run control panel applications or fiddle with printer settings.

Shell\Restrictions\Remove taskbar from Settings on Start menu

> Imposing this policy removes the last item from the Settings option on the Start menu. This stops users from fiddling with the taskbar properties.

Shell\Restrictions\Remove Find command from Start menu

> This policy removes the **Find** command from the Start menu. There is no need for users of the library terminals to root around the system looking for files, either data or applications. Removing **Find** from the start menu avoids any temptations.

Shell\Restrictions\Hide all items on desktop

> For this example, this policy is a killer. It removes all desktop settings including Network Neighborhood, My Computer, and the Recycle Bin. The desktop is barren.

System\Restrictions\Run only allowed Windows application

> This is the final policy implemented, and it stops all applications from being run except those registered in "List of allowable applications." The only two applications listed are the library application and Internet Explorer. This supplies ultimate control of the workstation, with the other policies simply used to tidy up the taskbar and desktop.

The next step is to edit the default system policy. We add entries for each of the 10 library workstations and make **Remote update** the only active setting (under *Network\System policies\update*). We now change the part **Update mode** to *Manual* and supply a pathname in the appropriate field. We must also include the name of the new policy we intend to use, in this case *LibWorkStations.POL*. As we have saved the new policy file in the share *LibData*, we use a UNC path; the path looks like the following:

```
\\iago\LibData\LibWorkStations.pol
```

We now save the default system policy, and we are ready to go. There is, however, a small problem. Three logons have to take place before we see the effect of the new policy. Why? Remember the order in which settings are loaded and used. In this case, it takes the first logon to load the policy settings that point to the new policy file *LibWorkStations.POL*. The second logon uses the Registry settings established from the first logon to find the new policy and load it. Finally, the third logon uses the settings established from the second logon to implement the new policy.

User Profiles

A *user profile* is a collection of user-specific settings that define the user's working environment. These settings include such items as the wallpaper, screen resolution, color schemes, application settings, and network connections. Every time a user logs onto an NT machine or domain, the profile for the user is deployed. When users log on to a domain account, they are supplied with server-based profiles called *roaming* profiles. These profiles appear to follow them from domain machine to domain machine, giving them a consistent personal working environment made up of three specific areas: Registry details, directories containing user-specific links and files, and directories containing links and files specific to a workstation or server.

Registry Details

Every user has a separate hive file that contains settings loaded into the Registry when he or she logs on. This file is called *ntuser.dat* and is located in the user's profile directory. Refer to Chapter 6, *NT Internals and Managing Users,* to remind yourself of the contents of the *ntuser.dat* hive.

User Profile Directories

Profile directories are stored at the location defined by the profile path setting supplied for each user through the *User Manager* or *User Manager for Domains,* depending on the profile type. The default location for profiles is *%systemroot%\profiles*. You can expect to see two default directories:

profiles\Application Data
> Repository for specialist settings required by NT applications. It is up to the individual applications to make use of this directory.

profiles\Desktop
> Any extra items that sit on the desktop that are not supplied by NT as default. For instance, My Briefcase and the user's own shortcuts appear here.

All of the following hold shortcuts to related items or files, or both:

profiles\Favorites

Favorite locations used, for instance, by Internet Explorer.

profiles\NetHood

Network Neighborhood items.

profiles\Personal

Program items. Word uses this as a default location for document storage.

profiles\PrintHood

Printer-related items.

profiles\Recent

Most recently worked-on documents.

profiles\SendTo

Items that files can be sent to, such as disk drives, notepad, or paint.

profiles\StartMenu

Items that form the Start menu, such as programs.

profiles\Templates

Template files. Again, applications such as Word make use of this folder to store user-defined templates.

NOTE   All the directories of a profile are downloaded from the machine specified to hold the profiles (usually a server of one sort or another) to a workstation when a domain user logs into a domain. As these directories can be used to store data files as well as shortcuts, it is quite possible that they can grow to such a size as to start affecting the logon and logoff times. For instance, Word 97 uses the *profiles\Personal* directory as the default location to store its documents. Over a period of time, a user stores Word documents, and the size of this directory increases. Eventually, depending on your type of network, the directory reaches such a size that it starts to affect the time taken to both log on and log off (the profile is copied back to a central location on logoff). Not only this, but if profile caching is on, then large amounts of local disk space get wasted. Keep this in mind when setting up applications, especially Word. You may want to change the location of file storage for the application if it defaults to a profile directory.

Each new profile is created from a copy of a default profile directory called *Default user,* which is also located in the *%systemroot%\profiles* directory. This is also where the template for each *NTuser.dat* hive is stored.

The Machine-Specific Directories

Every NT workstation and server contain a directory called the *All Users* directory. This directory is used to store items common to all users on the local machine. These items are represented as either desktop items or Start menu items. To reflect this, the *All Users* directory contains two subdirectories called *Start Menu* and *Desktop*. The *Start Menu* directory's purpose is to add machine-specific items to the *Start menu*, which by default contains a common program directory containing links to the administrative tools. The *Desktop* directory's role is to contain links and files for those items making up the desktop. The path for the *All Users* directory is once again *%systemroot%\profiles*.

To make things a bit clearer, let's look at an example. If, as an administrator, you create a shortcut, say to the floppy drive, and wish all successive users to see this icon on the desktop, then you need to put the shortcut into the *All Users\Desktop* directory. The icon will appear on the desktop for all users. If you do not put the icon in the *All Users\Desktop* directory, but place it straight onto the actual desktop, then only you as the administrator will ever see the icon. When you log out, the shortcut is saved to the administrator's personal desktop folder and thus cannot be loaded to the desktop by any other user.

Local and Roaming Profiles

Local profiles are profiles that are stored locally on a workstation. These profiles are used in two differing contexts: The profile is associated with a local user account, or the profile is a cached copy of a domain user profile. The first case is straightforward: A user account created locally on a workstation or server has a profile associated with it. This profile is accessible only from the workstation or server on which it was created. The second case is slightly more complex. When a user logs onto a domain with a server-based profile, termed a *roaming* profile, the profile is copied to the workstation or server from which the user is logging on. This copy is then used. If a user logs onto a domain and, for one reason or another, the roaming profile is unreachable, then the locally cached copy of that user's profile is used instead. If, when the user next logs on to the domain, the roaming profile becomes available, NT compares the roaming profile with the locally cached copy and, depending on which is the most recent, either uses the roaming profile or gives the user the choice of using the cached local profile. Let's look at an example.

We have configured our system to allow cached copies of the roaming profile to be stored on a workstation, and our maintenance boys have just cut through the UTP cable that connects the workstation to a hub and thus the domain. A user now logs on, and the workstation tries to grab the user's profile from the PDC. As the PDC cannot be contacted, the workstation uses the locally cached copy of the user's profile. Our workstations have Word 97 installed locally, so our user does some work and then logs off. In the meantime, the network team fixes the cut cable, and the workstation is back in contact with the PDC. Our user returns to the workstation and logs back on. NT automatically compares the cached version of the user's profile with the copy stored on the PDC and realizes that the cached version is now the most recent. It asks our user if he or she wants to use the newer cached version or download the older server version. Our user opts to use the new cached version. If our user had opted to use the older version of the profile, then any changes he or she had made to the desktop, any work stored in the profile directories during the disconnection, would have been lost, over-written by the older profile. It is worth taking the time to explain to users the consequences of selecting one or other of the different versions of the profiles under such circumstances.

As stated in the first paragraph of this section, roaming profiles are server-based and are used to generate a consistent user environment regardless of the domain workstation or server from which a user logs on. The profile follows the user around the domain and provides a useful way in which an administrator can manage some aspects of the user's environment. One restrictive form of the roaming profile is the mandatory profile, a roaming profile that users cannot alter. To create a mandatory profile, you simply need to rename a user's *ntuser.dat* file to *ntuser.man*. The user can still make changes to whatever settings for which he or she has permissions, but these changes are not saved centrally so that each time a user logs back on he or she sees the enforced profile. In reality, NT just does not copy back the roaming profile that it has downloaded to the workstation when a user has logged on. It uses the *.man* extension as a simple flag to enforce the mandatory setting.

As roaming profiles are server-based, it is quite possible to use this centralization for information or application distribution. We have done this ourselves several times in a simple fashion. For instance, we run an administration PDC that handles, among other services, our administrative database. On creation of a new student database, we distribute a new shortcut to all secretarial and administrative personnel that need access to it. We do this by adding the new shortcut to the *Start menu\programs* directory of their profiles. On the next logon, they see the new link to the database. The following short Perl script demonstrates how simple it is to do this.

The syntax for calling the *additem.pl* script is as follows :

```
additem [/v] [/q] filename item_name profile_directory
```

where /v puts it in verbose mode, /q puts it in quiet mode, *filename* is a text file of selected usernames, *item_name* is the item to copy, and *profile_directory* is the destination user profile directory.

A typical call to this script is as follows:

```
E:\>additem.pl /v userlist.txt c:\tmp\student.lnk "\Start menu\programs"
```

where *additem.pl* is the Perl script, *userlist.txt* is a text file containing a list of target usernames, *student.lnk* is the shortcut to the database, and *Start menu\programs* is the destination profile directory for the shortcut.

Example 7-1. Adding an Item to a Profile Directory

```perl
#additem.pl
#The script takes a list of users, finds their profile path and adds
#an item, such as a link, to a destination profile directory.

# Grab the user's profile path
sub GetProfileHome {
    my $username = shift @_;
    my $directories = 0;
    map /\w*\s\w*\s*(\S*)/, grep {
    if (/^Logon script/) {
            $directories = 1;
            0;
        } else {
            $directories = 0 if /^Home directory/;
            $directories;
        }
    } qx(net user $username);
}


#Get the flags, filename, item to copy and profile directory
#from the command line

$filename = shift @ARGV;

$not_quiet = 1;

if($filename eq "/v") {
    $verbose = 1;
    $filename = shift @ARGV;
} elsif ($filename eq "/q") {
    $not_quiet = 0;
    $filename = shift @ARGV;
}

#Get the item path and the profile destination folder
$itempath = shift @ARGV;
$pfolder = shift @ARGV;

# Open the file containing the usernames and load them into an array
```

Example 7-1. Adding an Item to a Profile Directory (continued)

```
open(USERLIST, $filename) || die "unable to load $filename\n";

print "Retrieving usernames from $filename...\n" if $not_quiet;
while ($username = <USERLIST>) {
    chop($username);
    @users = (@users,$username);
    print "$username\n" if $verbose;
}

# For each user in the array we call the GetProfileHome function to
# extract their profile path. To this we add the item path and then carry
# out the copy.

ADDITEM: foreach $username(@users) {
print "Adding $itempath to the $pfolder of $username\n" if $verbose;

    foreach $path(GetProfileHome($username)) {
            $destination= "\"".$path.$pfolder."\"";
        qx(copy $itempath $destination);
            print "Item copied to - $destination\n\n" if $verbose;
        }

}
```

Creating a Profile

A user profile is created in one of two ways. It is either automatically copied from a default profile, or it is manually copied from a template profile.

Default Profile

The steps of automatic creation are as follows:

1. A new user logs on to a workstation with a domain account with no pre-configured roaming profile.

2. The local workstation's default user profile, Default User, is loaded.

3. The user logs out, and the profile details are copied to a predefined server location (as specified by the profile path associated with each user).

Note here that the roaming profile is actually based on the configuration of a workstation's default user profile, not the default profile stored on the authentication server. This can lead to problems if each workstation has a differently configured default user profile. Which profile is assigned to a user then depends on which workstation he or she happens to log onto first. There is a way to enforce a uniform default user profile across all the workstations of a given domain. To do this, you first create the new profile with which you intend all your users to start, then copy it to the *NETLOGON* directory of the PDC in a directory labelled *Default User*. Make sure *Everyone* has permission to use this directory. You can copy the newly created profile using the **User Profile** tab from the control panel application, **System**. Now when a new user logs on to the domain for the first time, the workstation downloads a copy of the *Default User* directory from the PDC and makes a new directory called *Default User (Network)*. It then uses this default user profile for the new user. When creating a network default profile, consider from where you intend to create it. Our workstations have quite different video capabilities than our servers, so we created our network default user profile on one of the workstations. This gave us more flexibility in the screen configuration than would have been possible by using the server profiles available.

Templates

An administrator can also create a number of template users with Registry details and program links that are preset to match a number of user types. A newly created user who fits into one of these predefined categories can have the correct template profile copied into his or her new profile directory. This is done manually by the administrator through the control panel application, **System**. **System** has a tab named **User Profiles** that allows an administrator to select an existing profile, in this case a template profile, and copy it to the profile location set up through *User Manager* or *User Manager for Domains*. Only one user profile can be created at a time using this method, but it is quite acceptable if you have low user turnover.

The Template File Format

Customizing the System Policy Editor (SPE) as a general-purpose Registry tool has many benefits. It allows the system administrator to control Registry settings for users and machines in a consistent and central manner. This customization depends on template files that define the customization options, interface, and actions taken when loaded into the SPE. Because policies must be enforced by the programs to which they refer (e.g., the Explorer shell), Microsoft intends that policy template files be created by developers of software packages to centralize control of Registry settings for new applications. This means that information about the format of template files is hidden away in Microsoft's Win32 Software Development Kit.

As mentioned earlier, you do not need to depend on Microsoft or any developer to provide a template file for you. If you understand how the Registry works, and how specific programs use the Registry, you can use template files and the SPE to make your own changes. The advantages to using the SPE and template files for altering the Registry are in the centralization and distribution of profile settings. By enacting system and user policies at logon time, changes can be distributed throughout a network environment without the need for an administrator to update each local machine or current user hive manually. Instead, the system automatically propagates change details in a central profile file. In addition, the template policy file and SPE program provide a simple user interface for interacting with complex and sometimes obscure Registry entries.

Profile template files (*.adm*) have a hierarchical structure that is used by the SPE to generate the tree list used to navigate the policy options. The template file is broken down into individual sections called *classes* that specify the root key within which the Registry changes are to be carried out. The categories and policies are typically grouped into either a *user*-specific or *machine*-specific section. A **class** statement marks each of these sections:

```
class [ machine | user ]
```

If machine is specified, then all Registry key references are in relation to the **HKEY_LOCAL_MACHINE** root. If user is specified, then all references are based on the **HKEY_CURRENT_USER** root. These root key differences are reflected in the icon to which the category and policies are added. If no class is specified, and if no other type information is provided in later category definitions, the default placement for all policies is within the **HKEY_LOCAL_MACHINE** key. There is traditionally only one class machine and class user declaration per file, with policies grouped under the appropriate heading.

Once the class of policy change is determined, you can begin to create the tree structure that the SPE presents to the user. This is done with the **category** command:

```
category name [keyname key]
...
end category
```

NOTE   If you have access to the Win32 documentation, you will find that it
            states that the **category** keyword requires the use of a **type** modi-
            fier to indicate which root key the entries in the category applies.
            This, in fact, is not readable by the Windows NT System Policy Edi-
            tor, which will throw an error if it is used. Instead, use the **class**
            statement as specified earlier to designate whether the following cat-
            egories apply to **user** or **machine.**

Each **category** entry in the *.adm* file creates a corresponding node in the SPE tree. The *name* value holds the display name for the category, which is presented to the user at each node. If the *name* field includes spaces, you must place it inside double quotes. The `keyname` option is used to indicate a Registry key that all policies contained within the category should use unless specified otherwise. This saves your placing the same Registry key name with every policy entry.

Category entries can be nested to create an overall hierarchy that is mimicked by the tree structure in the SPE. As an extended example of how a custom template file might be organized, consider the following code:

```
class machine
category "Computing Centre Machine Restrictions"
    category "Internet Terminal Policies"
        ...
    end category
    category "Library Terminal Policies"
        ...
    end category
end category

class user
category "Computing Centre User Restrictions"
    ...
end category
```

In this case, there are different custom policies we wish to implement for different types of machines. To organize the policies themselves, we have broken them down into machine- and user-specific policies, with the machine-specific policies being further broken down into different terminal-type policies. Remember, this organization does not mean that Internet terminal policies could not be enforced on library terminals; it is simply a way to organize the custom policies for easy browsing. You could use your own organization, perhaps based on machine model, for example. Remember, the categories are used for organizing your policies for ease in finding.

Of course, categories are used to organize only the policies you wish to implement. To add policies, you use the policy statement:

```
policy name [key registry key]
    ...
end policy
```

The `policy` declaration works much like the `category` keyword in that it demarcates the beginning and end of a specific policy. Creating a policy entry in the template file causes the SPE to generate a leaf in its tree view of the policy option list. This leaf is a check box with three states: selected, cleared, or greyed-out. The optional key declaration is used to indicate which Registry key the policy is to act on if no key has been declared before, for example, in a category declaration. Note that if you have not declared a target key before the policy statement, the key declaration is required. Child parts of the policy will adopt the most recent key declaration or may specify their own. The user interface elements that are displayed in the SPE appear in the lower window. The items appear unfocused if the specific policy to which the parts are associated is not currently selected. The order in which the parts appear is identical to the order in which they are declared in the template file.

Parts allow for specific actions to be carried out in regard to the Registry. Registry changes can involve everything from setting flags to defining strings or numbers; parts, in addition to simply allowing multiple actions to be carried out, allow further user input into the process. To define a part, use the part declaration:

```
part name type
    . . .
    [keyname key_name]
    valuename value_name
end part
```

The *name* parameter indicates what string the SPE should use to display with the policy part. The *type* parameter indicates what kind of part should be created. There are several options for part types, which will be discussed in turn: `checkbox`, `combobox`, `dropdownlist`, `edittext`, `listbox`, `numeric`, `text`. Depending on what type is declared, each part declaration has a type-dependent section. For example, if the *type* is text, there is no type-dependent data. On the other hand, if the *type* is `edittext`, then there are several parameters indicating the default value and length, which the `edittext` field created in the SPE will be able to use. These are described in the next section. After the name and type parameters are given, depending on what kind of part is declared, there may be type-specific data that must be provided.

In addition to and after the type-specific data, a part declaration includes an optional **keyname** and required **valuename** parameter. The **keyname** option is used to indicate on which Registry key the profile part is acting. This key name is required only if there is no key definition in a higher portion of the policy file hierarchy. If any more global key name declarations have been made, the local part declaration overrides this setting with the value of **key_name.** The **value_name** parameter is used to indicate on which Registry value the profile part is to act. This will be used by the type-specific parameters in customizing the setting of **value_name** in the Registry. As with the rest of the template file format, the part declaration is closed with an end part statement.

Part Types

Each part declaration must include with it information about the kind of customization interface the SPE should provide for the user. These interfaces are used to change the Registry settings of the key/value pair defined at that point in the hierarchy.

The simplest example of a part type is `text`. This takes no additional type-specific data and simply displays the `name` value as a line of static text. In this case, the `valuename` option is omitted from the part declaration altogether because it does not make sense in this context. The following is an example of a text policy part:

```
part "This is a test string" text
end part
```

If you have several parts to a policy that a user will need to set, you can use text to separate and label them into individual groups. Or, you might wish to provide more detailed explanatory text to the policy in general. You will need to create a new text policy part for each line of text in a multilined statement that would otherwise run wider than the available space as a single line.

For Boolean settings, you can use the `checkbox` type. This type presents a standard check box, which can be either selected or unselected. Unlike the standard policy check boxes, the part type `checkbox` does not have a third (or greyed-out) state.

The `checkbox` has five type-dependent data fields that can be provided in the template file to instruct the SPE how to alter the Registry according to the state of the check box.

The `valueon` and `valueoff` options are used to indicate what setting the Registry value should take when the checkbox is selected or deselected, respectively. If this value is not specified, then the default of 1 is used for a selected state, and 0 for an unselected state. These data fields can take both string and numeric values. When using numbers, you must specify the value as being **numeric**.

```
valueon "\\iago\users"
valueon numeric 256
valueoff ""
valueoff numeric 1024
```

In addition to individual values, you can also specify more complex actions to be carried out, depending on the state of the check box. These instructions are collected into elements known as actionlists, which are discussed in more detail later. You can specify these instructions by using the actionliston and actionlistoff commands. For example, the following example creates a check box with an action list:

```
part "This is an additional part" checkbox
    actionliston
        keyname system\currentcontrolset\services\...
        valuename foo
        value "\\iago\users"
        valuename bar
```

```
        value numeric 13
    end actionliston
    actionlistoff
        keyname system\currentcontrolset\services\...
        valuename foo
        value ""
        valuename bar
        value numeric 9
    end actionlistoff
    valuename testing
end part
```

Note that the `checkbox` part must still specify a default `value_name` at the end of the definition even though the values are explicitly defined in the action lists. The `keyname` option is necessary only if the key you wish to use is different from the key defined previously in the hierarchy. This can also be changed for each element in the action list.

If you want the checkbox to be selected by default, use the `defchecked` option:

```
part "This is an additional part" checkbox
    defchecked
    actionliston
    ...
```

Beyond simple check boxes, you can also allow the user to type in specific information by implementing edit boxes, drop-down lists, and combo boxes.

The edittext part allows you to create a field where the user can fill in a text string for the Registry value. You can specify a default string using the `default` option. In addition, you can set a maximum length for the string using the `maxlen` option. If you want to force the user to enter a value in order for the policy to be used, use the required command. Finally, if the Registry key requires text in OEM format, you can use the oemconvert option. The following is an example of an edittext entry:

```
part "This is a test part" edittext
    default "test"
    maxlen 20
    required
    valuename test
end part
```

If you want to provide more than one default option for the `edittext`, you can use a `combobox` instead. The combobox uses the same options as the edittext with the additional `suggestions` command:

```
part "This is a test part" combobox
    default "test"
    maxlen 20
    required
    suggestions
```

```
            option "second option" third
        end suggestions
        valuename test
    end part
```

Notice the use of quotes to separate out strings with spaces.

If you want to provide numeric options, there is a `numeric` part, which works in a similar manner to the edittext or combobox. The `default` option is used to indicate the initial numeric value for the field. `max` is used to indicate the maximum value the number can be (defaults to 9999). The `required` option is used in the same manner as that of the edittext and comboboxes—that of ensuring the user fills out this option for the policy to be enabled. By default, the part creates a spinner, which allows the user to move through the numbers one at a time. This is set using the `spin` command. The numeric value associated with this option is used as the increment value for the spin buttons. If it is set to 0, the spin buttons are not displayed. By default, the spinner control is set to 1. If you wish the number to be stored in the Registry value as a `REG_SZ` type instead of `REG_DWORD`, use the `txtconvert` option.

```
    part "This is a test part" numeric
        default 20
        max 100
        required
        spin 2
        valuename test
    end part
```

Two of the more complicated policy parts are the `dropdownlist` and `listbox` types. These two can be used to make a wider variety of predefined changes, which appear in selection lists.

The `listbox` part is used to control set values, which can be entered for a single key. Adding a listbox part to a policy file places a button in the SPE called **show** that opens up a dialog box with an **add** and **remove** button. Pressing the **add** button allows the user to add valuename/value pairs to the Registry key. The **remove** button can be used to remove any already installed values. By default, the values in the list box replace any and all entries underneath the Registry key to which you are pointing. This means that if there are already values underneath a key, they will be deleted before the new values are entered. Using the **additive** option allows the preexisting values to remain, with entries in the listbox only being appended to the key. To have the user specify both the value name and setting, you must use the `explicitvalue` option. If you want to use a running list of value names and only have the user supply the value settings, you can use the `valueprefix` option. This causes each new entry in the listbox to be the setting of a value with the name of the prefix with an incremented integer added. For example, if the prefix were `user`, then adding the entries `ajm39`, `tdr20`, and rjh39 would result in the Registry values user1, user2, and user3 to be added with the previous respective usernames. An example listbox part might be:

```
part "Test part" listbox
    additive
    explicitvalue
end part
```

Notice that it is up to the user to provide all the information in this part. Additionally, because the user is specifying the value or the values are being provided automatically using the valueprefix option, there is no need to provide a valuename option.

By far the most complex of the policy parts is the dropdownlist. This allows the user to select from a predefined list of items that can have either different values or action lists associated with them. Unlike the **listbox**, the dropdownlist by default deals only with a single Registry value, although action lists allow you to expand this to several values at once.

The following example shows the use of the dropdownlist with three entries. The first entry simply sets the value of valuename1 to value1. The second item changes the value of valuename1 to a numeric value, in addition to setting the value valuename2 to the setting of value3. The final item deletes the value valuename1 from the Registry entirely.

```
part "This is a test part" dropdownlist
    itemlist
        name item1 value value1
        name item2 value numeric 2
        actionlist
            valuename valuename2
            value value3
        end actionlist
        name item3 value delete
    end itemlist
    valuename valuename1
end part
```

In several policy parts, notice the use of constructs known as *action lists*. The format for these lists is as follows:

```
actionlist
    [keyname key_name]
    valuename value_name
    value value
    [keyname key_name]
    valuename value_name
    value value
end actionlist
```

The `keyname` option is used to designate different Registry keys. If one is not specified, the latest setting for the key is used. The settings for the **value** option are similar to the rest of the template file format where the argument is taken to be a string value unless proceeded by a `numeric` qualifier. In addition, you can specify that the entire valuename/value pair be deleted by using `value delete`.

An Example of the Template File in Use

Now that we have discussed the component parts of the profile template file, we can have a look at a simple example. The idea is to create a logon script whose actions are determined by a number of Registry settings. These settings are generated and configured through a series of policies that have been added into the system policy via the SPE. To achieve this the following needs to be observed:

We create a Perl script that is encapsulated in a batch file, as only batch or command files can be run as logon scripts. This Perl script reads a set of predefined Registry entries and then acts accordingly on the data it finds there. In this case, the script looks for two Registry keys, one of which tells it what additional scripts to run, while the other supplies information for additional drive mappings. The Registry keys are as follows:

```
HKEY_CURRENT_USER\Environment\Logon\Scripts
HKEY_CURRENT_USER\Environment\Logon\Maps
```

The `Scripts` key contains value names that represent the full path of any number of extra scripts the administrator cares to set up. The value itself represents any command-line parameters that need to be passed on to the associated script. Thus, a value name could be *d:\scripts\logon\postgrads.pl,* and a value could be *userlist.txt.*

The `Map` key contains value names that represent a drive letter, and the value represents the path to be mapped. There can be any number of these mappings. For instance, the value name could be *M:,* and the value could be *\\iago\users.* These keys and values are generated automatically by the template file, as described later in this example. Note that because the Perl script uses all built-in functions, there is no requirement for invoking the **use** *module* syntax.

Example 7-2 is a Perl script designed to follow the policies described above.

Example 7-2. Policy-Controlled Perl logon Script

```
# logon.pl
# perl SPE-LOGON

require "NT.ph";
```

Example 7-2. Policy-Controlled Perl logon Script (continued)

```
sub getDriveMappings {
    $index = 0;
    Win32::RegOpenKeyEx(&HKEY_CURRENT_USER,
                        'Environment\Logon\Map',
                        &NULL,
                        &KEY_ALL_ACCESS,
                        $handle) or die "unable to access Registry";
    while(Win32::RegEnumValue($handle, $index++, $valuename, &NULL, $type,
                              $value)) {
        `net use $valuename $value`;
        print "$valuename $value\n";
    }
    Win32::RegCloseKey($handle);
}

sub getScripts {
    $index = 0;
    Win32::RegOpenKeyEx(&HKEY_CURRENT_USER,
                        'Environment\Logon\Scripts',
                        &NULL,
                        &KEY_ALL_ACCESS,
                        $handle) or die "unable to access Registry";
    while(Win32::RegEnumValue($handle, $index++, $valuename, &NULL, $type,
                              $value)) {
        `perl $valuename $value`;
        print "$valuename $value\n";
    }
    Win32::RegCloseKey($handle);
}

&getDriveMappings;
&getScripts;
```

We now have the Perl script that knows about our policies, so the next stage is to create a template file to use with the SPE. The template file gives us not only the opportunity to implement our policies (that is, specify additional logon scripts and drive mappings), but to present to us a graphical interface from which to do it. Example 7-3 is a template file that does just that.

Example 7-3. Template File for Adding Policies to the User Class

```
class user
category "Logon Script Settings"
    policy "Scripts to Run"
    keyname "Environment\Logon\Scripts"
        part "Scripts" listbox
            explicitvalue
        end part
         part "The NAME of the ITEM represents the full path of the script" text
        end part
        part "Example - D:\scripts\logon\postgrads.pl" text
        end part
```

Example 7-3. Template File for Adding Policies to the User Class (continued)

```
            part "The VALUE of the ITEM represents command line arguments" text
            end part
            part "and is optional" text
            end part
        end policy
        policy "Drive Mappings"
        keyname "Environment\Logon\Map"
            part "Mappings" listbox
                explicitvalue
            end part
            part "The NAME of the ITEM represents the drive letter" text
            end part
            part "Example - M:" text
            end part
            part "The VALUE of the ITEM represents the path mapping" text
            end part
            part "Example - \\iago\users" text
            end part
        end policy
end category
```

Having created the template file, we need to incorporate it into our system policy. To do this we import it into the SPE as a policy template (refer to earlier sections of this chapter for details on how to do this). Having imported the new template file, we can now configure the new policies. Figure 7-2 and Figure 7-3 show the interface of the additional policies for the user class and one of the new policies being configured.

Note that the list box offers us a very convenient way of data entry, and if you examine the code, you will see just how easy it is to do.

Use of Policy Template Files

Why would you want to create your own policy template file? The policy template file as envisioned by Microsoft is a tool for developers to provide policy functionality in their programs. By implementing a set of policies based on the settings of the Registry and then distributing a template file for easy control over these Registry settings, developers can integrate their programs within the wider scope of NT policies. This means that for policies to work, programs must first look to the Registry, and voluntarily limit themselves based on the information they find. It may seem that unless you are writing a Windows program, you would have little need for such a tool. When seen as a general Registry tool, though, there are many possibilities for its use:

- When implementing Perl scripts, you may want to run different options based on either the current user or machine on which it is being run. One way to do this is to create a policy file that adds entries to the Registry, which your

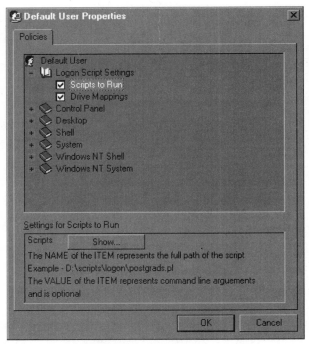

Figure 7-2. The additional policies for the user class

Perl script could then read and act on accordingly. By creating policies for different machines and groups of users, your customizations are propagated throughout the network as users log onto the system.

- Running Windows-based software in a client/server environment can still be difficult at times. Many programs expect to be able to write to the Registry at will upon installation, and they expect that information to be there the next time they run. If you are adding software to a server, simply pointing the user to the files does not mean that the environment will necessarily be set up correctly for the program to run. If the Registry changes made by a program are straightforward, you can propagate them to local workstations by creating a template file with the necessary changes and add them to the default computer policy, which will be added to the computer at next logon.

- Many times, programs do not come with their own policy files. Although this means that any customization will be limited, it is possible to control Registry settings to make sure that default values are enforced. Users will always be able to alter these during a session, but each time they log out and back in again they will find them reset.

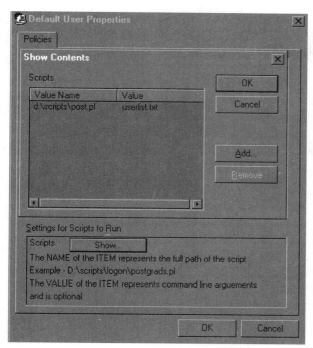

Figure 7-3. The scripts policy being configured

- Updating system files and drivers typically means that you have to sit down at each and every workstation. If instead you were to perform the installation on a template workstation and record changes that are made with a program such as *sysdiff*, you could load the files and changes to the Registry automatically to every machine when a user logs onto a machine, providing your own version of "zero administration."

The important thing to remember about policies is that they are general Registry changes that are carried out at logon. This provides the perfect opportunity to make any necessary system-wide changes to your workstations or user profiles. You are in no way limited to simply using policy templates as a tool for implementing already-defined policies. At the time of writing there were many changes in this area with regard to Windows 95 and NT. Microsoft's "Zero Administration" initiative is being billed as a solution to the problems of administering large installations of hardware and software. In addition to products Microsoft is releasing, software manufacturers in order to comply with new Logo requirements, will be required to build their applications with administration in mind—including policy templates. We hope these changes to operating system and application maintenance will make your job even easier.

8

Auditing and Windows NT

In many ways, this book is somewhat unbalanced in that the majority of it is spent discussing what is, in fact, a minority part of the administrator's job. Even though adding users to systems and getting their profiles set up are undoubtedly important, if your system is set up correctly, this should take only a very small part of your time. What you want to consume the majority of your time is sitting back and watching everything run smoothly.

Of course, *watch* is the operative term here. How do you watch a system? In fact, Windows NT does it for you—it is called the event log. By setting up the auditing of events, you can track the use (and abuse) of your network resources. If auditing is done correctly, you should be able to stay one step ahead of problems with security, resource loading, or system failure. Just as most of the work in dealing with users occurs in first getting them on the system, making sure auditing can be your eyes and ears requires some effort to set up.

Of course, auditing a system is not only about security. Many aspects of an active network need to be monitored to keep it running as smoothly as possible, in addition to watching over people's shoulders. You can put auditing to a multitude of tasks, but they can generally be broken down into three areas: resource monitoring, troubleshooting, and security.

Resource Monitoring

One of the best uses for the event logs, but one that is seldom put into effect, is to monitor resources. With computers distributed across a network, and with a limited number of common resources, it is important for administrators to keep track of resource usage. These resources can include file space quotas, print quotas, application usage, logon times, bandwidth, and more. It is possible, by setting up the proper auditing of events, to track how these resources are used both at the group and user levels. Careful analysis can reveal information about how individuals use their computers and where limited reserves are best moved to maximize the efficiency of the overall system.

Troubleshooting

In addition to resource monitoring and analysis, one of the basic uses of the event logs is troubleshooting. When a system goes down completely or simply has an intermittent quirk that affects the overall functionality, the event logs can often provide information about the current condition of any subsystems, and they can warn you when there is an existing or potential problem. The information can be as simple as telling you that a driver failed to load, thus pointing you in the right direction to look for the cause. Additionally, advanced subsystems sometimes even provide detailed information in the event log about the exact cause of a problem. If something is wrong, one of your first inclinations should be to go to the event viewer and see if any obvious problems have been reported.

Security

Ultimately, auditing always comes back to security. Auditing allows you to track users through a system, tracking inappropriate behavior so you can stop it in the future. Perhaps the biggest misconception about auditing, however, is the idea that it lets you know when someone has broken into the system. The reality is, of course, quite different, and it is easy to see why. If the system could *tell* you when security had been breached, then the system could just as easily have stopped whatever was happening in the first place. What the event log records is a series of decisions the security manager makes about granting or denying access to resources. Ultimately, it is up to the administrator to decide that, in fact, the secretary account rjh39 does not have administrator privilege to look through the personal email of the company CEO. Setting up a system to track suspicious activity means you have to know what to look for beforehand.

It is a depressing thought that if you ever have to use the event logs, in most cases, something has already gone wrong. It is not preventive medicine as much as a system for providing a series of clues about what might be happening. By automating and simplifying the task of keeping on top of events, however, you can more easily keep track of what is going on around your system.

The event logs, like any great tool, are very flexible. They can record whatever you want, but balancing the line between not recording the critical event that would tell you what had gone wrong and recording so much that you couldn't find it anyway is a fine one. What we hope to show you in the following sections is what you can log and how you can use that information to tell when something has gone wrong.

The Event Logs

Windows NT's event logging facility is, in fact, one of the better parts of the operating system. What most users fail to appreciate is the concept of a common event log format where all applications can record information about significant occurrences, be they successful or unsuccessful. NT provides a programming interface for placing information into logs, extracting information, and performing maintenance such as backups. This means that not only are the wide number of events the operating system provides available for tracking users through a system, but applications can create their own events for writing to the log as well. All these events can be audited, tracked, and examined using a single piece of software, whether it is the Event Viewer supplied with NT or any custom log viewer you wish to obtain or write yourself. You are not stuck using half a dozen proprietary log viewers for every piece of software you install.

Windows NT auditing is broken down into three logs:

System Logs

> The system logs record events produced by operating and hardware subsystems. Typical system log entries are problems with the network protocols or fixed disk drivers.

Application Logs

> The application log is used to record events produced by programs running on a system. The application log is where any custom events applications have created and registered with the system typically appear, although programs are not necessarily restricted to this log file.

Security Logs

> The security log is used to record events having to do with the use of permissions on a system. These events include not only the more traditional file access logs, but also events that deal with auditing itself and logon/logoff. The security log is sometimes confusingly called the *audit* log.

Unlike most of the system data an administrator deals with, the three event logs are not stored in the Registry itself. Instead, there are three binary files, *AppEvent.evt, SysEvent.evt,* and *SecEvent.evt,* that hold the application, system, and security logs, respectively. Traditionally, these files are kept, along with the registry hives, in *%systemroot%\system32\config.*

The exact location of these log files is stored in the Registry key:

```
HKEY_LOCAL_MACHINE\SYSTEM\CurrentControlSet\Services\EventLog
```

under three subkeys not surprisingly labelled `Application, Security,` and
`System.` In addition to the file location, the `logfile` Registry keys also hold additional information about how the system should handle each file. Table 8-1 lists the
most important of these values.

Table 8-1. Principal Values for the Log File Registry Keys

Value	Type	Description
File	REG_SZ	This value holds the path and filename for the log file itself. The default value is *%systemroot%**system32**config*\\ [*filename*], where *filename* is any one of *appevent.evt, sysevent.evt,* or *secevent.evt.*
MaxSize	REG_DWORD	This value indicates the number of kilobytes to which the log file should be limited. The default value for this key is 512KB.
Retention	REG_DWORD	This value holds the number of seconds that an event should be held until it can be overwritten by the system when the log has reached the *MaxSize* limit. The default value is 7 days, or 604800 seconds. If there are no records old enough to overwrite, the system generates a *log full* event. If this value is set to a very low number (i.e., 0) then the log will never become full because it will continually overwrite any events already in the file. If this value is set to 0xFFFFFFFF, then the log must be cleared manually.

In addition to the values in Table 8-1, you can also force the system to halt when
the security log file becomes full. Halting a system when a log file is full is obviously used only by the seriously paranoid. If you watch your log files daily or
have a system for alerting you when the log files approach their capacity, you
should never have a problem with full log files. If your security cannot tolerate
any un-audited activity, however, you can create the following entry in the
Registry to cause a system crash when the security log becomes full:

```
HKEY_LOCAL_MACHINE\SYSTEM\CurrentControlSet\Control\Lsa
    CrashOnAuditFail = 1 (REG_DWORD)
```

Setting `CrashOnAuditFail` to 1 causes the system to come to a blue screen
halt if the security log becomes full. Before the system halts, it changes the value
of `CrashOnAuditFail` to 2, which indicates to the system that on any subsequent reboot, only users in the Administrators group can log on until the value is
reset.

Registering Events

All programs wishing to log events with Windows NT must register themselves
under one of the three log file keys in the registry. Programs register their events
by placing a `source` subkey underneath the `logfile` key to which they want

their events to be written. For example, if you look at the `Application` key,
you might find the following subkeys:

```
Autochk
DrWatson
ntbackup
Perfctrs
```

These are all sources that applications have defined to provide information to the
operating system about how to decipher the events that the programs might throw.
Because events are typically defined beforehand, applications can decrease the
amount of time they spend writing to the log file by passing indices only to the event
thrown, along with a small set of unique data for that particular event. Each index
points to a more descriptive string stored in a separate file that explains what the data
means. Each of these source keys defines several values, one of which is the `Event-
MessageFile` (`REG_EXPAND_SZ`), which points to the message file where the
description strings are kept. Traditionally, the executable or dynamic link library
throws the events. For example, if you look at the `DrWatson` source key under
`Applications,` you will find under `EventMessageFile` the following path:

```
%systemroot%\system32\drwtsn32.exe
```

In addition to pointing to the event message file, the `source` keys in the Registry
can also store more information about the types of events that a program might
throw. These `source` key values include additional message files for the event
category and parameters, in addition to the number of categories and event types
supported by the event source. This leads us to the next topic: the format of
Windows NT events.

Event Format

Because each subsystem or application can generate its own events, Windows NT
defines a skeleton to which all events conform. An event can be broadly broken
down into three sections: header, description, and data. *Header information*
comprises fixed fields that provide details about the event source, in addition to
information for identifying and categorizing an event. The *description* is a combination of strings and data that attempts to provide a readable explanation of the
event in question. The *data* area of an event holds binary information that can be
used by troubleshooting programs (see Figure 8-1).

Event header information

All events provide information that can be used to organize the data available in the
log file. By forcing each event to detail certain known attributes, any program
wishing to evaluate the event log can sort and filter events according to these items.

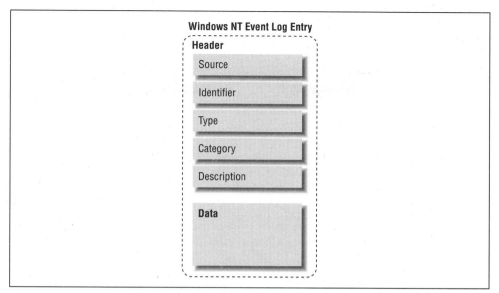

Figure 8-1. The format of a Windows NT event log entry

Source

The event source is the application or subcomponent that generated the event. These sources generally equate to one of the *source* keys in the event log Registry hierarchy. Because each source can define its own events, this represents a very important piece of information. Although not typical, it is certainly possible for events to look very similar but have completely different sources.

Identifier

The event identifier is used to hold an ID number unique to each source. If you recall, the `EventMessageFile` value stored under each source key in the Registry points to a file that holds a text description of each identifier. These files are typically executables or dynamic link libraries that have the strings embedded within the program resources.

Type

Event types are broken down into five mutually exclusive categories to which each event must be assigned:

- *Information.* These events are typically considered "successful." That is, they do not necessarily indicate that something has gone wrong, but declare that an operation has been carried out without a problem. For example, you will find log entries referring to the successful startup of the event log each time the operating system is rebooted.

- *Warning*. These events indicate that there is a non-critical error that could lead to problems in the future but does not inhibit the system from operating. For example, being unable to browse a server may throw a warning event.

- *Error*. These events are typically failures in an operating system service or driver that have a significant impact on data or the system functionality. For example, a disconnected external storage driver might throw an Error event if it can't detect the drive on its port.

- *Success Audit*. The security log stores events having to do with the results of attempts to use system objects like files, processes, or printers. If the security manager allows access to the object, and that access is being logged, it shows up as a success audit.

- *Failure Audit*. If the security manager refuses access to an object that is being audited, it throws a Failure Audit event.

Category

The event category allows a source to define the general organization of events it might throw. These categories start at one (1) and run sequentially. Like event identifiers, they are mapped to text strings within the message source. Either this source can be the same as for the event ID, or the originating program can register an additional source for the category text. By using the category information, events from a source can be grouped and sorted for easier perusal.

Description

In addition to the heading information provided for each event, there is a text description that provides more detailed information than the source provides about exactly what happened. For example, if there has been a problem accessing a file, the description includes information about exactly which file it was. The description information presented in the event viewer is a combination of data (such as filename) and message strings provided by a parameter message file. This message file can be the same as the other event message files (default), or the source can provide a separate file by setting its `ParameterMessageFile` Registry value to the message file path.

Data

In addition to string-based data, an event can also provide a binary data section that can be used to hold information that might be helpful in solving the problem. This data, however, is highly dependent on its source, and using this information will depend on knowing exactly what it is or having a program for analyzing this data. The data section of an event does not necessarily hold that much information. It is not intended to provide a tracking system to debug an errant program, for example. With thousands of possible events occurring on a system, keeping the data as small as possible is important.

Auditing and the UMD

Previous sections of this chapter describe the event logs used by NT and the format of records they can contain. One of these event logs, the security log, is configured and activated through the UMD. Events can be generated in one of two ways, either through the success of an action or through its failure. The range of the security events that can be audited stretches from system-wide events, such as logging on or off, to very localized actions, such as attempting to open an individual file. The UMD makes available a number of options for auditing, giving the administrator or a user from the domain admin[*] group the ability to track some, or all, of those event types. NT groups these actions into categories that are described in Table 8-2. The resulting selections make up the audit policy that, if configured on a PDC, acts as the policy for all the servers across the same domain. Before you rush ahead and create your policy, make sure you have read the previous sections so that you are aware of some of the issues associated with doing so. For instance, merrily selecting all the options available to you from the audit window generates a mass of records in the security log. If the system is set to crash when the security log becomes full, you will find yourself regularly surprised by the "blue screen of death." Reboot required.

Creating the audit policy

The audit policy is created only through the UMD and is achieved by selecting **Policies→Audit** and then clicking on the check boxes of your choice. Table 8-2 shows you to which category the audit dialog box options belong and which events are audited when an option is activated.

Table 8-2. Security Event Categories

Category	Description
LOGON/LOGOFF *Dialog*: Logon and Off *Events*: Successful Logon, Unknown Username or Bad Password, Account Currently Disabled, Logon Type Restricted, Password Expired, Unsuccessful Logon, User logoff	These events deal with a single attempt, be it successful or not, to log onto the system. Details recorded include the type of logon request, such as a network, interactive, or service connection.
OBJECT ACCESS *Dialog*: File and Object Access *Events*: Object Open, Handle Closed	This category tracks events that deal with access to restricted objects such as printers, files, and directories. It does not respond directly to object access but allows the auditing of the object to be established. Setting up the auditing of these objects is described later in this chapter.

---

[*]Only the Administrator or members of the domain admin group can set an audit policy.

Table 8-2. Security Event Categories (continued)

Category	Description
PRIVILEGE USE *Dialog*: Use of User Rights *Events*: Special Privilege Assigned, Privileged Service Called, Privileged Object Operation	Events in this category are used to track the use of privileges granted through the user rights policy, as well as the action of granting rights to a special privilege. An example of the latter is bypass traverse checking. Once granted, every traverse generates an entry in the event log. This would soon fill up the log, so NT takes a more practical approach and simply generates an entry in the log when the privilege is granted or revoked.
ACCOUNT MANAGEMENT *Dialog*: User and Group Management *Events*: User Account Created, User Account Changed, User Account Deleted, Global Group Member Added, Global Group Member Removed, Local Group Created, Local Group Member Added, Local Group Member Removed, Local Group Changed, Local Group Deleted	Events generated by this category refer to high-level changes made to the Registry. They do not comment on details of any changes made, only on the type of that change. For instance, making a change to a user's property generates a User Account Changed entry, but does not supply you with the details of that change.
POLICY CHANGE *Dialog*: Security Policy Changes *Events*: User Right Assigned, User Right Removed, Audit Policy Change	This category tracks high-level security policy changes, such as user right additions and audit policy changes.
SYSTEM EVENT *Dialog*: Restart, Shutdown, and System *Events*: System Restart, System Shutdown, Authentication Package Load, Logon Process Registered, Some Audit Event Records Discarded, Audit Log Cleared	This category covers events that reflect actions that affect the security of the system as a whole. This includes the security audit log.
DETAILED TRACKING *Dialog*: Process Tracking *Events*: New Process Has Been Created, Process Has Expired, Handle Duplicated, Indirect Access To Object	This category tracks process actions including process creation and indirect access to objects. Auditing these events gives an administrator the information required to determine the source of some forms of security breaches. For instance, it can help determine whether an incident, such as the attempted access of a restricted file, is, in fact, a rogue program or a rogue user.

Although the audit dialog box shows options for success or failure of an event, some of the events, such as those in the Account Management and Policy Change categories, have no failure state and therefore do not write a failure record to the event logs. The failure is tracked at a lower level, as Microsoft likes to term it, "at the finer granularity of auditing." The low-level tracking is carried out by events in the Object Access category.

WARNING   When trying to track Account Management and Policy Change
events, it is important to realize that only successful events have entries placed into the security event log. As failures are handled by
the low-level tracking category Object Access, you must make sure
that not only have you activated this category but that you have re-
quested it to track failures. Do not be lulled into a false sense of security by the fact that there is a failure option against the Account
Management and Policy Change categories; they have no effect.

Example 8-1 is an example of the record entry of the Object Open event in the
security event log.

Example 8-1. Event Log Record of an Object Open Event

```
Date    : 1/30/97Event ID: 560
Time    : 9:45:25 PMSource:Security
User    : ajm30Type:Failure Audit
Computer: IAGOCategory:Object Access

Object Open:
 Object Server:Security Account Manager
 Object Type:SAM_DOMAIN
 Object Name:JESUS
 New Handle ID:-
 Operation ID:{0,211609}
 Process ID:2154789024
 Primary User Name:SYSTEM
 Primary Domain:NT AUTHORITY
 Primary Logon ID:(0x0,0x3E7)
 Client User Name:ajm30
 Client Domain:JESUS
 Client Logon ID:(0x0,0x310A9)
 AccessesReadPasswordParameters
    CreateUser
    LookupIDs

Privileges-
```

This record was generated when a unauthorized user, ajm30, tried to create a new
user using the **net user** command. Although the Object Open event does not
belong to the Account Management category, this is the type of record you
should be looking for if you are interested in extracting audit information for
unsuccessful Account Management. Out of interest, the Privileged Object Operation event (Privilege Use category) also wrote a record to the log, indicating that
an attempt to use a privileged object occurred, but this record gives the object
handle number rather than a readable description of the object in question.

Auditing on Files and Objects

Being able to audit files and objects gives the fine control required to produce a comprehensive audit policy. It offers the administrator the flexibility not only to select the object to be audited, but to control the logging of the types of actions that can be applied to that object. Before you go about setting up this form of auditing, remember that you must first have configured your audit policy to track Object Access events (see earlier explanation).

To set the audit details of a file, you first need to access its properties option. To do this, find the file through either Windows NT Explorer or the desktop GUI (also called Explorer), and right-click on it. Select **Auditing** from the **Security** tab of the **Properties** dialog box. Next you need to add a user or group to the **Names** window and set the associated audit events. Like the Audit Policy configuration, the **Events to Audit** section of this dialog box allows for the tracking of a success and/or failure event. Table 8-2 and 8-4 show which events are available for auditing and which actions generate these events with respect to files, directories, and printers.

Table 8-3 lists the types of access that can be set for auditing on files or directories. Associated with each access type is the action that generates the event. For instance, you can see that if you set the **Read** option for auditing on a particular file, then the action of displaying that file generates an audit event that is written to the event log.

Using Table 8-3 you can see that if you select the audit option Read for a file, then the following actions generate an event record in the security event log:

- Displaying the file's data
- Displaying the file's attributes
- Displaying the file's owner and its permissions

Directory auditing has an extra feature not found with file auditing. This feature allows the administrator to set a local audit policy and force that policy onto either all files or all subdirectories, or indeed both files and subdirectories that reside within a directory. These extra options are **Replace Auditing on Subdirectories** and **Replace Auditing on Existing Files**; they are found above the common option settings in the audit dialog box associated with a directory.

Table 8-3. Access Types and Audit Actions for Files and Directories

Access Types	Actions That Generate Audit Events
Read	Displaying file data Displaying directory filenames Displaying attributes for both files and directories Displaying owner and permissions for both files and directories
Execute	Displaying attributes for both files and directories Executing a file Moving to a directory's subdirectories
Write	Displaying owner and permissions for both files and directories Changing attributes for both files and directories Creating files and subdirectories Changing a file's data
Delete	Deleting files and directories
Change permissions	Changing permissions for both files and directories
Take ownership	Taking over the ownership of both files and directories

Setting up a printer for auditing is done in exactly the same way. Some types of access are different, and some are removed. Table 8-4 matches access types with events that can be audited for a printer.

Table 8-4. Actions and Audit Options for a Printer

Access Types	Actions That Generate Audit Events
Print	Printing a document
Full control	Modifying job settings for a document Pausing or restarting the printer Deleting or moving a document Setting a printer for sharing Modifying the priorities of a printer
Delete	Deleting a printer
Change permissions	Modifying the permissions of a printer
Take ownership	Taking over the ownership of a printer

Auditing and the Registry

As you will recall from earlier chapters, the Registry is organized into keys and values. These can be equated to directories and files, the difference being that only keys can be audited. The main reason for auditing the Registry is to monitor access to it by applications and users. As we are primarily interested in users, we need to look for events generated by user action. The most common reason that an administrator would want to audit the Registry is to provide a means of tracking any unauthorized attempts, successful or not, to remove or change security-related values.

Setting up Registry auditing takes the same form as directory auditing, except that to configure the local policy you need to run the Registry editor, *regedt32*. Again, you must have already activated auditing through the UMD and have, as a minimum, selected the failure option of File and Object Access. Fire up *regedt32* and find the key you want to audit. With the key highlighted, select from the main menu **Security→Auditing** and the Registry key auditing dialog box appears. Its layout is very similar to that of the equivalent directory dialog box. Adding users to the **Name** list is done in the usual way, and there is also an option to force this local policy on all keys arranged below it. Table 8-5 lists the access types and associated audit events.

Table 8-5. Access Types and Audit Events for Registry Auditing

Access Type	Actions That Generate Audit Events
Query value	Attempting to read a Registry key value
Set value	Attempting to modify a Registry key value
Create subkey	Attempting to create a new subkey under the Registry key that is being audited
Enumerate subkeys	Attempting to read the subkeys of the Registry key under audit
Notify	Tracking notification events from the selected Registry key
Create link	Attempting to create a symbolic link to the Registry under audit
Delete	Attempting to delete the selected Registry key
Write DAC	Attempting to access the selected Registry key to modify the security permissions of that key
Read control	Attempting to access the selected Registry key to read the security permissions of that key

Let's look at an example to see how we can create a local audit policy for a particular key and why we would want to do this. The key we will use is:

```
HKEY_LOCAL_MACHINE\SYSTEM\CurrentControlSet\Services\Eventlog\System
```

As mentioned earlier, this key contains information about the system event log including where it is stored, its size, and its retention time. As information about the security event log, it may well command the attention of an individual who has been abusing the system. It is therefore in the administrator's interest to make sure that the audit trail is properly established.

For this example we will monitor two groups: Everyone and Administrators.

The Everyone group

We are looking to set up an audit policy that tells us when a user tries to probe this key, but in a selective way. Although this key is seldom accessed, many others are accessed more regularly, so simply selecting all options would generate quantities of unnecessary event records.

Query Value

We use this option with only a failure set to throw an event. A member of the group **Everyone**, who is not a member of the **Administrator** group, should not be able to carry out this action successfully. We bother with this event so that we can monitor a user who tries to carry out an action that can be considered outside the bounds of normal use. Once found, the user can be watched more closely or put straight up against the wall.

Read Control

This is set to do much the same job as Query Value; it throws an event when an attempt is made to read the permissions for the key. We should monitor both success and failure here to give us a clue not only to the fact that someone is probing the key but also, if successful, whether they have modify capabilities.

Write DAC

Monitoring this action for both success and failure gives us the information that someone is trying to modify, or has been successful in modifying, their access rights to the key. If they are indeed successful, then a breach of security has occurred, and we need to start worrying about the state of this key's values, as well as that of most other keys.

The Administrators group

We assume that the Administrators group has full control over this key. All the options used are set to throw an event on both success and failure. Although there should be no failures as the administrators have full control, it is still worth checking this just to make sure that nothing has gone astray. Auditing is not about checking to see if what a user actually does works; it is about recording whether they succeeded or failed at gaining access to the object from the security manager. The audit policy we set up here is to look only at creations and modifications to the key and its values.

The options activated are Set Value, Create Subkey, and Create Link.

The difference between the two policies is that one is a security policy and the other is a monitor policy. One tells us when a user tries to probe for information, and the other simply supplies us with data about Registry changes.

Ultimately, setting up policies is governed by how security conscious you are, how big you want your event logs, and possibly how much trouble you would get yourself into if you are not sufficiently covered.

The Event Viewer

The Event Viewer is the basic tool supplied with NT to allow viewing of the records stored in the three event logs that the system generates. The Event Viewer provides the administrator with the following functionality:

- Select an event log and display its contents

- Look at an individual record and display its data

- Allow manual clearing of the individual logs

- Set retention strategy and log size

- View event logs on other servers or NT workstations

- Filter, find, and organize event records to the screen

- Archive and retrieve event logs

Select an eventlog and display its contents

To do this you simply select **Log→System** from the Event Viewer's main menu, then highlight one of the three log files available. Having selected an event log file, you are presented with a sequential list of record entries for that log.

Look at an individual record and display its data

A record entry in the event log consists of date, time, source, category, event, user, and computer. This is, in fact, most of the header information stored with every record, and it gives you a quick visual guide to the log entries. To look at an individual record's details, select it either by double-clicking on it or by highlighting it and pressing ENTER. A dialog box for that record is displayed showing header information, description, and data. These details are documented earlier in the chapter.

Allow manual clearing of the individual logs

To clear the logs, select **Log→Clear All Events** from the main menu. NT checks that you mean to do this and gives you the option of saving the contents of the log before all the records are removed. The EventLog service automatically writes a record at the start of the clean log to indicate that a clear log event has occurred. The **Clear All Event** option clears only the currently selected log.

Set retention strategy and the log size

You can configure the Event Viewer to handle the automatic removing of records from a particular log. To do this, select **Log→Log Settings**... and choose from one of the three options available to you for managing the removal of records.

Overwrite Events as Needed

> This option ensures that the event records are still written to the log file once the file is full. It works by replacing the oldest record with the new one. It is the default.

Overwrite Files Older Than [ ] Days

> This option allows you to set the number of days that a record is stored in the event log, after which it is automatically removed. Strangely enough, the value stored internally is in seconds not days, so it is possible, if unnecessary, to set the time for record removal to be a second.

Do Not Overwrite Events (Clear Log Manually)

> As it says, this option disables any automatic clearing action, relying on a manual clearance of the log instead. A little warning is warranted here: If you have set the Registry Value `CrashOnAuditFail` to 1, make sure you do something with the log before it does fill up. Crashing the machine because there has been an attempt to breach the security is one thing, but crashing regularly because you keep forgetting to clear out or archive the log file is another, and probably a hangable offense at that.

From here you can also set the log file size. The default is 512K, but this can be set above 40MB if you want.

View event logs on other servers or NT workstations

From the main menu select **Log→Select Computer** and either select a computer from the Select Computer list box or type a computer name in the data entry field. Remember to use a UNC name such as *iago*. If you have permission, the event viewer now displays the event logs from the other machine. Do not forget that the servers on a given domain use the same audit policy as the PDC, whereas workstations use their own local ones.

Organize, find, and filter event records to the screen

When you are presented with a large set of data, finding all the records that interest you can be extremely difficult. The Event Viewer offers you three ways in which to organize the records that make up an event log.

Oldest/Newest records

The simplest way to organize the records of a log is to view them in date and time order. By default, the Event Viewer shows the latest record at the top of the record list. You can reverse this by selecting **View→Oldest First**.

Find a record

The Find facility allows you to set up a search pattern and then look through an event log, stopping at each matching record. To set up the Find you first need to bring up its dialog box. To do this, select **View→Find**. A number of options are available to you for creating a search pattern. You can include one or all types (Information, Warning, Error, Success Audit, and Failure Audit), the source of the event, its category, its event ID, who generated it, from which computer it was generated, and even the event's description.

Filter the records

This is a very useful feature of the Event Viewer. It can filter the records of an event log according to a pattern and display only those matching records as a record list. The options for setting up the filter pattern are the same as for the Find, except that you can also decide from which day and time you want to start and stop the filtering process. To set up filtering select **View→Filter Events**.... The option **View→All Events** reverses the filtering option, showing all the events in the selected event log.

Archive and retrieve event logs

The Event Viewer allows you to archive event logs in a fairly basic manner, by selecting **Log→Save As**... and then saving the log in one of three formats: as an event log, as a text file, or as a comma-separated file. To view an archived file, use the **Log→Open**... option, noting that you can view only files saved with the *.evt* extension. Event files are stored as binary files, and as the Event Viewer cannot import other file types, you are not able to read any text or CSV files you may have created with the **Save As** option. Chapter 9, *Auditing with Perl*, gives an example of event log filtering through a Perl script, but here is a small taste of things to come.

The following Perl script can be used to make a backup of an event log. The syntax is as follows:

```
backlog eventlogname filename
```

eventlogname is the event log you want to back up, and the *filename* is the name you wish to give to the archived log. For instance, you might use the following command to back up the security event log:

```
D:\perl\scripts>backlog security sec0197.evt
```

The script uses the built-in WIN32 functions the same way as Registry functions are used in earlier chapters. An event log is opened, a copy made and then closed.

Example 8-2. Backing Up an Event Log

```
# Backlog.pl
Win32::OpenEventLog($log,$ENV{COMPUTERNAME},$ARGV[0]) or die
"Cannot open event log\n";
Win32::BackupEventLog($log,$ARGV[1]) or die "Cannot create backup\n";
Win32::CloseEventLog ($log);
```

A Useful EventLog Script

As with all the tools that Microsoft supplies, we always seem to need another way of doing something. In this case, having a command-line utility to set event logging features would be quite useful. The script here uses Perl's built-in Registry functions to change the CrashOnAuditFail, File, MaxSize, and Retention settings for the three event logs: application, system, and security. If you have not done so, you should go back and take a look at Chapter 6, *NT Internals and Managing Users,* for how to use the Registry functions in Perl.

The script command line is as follows:

```
eventlog [/c on|off|reset] [log [/s size] [/r retention] [/f
    filename]] [log ...]
```

If the script is run without any arguments, it prints out the setting for the `CrashOnAuditFail` Registry value. Additionally, if only a log name is provided, then it prints out the crash information in addition to the file, size, and retention settings for that particular log.

```
D:\perl\scripts>eventlog system
CrashOnAuditFail set to: 0
Path set to: %SystemRoot%\system32\config\SysEvent.Evt
MaxSize set to: 512 KB
Retention set to: 168 HRS
```

Any number of log files can be placed on the command line, with the new options for that log following. The size is accepted in kilobytes and retention in hours, and the filename can either be a fully qualified path or be based on an environment variable such as *%systemroot%*. Notice that the routine indicates the actual value in bytes and seconds that the new registry settings will have, even though it converts from kilobytes and hours from the command line and for returning set values. The script can, of course, be changed to work in other increments that you find more convenient.

```
D:\perl\scripts>eventlog system /s 1024 /r 168
Setting system MaxSize to 1048576.. Done.
Setting system Retention to 604800.. Done.
```

```
CrashOnAuditFail set to: 0
Path set to: %SystemRoot%\system32\config\SysEvent.Evt
MaxSize set to: 1024 KB
Retention set to: 168 HRS
```

The `CrashOnAuditFail` value is global to all the event logs, so it can be changed on its own. In addition to turning the crash feature on and off, you can also use this command to reset the system from the command line after a crash has occurred.

```
D:\perl\scripts>eventlog /c reset
Setting CrashOnAuditFail value to 1.. Done.
CrashOnAuditFail set to: 1
```

Example 8-3. Changing Event Log Settings with Perl

```
# eventlog.pl
# This script is for altering the crash on audit fail,
# maximum size, and retention settings.

# this is required for the Registry functions

require "NT.ph";

# since the CrashOnAuditFail registry setting is in a separate key
# we have set up a different function to handle it from the
# other settings. The key value is created if it does not exist.

sub SetCrashValue {
    $setting = shift @_;
    print "Setting CrashOnAuditFail value to $setting";
    Win32::RegOpenKeyEx(&HKEY_LOCAL_MACHINE,
        'SYSTEM\CurrentControlSet\Control\Lsa',
        &NULL,
        &KEY_ALL_ACCESS,
        $hkey) ?
        print '.' : die "Unable to open Crash Control Key\n";

    Win32::RegSetValueEx($hkey,
        'CrashOnAuditFail',
        &NULL,
        &REG_DWORD,
        $setting) ?
        print '.' : die "Unable to set value\n";

    Win32::RegCloseKey($hkey);
    print " Done.\n";
}

# This function is used to set the eventlog source settings
# it is passed the log (i.e. system, security, application),
# the value (File, MaxSize, Retention) and the new setting.

sub SetLog {
    $log = shift @_;
    $value = shift @_;
```

Example 8-3. Changing Event Log Settings with Perl (continued)

```
        $setting = shift @_;
        print "Setting $log $value to $setting";
        Win32::RegOpenKeyEx(&HKEY_LOCAL_MACHINE,
            "SYSTEM\\CurrentControlSet\\Services\\EventLog\\$log",
            &NULL,
            &KEY_ALL_ACCESS,
            $hkey) ?
            print '.' : die "Unable to open $log Key\n";
        Win32::RegSetValueEx($hkey,
            $value,
            &NULL,
            &REG_DWORD,
            $setting) ?
            print '.' : die "Unable to set $value\n";

        Win32::RegCloseKey($hkey);
        print " Done.\n";
    }


# This is used to print settings for CrashOnAuditFail and
# if passed a log name, the settings for that event log.

sub DisplayLogInfo {
    Win32::RegOpenKeyEx(&HKEY_LOCAL_MACHINE,
        'SYSTEM\CurrentControlSet\Control\Lsa',
        &NULL,
        &KEY_ALL_ACCESS,
        $hkey) or
        print "Unable to open Crash Control Key\n";

    Win32::RegQueryValueEx($hkey,
        'CrashOnAuditFail',
        &NULL,
        $type,
        $crash) ?
        print "CrashOnAuditFail set to: ",ord($crash),"\n" :
        print "CrashOnAuditFail read fail - value may not exist\n";

    Win32::RegCloseKey($hkey);
    if($log = shift @_) {

        Win32::RegOpenKeyEx(&HKEY_LOCAL_MACHINE,
            "SYSTEM\\CurrentControlSet\\Services\\EventLog\\$log",
            &NULL,
            &KEY_ALL_ACCESS,
            $hkey) or print "Unable to open $log Key\n";
        Win32::RegQueryValueEx($hkey,
            'File',
            &NULL,
            $type,
            $path) ?
            print "Path set to: ",$path,"\n" :
            print "Path read failure - value may not exist\n";
```

Example 8-3. Changing Event Log Settings with Perl (continued)

```perl
        Win32::RegQueryValueEx($hkey,
            'MaxSize',
            &NULL,
            $type,
            $size) ?
            print "MaxSize set to: ",unpack("L",$size)/1024," KB\n"
            : print "MaxSize read failure - value may not exist\n";

        Win32::RegQueryValueEx($hkey,
            'Retention',
            &NULL,
            $type,
            $sec) ?
            print "Retention set to: ",unpack("L",$sec)/3600," HRS\n"
            : print "Retention read failure - value may not exist\n";

        Win32::RegCloseKey($hkey);
    }
}


# This is where all the command parsing takes place. It simply
# loops through all of the command-line arguments, calling the
# appropriate subroutine as necessary.

while ($command = shift @ARGV) {
    if($command eq '/c') {
        $command = shift @ARGV;
        if($command eq 'on' or $command eq 'reset') {
            SetCrashValue(1);
            next;
        } else {
            SetCrashValue(0);
            next;
        }
    } elsif ($command eq '/s') {
        $command = shift @ARGV;
        SetLog($log,'MaxSize',$command*1024);
        next;
    } elsif ($command eq '/r') {
        $command = shift @ARGV;
        SetLog($log, 'Retention', $command*3600);
        next;
    } elsif ($command eq '/f') {
        $command = shift @ARGV;
        SetLog($log, 'File', $command);
    } else {
        $log = $command;
    }
}


DisplayLogInfo($log);
```

It is important to notice that this script is used to set options for the event logs, but it does not, in fact, use any of the built-in event log functions that Perl provides. In the next chapter we will look more specifically at the event log functions provided in Perl with the aim of creating more command-line utilities that can be used in place of programs such as the *eventvwr*.

Archived event logs are most useful if they have been stored in their native format. Otherwise, you lose information such as the entire data section of all events. Even though event logs can be saved as text files, this is not really recommended practice. By creating utilities that can open, filter, and search native event log files into text output, you can keep the information of the native format while using the flexibility of other text-based tools from the command line—a job for which Perl is eminently suited. This, of course, requires the use of the event log functions that Perl provides, in addition to the more common features.

9

Auditing with Perl

Once you have established an audit policy and configured those objects you are interested in, you need to concentrate on archiving and event filtering. The archiving strategy you implement should take into account the following:

- The maximum size of the event logs
- Whether the Crash on Full option is set
- The number of objects under audit
- Which events generate an entry in the event logs
- The time designated to keep the archived files
- How safety conscious you are

Archiving the event logs needs to be both a regular and an automated process in order to maintain the audit trail's consistency and security. To achieve this, an administrator needs to have put in place either a disciplined work regime of archiving through the GUI or an application/script that is run automatically by the operating system at given intervals. Once archived, these audit trails can be analyzed to provide information of either a security or monitoring nature. They should not be tucked away and left to collect disk dust. Remember, you can get out of an archive only what you put in, so make sure your audit policy is up to its task.

In this chapter, we present a solution for a typical situation by using Perl and its built-in event log APIs.

Event Log APIs

The built-in Perl APIs are the key to getting a handle on event log information as well as supplying the tools to manipulate these logs from the command line. The examples in this chapter use most of the event log APIs; each one is described before use. The following Perl scripts demonstrate how to set up event log backups, including source registration, event log filtering, and automatic alarm warnings, which include service registration.

Registering a Source

Registering a source is the process of informing NT through registry settings about programs that will generate auditing events. Why do you need to register a source? Well, actually you do not, but by doing so you can give the event record you intend to write some added details, giving more information about actions carried out by your scripts. To register an event source (that is, the application or script that writes an event record), you need to add a key and associated value to the Registry. We want to register the script *BackLog.pl* as a source with the application event log, so we first open the key:

```
HKEY_LOCAL_MACHINE\SYSTEM\CurrentControlSet\Services\EventLog\Application
```

Having opened this key, we then add a new subkey `Backlog` and create the associated value `TypeSupported`. This value is of type `REG_DWORD` and has a hexadecimal setting of 0x07. This value indicates which of the event types the source supports. Table 9-1 shows the event types and their associated values.

Table 9-1. Event Types

Event Types	Values
EVENTLOG_SUCCESS	0x0000
EVENTLOG_ERROR_TYPE	0x0001
EVENTLOG_WARNING_TYPE	0x0002
EVENTLOG_INFORMATION_TYPE	0x0004
EVENTLOG_AUDIT_SUCCESS	0x0008
EVENTLOG_ AUDIT_FAILURE	0x0010

0x07 is arrived at by considering all the event types the source supports and OR'ing them together. In this case, the first four values OR'd together result in 0x0007.

Another value can be set here, `EventMessageFile`. This value is of type `REG_EXPAND_SZ` and is the name of the executable that holds the description record. The description record holds string values that explain the meaning of event IDs. This record is dependent on the eventID number and is defined by the application itself. Creating your own description records is outside the scope of this book, but there is nothing to stop you from making use of the records defined by other applications. For instance, the file *MsAuditE.dll* is used in Example 9-2, and so the value `EventMessageFile` is included and set to point to this executable in Example 9-1.

Example 9-1 shows how to register a source using Perl—in this case, the *backlog* script we will build later. The Win32 Registry APIs are described in Chapter 7, *Controlling the User*. No Win32 Event Log APIs are used in this short script.

Example 9-1. Sreg.pl

```
#SReg.pl
#Registers a new application source with the EventService

require "NT.ph";

# Open the key HKEY_LOCAL_MACHINE and return a handle to the subkey
# Application

Win32::RegOpenKeyEx(&HKEY_LOCAL_MACHINE,

'SYSTEM\CurrentControlSet\Services\EventLog\Application',
            &NULL,&KEY_ALL_ACCESS,$hkey) or die "FAILED to open key\n";

# Using the returned handle from RegOpenKeyEx, $hkey, create a new
# subkey BackLog the handle $backlog pointing to it
Win32::RegCreateKey($hkey,'BackLog',$backlog);

# Using $Backlog, create a new value TypeSupported. The 7 represents
# what types the source can use when writing an event record
Win32::RegSetValueEx($backlog,'TypeSupported',&NULL,&REG_DWORD,7);
Win32::RegSetValueEx($backlog,'EventMessageFile',&NULL,&REG_EXPAND_SZ,
        '%SystemRoot\System32\MsAuditE.dll');

# Close the open keys
Win32::RegCloseKey($backlog);
Win32::RegCloseKey($hkey);

print "Source - BackLog - Registered\n";
```

Event Log Backup

The next script we must write is the one to archive the event logs. This needs to open each log in turn, make a backup of it using some incremental naming method, clear it, and then write a record to the clean log indicating that it was cleared by this particular Perl script. This will then tell any of the administrators who view the log subsequently that it was cleared as part of a backup, rather than for any other reason. Having made the backup, the event log is closed.

Example 9-2 uses four API functions:

Win32::OpenEventLog()

```
Win32::OpenEventLog($handle, $server, $source)
```

This call opens an event log supplied by `$source` on the machine `$server`, and returns the file handle `$handle`.

Win32::ClearEventLog()

```
Win32::ClearEventLog($handle, $filename)
```

This call not only clears the event log pointed to by `$handle`, but also backs it up to the file `$filename` and writes a cleared log event record to the newly cleared log. Alternatively, to make a backup of the log without clearing it, you can use the `BackupEventLog` API.

Win32::BackupEventLog()

```
Win32::BackupEventLog($handle, filename)
```

This call is identical to `ClearEventLog` except that after backing up the log, it does not clear it.

Win32::WriteEventLog()

```
Win32::WriteEventLog($server, $source, $eventType, $category,
        $eventID, $reserved, $data, $message1, …)
```

This call writes an event record to the event log supplied by `$source`. Table 9-2 lists the parameters used and presents a short description.

Table 9-2. Parameters of WriteEventLog

Parameter	Description
$server	This is a string that holds the name of the computer. An example is *IAGO*.
$source	This is a string that holds the name of the source. An example is 'System'.
$eventType	This is an integer and should be one, or more than one, of the predefined types OR'd. These types are documented in Table 9-1.
$category	This is an integer representing some internally defined category to the source.
$eventID	This is an integer and is one predefined by the source application or, if you are using your own source, anything that makes sense to you.
$reserved	This call is not used
$data	This is proprietary binary data and can be used only if you know exactly what the source is returning.
$message1, $message2…	This is a string and is used to supply text information for the record. If the value `EventMessageFile` is present, then, depending on the number of fields in the description record, there should an equal number of messages.

Win32::CloseEventLog()

```
Win32::CloseEventLog($handle)
```

This call closes the open event log pointed to by `$handle`.

Example 9-2 uses the following syntax:

```
backlog path
```

where *path* is the path to the directory where you want to store the archived files. For example, you may wish to store the archive files in a directory called *EventBackups*:

```
E:\>backlog d:\EventBackups
```

Example 9-2. BackLog.pl

```perl
# Backlog.pl
# Backs up the Event logs with an auto incremental name,
# clears the Event logs, and writes an event record to the
# application Event log

require "NT.ph";

# If the argument is left blank use the current directory
if ($ARGV[0] eq "") {
    $ARGV[0] = ".";
}

# If the directory does not exist ask to create it
if (!-d $ARGV[0]) {
    print "$ARGV[0] does not exist create? [y/n] : ";
    if (<STDIN> =~ /^y/i) {
    qx(mkdir $ARGV[0])
    } else {
        die "No backups carried out\n";
    }
}

# Set the log names and get the date
@eventlogs = ("system","security","application");
($sec,$min,$hour,$day,$month,$year) = localtime(time);
$month++;

# Fire each log, loop around using the day, month, and a letter to
# create a unique name for the backup file
foreach $log(@eventlogs) {
    $log =~/(\w{3})/;
    $backlog = $ARGV[0]."\\".$1.$day."_".$month."a";

# If the backup file exists, increment the end letter and try again
    while (-e $backlog) {
        $replace = chop($backlog);
        $backlog = $backlog.++$replace
```

Example 9-2. BackLog.pl (continued)

```
    }

# Open the event log
    Win32::OpenEventLog($logopen,$ENV{COMPUTERNAME},$log);

# Make a backup and then clear the log
    if (Win32::ClearEventLog($logopen,$backlog)) {
        print "$log backed up to - $backlog\n"
    } else {
        Win32::WriteEventLog($ENV{COMPUTERNAME}, "BackLog",&EVENTLOG_ERROR_TYPE,
                        &NULL,517,&NULL,&NULL,"BACKLOG - backup FAILED",
                        "","",$ENV{USERNAME},$ENV{USERDOMAIN},"");
                        die "BACKLOG FAILED TO CREATE BACKUPS\n";
    }

# Close the log
    Win32::CloseEventLog($logopen);

}# End of FOREACH

# Write a record to the application event log to indicate a successful
# backup has been done
Win32::WriteEventLog($ENV{COMPUTERNAME},"BackLog",&EVENTLOG_INFORMATION_TYPE,
                    &NULL,517,&NULL,&NULL,"BACKLOG - backup completed",
                    "","",$ENV{USERNAME},$ENV{USERDOMAIN},"");
```

Having registered *Backlog* as a source and built the script, we now want to collect the data. As mentioned earlier, we want this to be an automated process, and the easiest way to do this is to use the   command. This command allows you to schedule the running of an executable, batch, or command file at a given time on a given day. For our purposes, we wish to run Backlog every midnight, giving us a block of data in units of a day. To do this, we need to run the following *at* command :

```
    AT 00:00 /every d:\backlog.cmd
```

at is the command, `00:00` is midnight, `/every` tells *at* to run the command every day, and *d:\backlog.cmd* is the command file that calls the Perl script with its parameters. We have had more success with the *at* command when calling Perl scripts in an encapsulating command or batch file.

Backlog.cmd contains the line:

```
    d:\perl scripts\backlog d:\eventbackups
```

Filtering an Event Log

Up to this point, the scripts we have looked at concentrated on the administration and maintenance of event logs. Although we hope you never have to use your event logs in anger, being able to search your logs and find out what is going on is essential. The following script is used to search both the three main event logs any backup logs you might have created. It is by no means a complete filter tool for event logs, but it is a good example of what is possible with Perl.

The *logjam* script takes a series of arguments from the command line and searches through the specified log for a matching event. When a matching event is found, the elements of the event are sent to the output, which can either be the standard output or a file. The options for the command are as follows:

/l *log*

This command is used to designate which log should be searched. This can include the three primary logs (application, system, and security), or it can be a filename to a backup event log. This should be provided before any **/a** argument

/f *filename*

This command indicates that the output of the script should be sent to filename.

/i *filename*

By using the /i option, you can designate a filename for the input arguments to the script. This allows more complex searches to be carried out repeatedly without retyping.

/m *key value*

The /m option is used to indicate an element you wish to match in an event. The key name must be one available in the `%event` hash created from reading the event log. The key names are as follows:

computer

The name of the computer that generated the event

sid

The security ID of the user under which the event was generated

data

Event-specific data; typically binary information

Strings

Character strings associated with the event

recnum

The record number of the event

id

The event identification number of the event, as specified by the event generator `type`

> The type of event that occured (Information, Warning, Error, Success Audit, Failure Audit)

`tgen`

> The time the event was generated

`twrite`

> The time the event was written to the log file

`account`

> The account (or username) under which the event was generated

`category`

> The category of the event as specified by the event generator.

> `/t [before | after]` *hh:mm:ss dd:mm:yy* `[`*hh:mm:ss dd:mm:yy*`]`

> Because it is unlikely you will know exactly what second an event you are looking for occurred, you can specify a range of times for which to search. If before or after are provided, you need to specify only one time. Or, you can provide a range of dates on which to search.

`/d csv | del`

> By default, *logjam* placed spaces between all the event keys during output. If you would like to use another delimiter, you can specify that using the /d option. Used with csv, the output file is comma-separated.

`/a`

> Because there may be more than one set of values on which you want to search, you can use the /a option to force a search on all the options at that point in parsing the command line. You can then proceed to reset the key-value pairs to search for another event. For example:

```
D:\perl\scripts>logjam /l application /d csv /m id 105 /a /m id 108
,0,JUDAS,,105,3,,ReachOut,ReachOut ,855411636,855411636,65540
,0,JUDAS,,105,18,,ReachOut,ReachOut ,855412837,855412837,65540
,0,JUDAS,,105,22,,ReachOut,ReachOut ,855412958,855412958,65540
,0,JUDAS,,108,4,,ReachOut,ReachOut ,855411714,855411714,65540
,0,JUDAS,,108,15,,ReachOut,ReachOut ,855412554,855412554,65540
```

In this case, after searching for all events with an ID of 105, the script then resets the ID key to 108 and searches for this value in the application log. The long numbers (855...) are the event generation and write time stamps in seconds since 1970.

Even though it is simple in what it can do, the *logjam* script does show off some fundamental elements needed for working with event logs in Perl. In addition to the backup and write API functions discussed in the previous section, there are a couple of new event log functions for reading events from event logs as well as opening up previously backed-up logs.

Win32::OpenBackupEventLog()

```
Win32::OpenBackupEventLog($handle, $computer, $file)
```

`$handle` is the returned handle to the backed-up event log that can then be used for subsequent reads. `$computer` is the argument used to pass the name of the computer on which to open the log, and `$file` is used to pass the name of the event log file you wish to open. The function returns true if it is able to open up the event log file; otherwise, it returns false. Note that these backup files should be in the native binary event log format. This reinforces the view that you should always keep your backups in their binary form. If needed, you can always use a program such as the Event Viewer or *logjam* to convert them to another format. Once you have an event log opened, you can begin to read elements using the following function:

Win32::ReadEventLog()

```
Win32::ReadEventLog($log, $flag, $rec, $evtHeader, $source,
                    $computer, $sid, $data, $strings)
```

Table 9-3 defines each of the arguments for this function.

Table 9-3. Argument Definitions for ReadEventLog

Argument	Value
$log	This is the logfile handle returned by either the *OpenEventLog* or the *OpenBackupEventLog* functions.
$flag	This argument is used to indicate the way the log should be read. EVENTLOG_SEQUENTIAL_READ is used to indicate that the log should be read record by record with each subsequent call to the *ReadEventLog* function. Used with EVENTLOG_FORWARDS_READ and EVENTLOG_ BACKWARDS_READ flags, you can designate in which direction subsequent calls to the read function should move. EVENTLOG_SEEK_READ is used to read a particular log entry. When $flag is set to this value, the $rec argument is used to indicate what record to read.
$rec	The $rec argument is used to designate which record to read if the EVENTLOG_SEEK_READ flag is set. If the read method is sequential, then this value is ignored.
$evtHeader	The $evtHeader argument is a return value holding the header information for the event read. This is in a packed format, and the relevant information must be extracted.
$source	This argument is a return value holding the source of the event read.
$computer	This is a return value indicating the name of the computer that generated the event

Table 9-3. Argument Definitions for ReadEventLog (continued)

Argument	Value
$data	The $data argument is a return value that holds the data section of an event entry. This is typically in a proprietary format, so you must either know exactly what format the data is in or have extra software that can handle it.
$strings	The $strings argument is a return variable that holds the strings used in the description section of an event log entry. This string does not include the descriptive elements that are included in the event viewer because these come from each source's message file.

As with the *OpenBackupEventLog*, the *ReadEventLog* function returns true if it was able to return an event and false otherwise. As you will see in the script itself, using the *ReadEventLog* does not automatically return all the individual elements of an event entry. In particular, the $evtHeader argument is a packed value from which you must extract the information inside.

Example 9-3. Perl Script logjam.pl to Search Through the Event Logs

```perl
# NT.ph is required for the predefined routines such as
# &EVENTLOG_SEQUENTIAL_READ.

require "NT.ph";

# required for the date conversion functions

use Time::Local;

# getStrDate returns the string version of a time based on the
# number of seconds since 1970.

sub getStrDate {
    my $epoch = shift @_;
    my ($tSec, $Min, $tHour,
        $tMDay, $tMon, $tYear,
        $wday, $yday, $isdst) = localtime($epoch);

    return("$tHour:$Min:$tSec $tMDay/",++$tMon,"/$tYear");
}

# getEpochDate is the reverse of the previous function in that it
# takes a string date, and converts it to an epoch value. This is
# used to make time comparisons easier

sub getEpochDate {
    $string  = shift @_;
    $string =~ /(\d{2}):(\d{2}):(\d{2})\s(\d{2})\/(\d{2})\/(\d{2})/;
    $time = Time::Local::timelocal($3,$2,$1,$4,$5,$6);
    return($time);
}

# this is where all of the work is done. After shifting all of the
```

Example 9-3. Perl Script logjam.pl to Search Through the Event Logs (continued)

```perl
# arguments into their appropriate variables, the function checks
# too see whether the log source is one of the three standard, or
# a backup file and opens it up accordingly. Note that the %search
# hash is passed in by reference.

sub searchEvents {
    my $source = shift @_;
    my $sHashRef = shift @_;
    my $delimiter = shift @_;
    my %search = %$sHashRef;
    if($source ne 'application' and $source ne 'system'
        and $source ne 'security') {
        Win32::OpenBackupEventLog($openlog,
                                  $ENV{COMPUTERNAME},
                                  $source)
            or die "unable to connect to backup log $source";
    } else {
        Win32::OpenEventLog($openlog,
                            $ENV{COMPUTERNAME},
                            $source)
            or die "unable to open $source log";
    }
    my $flag = &EVENTLOG_FORWARDS_READ | &EVENTLOG_SEQUENTIAL_READ;

    # this is the loop where each of the events in a log is
    # compared against the arguments provided. Notice that
    # those variables we are concerned with are placed in the
    # %event hash. This structure can later be easily compared
    # with the %search hash passed into the function.

    while ( Win32::ReadEventLog($openlog,
                                $flag,
                                0,
                                $evtHeader,
                                $event{'source'},
                                $event{'computer'},
                                $event{'sid'},
                                $event{'data'},
                                $event{'strings'} )) {
        # this very long line is used to unpack the header information
        # into its respective variables. Note again the use of the
        # % event hash.

        ($length, $reserved, $event{'recnum'},
         $event{'tgen'}, $event{'twrite'},
         $event{'id'}, $event{'type'}, $nStrings,
         $event{'category'}, $rFlags, $clRecNum,
         $strOff, $sidLen, $sidOff, $dataLen,
         $dataOff) = unpack "L16",$evtHeader;

        # since user info is passed as an sid, we must convert it
        # to a readable format. This is done with LookupAccountSID.
```

Example 9-3. Perl Script logjam.pl to Search Through the Event Logs (continued)

```
    # In this case, the PDC is hard-wired into the function call.

    Win32::LookupAccountSID('iago', $event{'sid'}, $event{'account'},
                            $domain, $sidtype);

    # This is the loop which compares each of the keys in the
    # %search hash to their respective keys in the %event hash
    # created from the event just read from the log. Since the
    # %search hash may not include all keys, there is no need
    # to loop through every possible key. If a key
    # exists in the %search hash, and its value does not equal
    # the corresponding key in the %event hash, the loop is
    # immediately stopped, and the event not added to the output.

KEY: foreach $key(keys %search) {

        # the time matching is based in event generation
        if ($key eq 'begintime' or $key eq 'endtime') {
            if($event{'tgen'} >= $search{'begintime'}
               || $event{'tgen'} <= $search{'begintime'})
            {
                $match = 1;
                next;
            } else {
                $match = 0;
                last;
            }
        } elsif($key eq 'strings') {

            # in this example it is sufficient to match any word
            # in the strings key. The strings key is also known
            # as the description in the event viewer (minus the
            # built in strings added by the source).
            @words = split("\s+",$event{'strings'});
            foreach $word(@words) {
                if($word eq $search{'strings'}) {
                    $match = 1;
                } else {
                    $match = 0;
                }
            }
            last KEY if not $match;

        # for all other keys, a direct mapping can be done

        } elsif ($event{$key} eq $search{$key}) {
            $match = 1;
            next;
        } else {
            $match = 0;
            last;
        }
```

Example 9-3. Perl Script logjam.pl to Search Through the Event Logs (continued)

```perl
        }

        # if the event has gotten this far without a mismatch,
        # it is sent to the output.

        foreach $key(sort keys %event) {
            $output .= $event{$key}.$delimiter;
        }
        chop($output);
        print $output,"\n" if $match;
    }
    Win32::CloseEventLog($openlog);
}

# a default delimiter is selected as space

$del = ' ';

# this is the loop where all of the command line arguments are taken
# and use to build up the options and search hash

while($command = shift @ARGV) {
    if($command eq '/m') {
        $key = shift @ARGV;
        $value = shift @ARGV;
        $match{$key} = $value;
    } elsif($command eq '/l') {
        $log = shift @ARGV;
    } elsif($command eq '/f') {
        $file = shift @ARGV;
        open(OUTPUT,">$file") or die "unable to open $file";
        select(OUTPUT);
    } elsif($command eq '/i') {

        # this option takes the input file, and after splitting each
        # line, adds the arguments to the @ARGV array

        $file = shift @ARGV;
        open(INPUT,$file) or die "cannot open $file for input";
        while(<INPUT>) {
            chomp;
            @newargs = split('\s+',$_);
            @ARGV = (@ARGV,@newargs);
        }
    } elsif($command eq '/t') {

        # this option sets the time limits to search for

        $arg = shift @ARGV;
        if( $arg eq 'after') {
            $str = shift @ARGV;
            $match{'begintime'} = getEpochTime($str);
```

Example 9-3. Perl Script logjam.pl to Search Through the Event Logs (continued)

```perl
        $match{'endtime'} = time;
    } elsif( $arg eq 'before') {
        $str = shift @ARGV;
        $match{'endtime'} = getEpochTime($str);
        $match{'begintime'} = 0;
    } else {
        $beginstr = shift @ARGV;
        $endstr = shift @ARGV;
        $match{'begintime'} = getEpochTime($beginstr);
        $match{'endtime'} = getEpochTime($endstr);
    }
} elsif($command eq '/d') {

    # this command used to set the delimiter to a comma for csv

    $arg = shift @ARGV;
    if($arg eq 'csv') {
        $del = ',';
    } else {
        $del = $arg;
    }
} elsif($command eq '/a') {

    # this is used to run the search command
    # before loading up the next match variables

    searchEvents($log,\%match,$del);
    }

}


# this runs the search for the last set of variable,
# or if there is only one set given

searchEvents($log,\%match,$del);
```

As mentioned before, many things could be done with our event log filter script to make it more useful. The matching done is very basic, and there is no facility for the inclusion of Boolean operations or regular expressions. In addition, some of the more powerful report-formatting capabilities of Perl are not exploited for output to a file or the screen. For example, you could generate HTML output for remote administrative monitoring. The practical elements of opening the log, reading entries, and sending them to output are all there. For example, to compute how many users log in over a week, we simply look for all logon events (ID = 528) over a week's time:

```
logjam /l security /f out.txt /m id 528 /t "00:00:00 01/02/97"
    "00:00:00 08/02/97"
```

The number of lines in the resulting output could then be counted to find the total number of logons for that week. You will quickly find that in order to do something useful with your data, you will need more powerful means of analysis. In this case, outputting the results of a filter into a CSV file, then importing them into a program such as Excel, allows you not only to filter, but also to analyze and chart what is going on.[*] Of course, using the built-in OLE capabilities of the Win32 version of Perl, you can push your data straight into an Excel worksheet.

Outputting filtered log entries to Excel

Perhaps one of the most underused elements of Perl is its ability to interact with OLE objects such as Microsoft Word and Excel, thus obviating the need for cumbersome translations from CSV files to Excel worksheets. Within Perl it is possible to simply place the data straight into an Excel worksheet. To do this, the first thing necessary is to include the OLE module:[†]

```
use OLE;
```

To incorporate output to Excel into the *logjam* script, we moved the opening and closing of the output file to the filtering subroutine, passing the value of the output file argument

```
} elsif($command eq '/f') {
    $out = shift @ARGV;
...
searchEvents($log,\%match,$del,$out);
```

Once the filtering subroutine has the output filename, we can test to see whether the output should be to Excel and then open up the proper output accordingly. In the case of output to Excel, we use the *CreateObject* method to create a running instance of Excel and then ask it to open up our output file. Note that in this case you must create the Excel worksheet you wish to use.

```
if($output eq 'excel') {
    $excel = CreateObject OLE 'Excel.Application.5' or die "unable to open Excel";
    $excel->Workbooks->Open('D:\perl\scripts\out.xls') or
        die "unable to open Excel workbook";
} else {
    open(OUTPUT,">>$output") or die "unable to open $output";
    select(OUTPUT);
}
```

Once we have opened up Excel and have found a matching record, we can begin to enter information into the worksheet using the following method. Note that the $j and $i indices are used to move through the cells as we add keys from an event and as we add more events to the worksheet.

---

[*] Colored pictures always impress the suits in management.

[†] The libwin32 package in the 5.004 build specifies the syntax of: use Win32::OLE.

```
if($output eq 'excel') {
    $j = 1;
    foreach $key(sort keys %event) {
        $excel->Workbooks(1)->Worksheets('Sheet1')->Cells($j++,$i)->
            {Value} = $event{$key};
    }
} else {
    foreach $key(sort keys %event) {
        $output .= $event{$key}.$delimiter;
    }
    chop($output);
    print $output,"\n" if $match;
    $output = "";
}
```

Finally, when we have completed running through the filter, we must close down whatever output we have been using. This is a very important element of the script. Failing to close down Excel will leave a running copy on your system! Although this will not necessarily take up processor cycles, it will eat into your virtual memory and will require using the Task Manager to close down. This is important to remember if your program has crashed during execution without shutting down Excel. After a few aborted attempts at running Excel through Perl, you would have several copies of Excel running on your system. When Perl runs Excel it does not create any visual cue. This means that you definitely need to keep track of what is going on and periodically check the Task Manager process tab to see that all copies have been closed down. If you ever get the error that your file is in use by another application, you can bet that you have a rogue copy of Excel somewhere.

```
if($output eq 'excel') {
    $excel->Save();
    $excel->Quit();
} else {
    close($output);
}
```

With the filtered events in Excel, you can begin to look at more complex information such as average logon times and usage by machine, to name two. Of course, if you have serious reporting needs, more powerful tools are available for generating reports about event logs and other NT system diagnostics. One such program is Seagate's Crystal Reports, which comes with the NT 4.0 Server Resource Kit. As we mentioned before, if you are working with NT in any serious fashion, the Resource Kit is something you *must* get. Generating reports from the event log can be extremely useful for understanding how your setup is working and identifying where trouble spots may lie. To react to an event in real time, you will need some method of having the system notify you when something has gone wrong.

Blating on an Event

The next example uses a public domain utility called *blat* to send off a mail message when the event log has reached a critical size. The script *loggauge* periodically reads the log file, checking its current size against its maximum possible size as set in the Registry. Once the logfile has reached a specified percentage of the maximum size settings, the script sends off a mail message to the administrator warning him or her of the current size. This message then allows the administrator to perform a manual backup of the log file before it reaches full capacity. If you have set the `CrashOnAuditFail` setting for the event log, you certainly need some means of making sure you are not letting your system crash because you simply forgot to clear the log. By allowing the system to mail you a message, you can make sure you are notified in a timely manner. If you want a completely hands-off approach, you can even have the script run the *backlog* backup and clear script developed at the beginning of the chapter, which would ensure that all log events were properly backed up.

The command line options for *loggauge* are:

```
loggauge eventlog percent seconds
```

where `eventlog` is the log to monitor, `percent` is the level at which the program should send a warning message, and `seconds` are the number of seconds to sleep before checking the size of the logfile. You should balance the level at which you are warned and the seconds between checks to make sure that you have adequate time to act on the logs before they are full, but that you are not inundated with email once it reaches the set level.

Example 9-4. Mailing a Message when the Event Log is Near to Full

```
#LogGauge checks an event log to see how full it is. If it becomes greater
#than a given percentage then a mail message is sent to the administrator.

require "NT.ph";
#Get the parameters, event log, percentage level, and sleep time

$log = shift @ARGV;
$level = shift @ARGV;
$snooze = shift @ARGV;


#Start the infinite loop. Open the appropriate key and extract the event
#log path and the event log's maximum file size.
while (1) {Win32::RegOpenKeyEx(&HKEY_LOCAL_MACHINE,

"SYSTEM\\CurrentControlSet\\Services\\EventLog\\$log",
                        &NULL, &KEY_ALL_ACCESS, $hkey);
    Win32::RegQueryValueEx($hkey,'File',&NULL, $type, $path) or die;
    Win32::RegQueryValueEx($hkey,'MaxSize',&NULL, $type, $size) or die;
    Win32::RegCloseKey($hkey);
```

Example 9-4. Mailing a Message when the Event Log is Near to Full (continued)

```
#Convert the %SystemRoot% to the actual root i.e., d:\winnt
    $ExpandedPath = Win32::ExpandEnvironmentStrings($path);
#Grab the file information
    @fileinfo = stat $ExpandedPath;
#Calculate the % used
    $percent = $fileinfo[7] / unpack("L",$size) *100;
#Call 'blat' if $percent is greater than $level mailing the file
#EvtWarning.txt to the administrator.
    if ($percent > $level) {
        qx(blat EvtWarning.txt -s \"EventLog Critical - $percent\" -t
            admin\@jesus.cam.ac.uk -q);
    }
#Sleep before testing again
    sleep($snooze) or die;
}
```

The one element really important here is the *blat* command. *blat* is a public
domain mail program for NT that allows you to send a file as an email message
using an SMTP machine. You can get *blat* from several locations, but the principal
archive is at:

http://gepasi.dbs.aber.ac.uk/softw/blat.html

The archive includes instructions for installing it for your particular setup. Once
you have it set up, you can send a file as follows:

```
blat filename -s "subject" -t name@address -q
```

Of course, to run the program when you are not logged in, you need to have it
running as a service. The resource kit provides a utility for running an application as a
service called *srvany;* it must be installed as a service before it can be run. In order to
get the *loggauge* script to run as a service, you need to perform the following steps:

1. Move the *srvany.exe* file to a locally accessible path (*d:\winnt\system32*), and
   then issue the command:

   ```
   D:\>instsrv Loggauge d:\winnt\system32\srvany.exe
   ```

   This will create a service entry called Loggauge in the service control applet
   under control panel.

2. To quickly get the service running, from the services applet in the control
   panel, you can set the Loggauge startup type to manual. Then, in the
   command-line options field, enter the following, replacing the paths with the
   proper pointers:

   ```
   /D d:\\perl\\scripts perl loggauge.pl security 95 300
   ```

   The /D option takes the following path and uses it as the working directory
   for the program. The file then takes the next argument (in this case, perl) and
   runs it with the arguments that follow. Note: Be sure that the text file required
   for *blat* is in the working directory.

3. After pressing the Start button you should have a running email warning for when your event logs are approaching full.

If you want to, you can set up a more permanent entry for your *loggauge* service using the Registry and setting the service startup to automatic, which is spelled out in the instruction guide for the *srvany* utility. In the above example, you need to restart the service manually each time the computer restarts.

The same techniques presented here can be used with the *logjam* script to periodically search the eventlogs for suspicious events and to email you if they occur. By using a combination of eventlog and file monitoring tools, command-line mailers, and the *srvany* service, you can set up your system to warn you automatically when potential problems arise.

Just because Microsoft provides all its tools in a graphical form or hides them behind the Win32 API, does not mean that you, as an administrator, cannot create your own customized utilities for dealing with the underlying elements of the NT operating system. By using the Perl Win32:: functions, along with the Win32 modules that come with the distribution of Perl or are available over the Internet, you will find that you have almost as much flexibility as any native programmer.

Conclusion

Our goal in this book has been to ease the process of user administration in a Windows NT environment. Whether you are using NT's built-in tools, utilities available from third parties, or your own scripts, you will find that there are many ways to make life easier. We hope that the ideas and techniques we have presented in this book will help you achieve your own kind of "Zero Administration" network. While true zero administration is neither achievable nor necessarily desirable, automating as much of your day-to-day tasks as possible allows you do more than just run in place. The techniques and processes shown in this book should allow you to free your time for the more important strategic roles of administration, the ones that have the most impact on the productivity of your organization.

The next incarnation of Windows NT and Windows 98 will include Microsoft's ideas of "Zero Administration" in the form of policies, application design, directory services, and much, much more. Some of these changes may very well change the tasks we have presented here or may even completely eliminate the need for them. However, even as NT becomes easier to administer, the need for customization and automation will always exist. Every network has its own needs that can be dealt with only after once a system has been installed. As the administrator, it will be your job to take the tools available and craft a user-friendly, stable, and productive computing environment. Good luck!

Index

About the Author

Ashley Meggit is the computing officer for Jesus College of Cambridge University, where **Timothy Ritchey** is a Ph.D. candidate. Both have extensive programming and administrative experience, and Mr. Ritchey has written or contributed to several computing books, including *Internet Security Professional Reference* from New Riders.

Colophon

Our look is the result of reader comments, our own experimentation, and feedback from distribution channels. Distinctive covers complement our distinctive approach to technical topics, breathing personality and life into potentially dry subjects.

The animal featured on the cover of *Windows NT User Administration* is an octopus, an eight-legged cephalopod mollusk most closely related to the nautilus, squid, and cuttlefish. The common octopus is about 2–3 feet long. Its brain is the most complex of the invertebrates', with long- and short-term memories, providing it with the ability to solve problems by trial-and-error methods—a trick that comes in handy when evading or robbing fishermen's traps. An octopus also has complex eyes, with vision approximately as acute as a human's. Their suckers' touch is very sensitive.

One of the octopus's defense mechanisms is the release of a purple-black ink cloud as smoke screen or decoy. They can also change color for camouflage (as well as to reflect mood change) and dart away by jetting water through their siphon. This ability keeps the octopus from being an easy target, though they have no exterior hard shell. This lack of solid body matter also allows octopuses to squeeze into very small spaces.

The male octopus usually dies soon after mating; the female usually dies soon after laying a large number of eggs and caring for them until they hatch. Only a few young out of what may be more than 200,000 eggs will survive to adulthood. The lifespan of an octopus is short, ranging from 6 months to 3 years, depending on species and water temperature.

Edie Freedman designed the cover of this book, using a 19th-century engraving from the Dover Pictorial Archive. The cover layout was produced with Quark XPress 3.32 using the ITC Garamond font.

The inside layout was designed by Nancy Priest and implemented in FrameMaker 5.0 by Mike Sierra. The text and heading fonts are ITC Garamond Light and Garamond Book. The illustrations that appear in the book were created in Adobe Photoshop 4.0 and Macromedia FreeHand 7.0 by Robert Romano.

Whenever possible, our books use a durable and flexible lay-flat binding. If the page count exceeds the limit for this type of binding, perfect binding is used.

Windows NT Administration

Windows NT in a Nutshell

By Eric Pearce
1st Edition June 1997
364 pages, ISBN 1-56592-251-4

Anyone who installs Windows NT, creates a user, or adds a printer is an NT system administrator (whether they realize it or not). This book features a new tagged callout approach to documenting the 4.0 GUI as well as real-life examples of command usage and strategies for problem solving, with an emphasis on networking. Windows NT in a Nutshell will be as useful to the single-system home user as it will be to the administrator of a 1,000-node corporate network.

Windows NT User Administration

By Ashley J. Meggitt & Timothy D. Ritchey
1st Edition November 1997
218 pages, ISBN 1-56592-301-4

Many Windows NT books introduce you to a range of topics, but seldom do they give you enough information to master any one thing. This book (like other O'Reilly animal books) is different. *Windows NT User Administration* makes you an expert at creating users efficiently, controlling what they can do, limiting the damage they can cause, and monitoring their activities on your system. Don't simply react to problems; use the techniques in this book to anticipate and prevent them.

Windows NT SNMP

By James D. Murray
1st Edition February 1998
464 pages, Includes CD-ROM
ISBN 1-56592-338-3

This book describes the implementation of SNMP (the Simple Network Management Protocol) on Windows NT 3.51 and 4.0 (with a look ahead to NT 5.0) and Windows 95 systems. It covers SNMP and network basics and detailed information on developing SNMP management applications and extension agents. The book comes with a CD-ROM containing a wealth of additional information: standards documents, sample code from the book, and many third-party, SNMP-related software tools, libraries, and demos.

Essential Windows NT System Administration

By Æleen Frisch
1st Edition February 1998
486 pages, ISBN 1-56592-274-3

This book combines practical experience with technical expertise to help you manage Windows NT systems as productively as possible. It covers the standard utilities offered with the Windows NT operating system and from the Resource Kit, as well as important commercial and free third-party tools. By the author of O'Reilly's bestselling book, *Essential System Administration*.

Windows NT Backup & Restore

By Jody Leber
1st Edition May 1998 (est.)
250 pages (est.), ISBN 1-56592-272-7

Beginning with the need for a workable recovery policy and ways to translate that policy into requirements, *Windows NT Backup & Restore* presents the reader with practical guidelines for setting up an effective backup system in both small and large environments. It covers the native NT utilities as well as major third-party hardware and software.

Windows NT Server 4.0 for NetWare Administrators

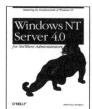

By Robert Bruce Thompson
1st Edition November 1997
756 pages, ISBN 1-56592-280-8

This book provides a fast-track means for experienced NetWare administrators to build on their knowledge and master the fundamentals of using the Microsoft Windows NT Server. The broad coverage of many aspects of Windows NT Server is balanced by a tightly focused approach of comparison, contrast, and differentiation between NetWare and NT features and methodologies.

O'REILLY™

TO ORDER: **800-998-9938** • *order@oreilly.com* • *http://www.oreilly.com/*
OUR PRODUCTS ARE AVAILABLE AT A BOOKSTORE OR SOFTWARE STORE NEAR YOU.
FOR INFORMATION: **800-998-9938** • **707-829-0515** • *info@oreilly.com*

Windows NT Administration

Windows NT Desktop Reference

By Æleen Frisch
1st Edition January 1998
64 pages, ISBN 1-56592-437-1

A hip-pocket quick reference to Windows NT commands, as well as the most useful commands from the Resource Kits. Commands are arranged ingroups related to their purpose and function. Covers Windows NT 4.0.

MCSE: The Core Exams in a Nutshell

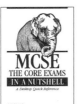

By Michael Moncur
1st Edition May 1998 (est.)
300 pages (est.), ISBN 1-56592-376-6

MCSE: The Core Exams in a Nutshell is a detailed quick reference for administrators with Windows NT experience or experience administering a different platform, such as UNIX, who want to learn what is necessary to pass the MCSE required exam portion of the MCSE certification. While no book is a substitute for real-world experience, this book will help you codify your knowledge and prepare for the exams.

MCSE: The Electives in a Nutshell

By Michael Moncur
1st Edition June 1998 (est.)
550 pages (est.), ISBN: 1-56592-482-7

A companion volume to *MCSE: The Core Exams in a Nutshell*, *MCSE: The Electives in a Nutshell* is a comprehensive study guide that covers the elective exams for the MCSE as well as the Internet requirements and electives for the MCSE+Internet. This detailed reference is aimed at sophisticated users who need a bridge between real-world experience and the MCSE exam requirements.

Managing the Windows NT Registry

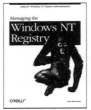

By Paul Robichaux
1st Edition April 1998
470 pages, ISBN 1-56592-378-2

The Windows NT Registry is the repository for all hardware, software, and application configuration settings. This is the system administrator's guide to maintaining, monitoring, and updating the Registry database. A "must-have" for every NT system manager or administrator, it covers what the Registry is and where it lives on disk, available tools, Registry access from programs, and Registry content.

Learning Perl on Win32 Systems

By Randal L. Schwartz, Erik Olson &
Tom Christiansen
1st Edition August 1997
306 pages, ISBN 1-56592-324-3

In this carefully paced course, leading Perl trainers and a Windows NT practitioner teach you to program in the language that promises to emerge as the scripting language of choice on NT. Based on the "llama" book, this book features tips for PC users and new, NT-specific examples, along with a foreword by Larry Wall, the creator of Perl, and Dick Hardt, the creator of Perl for Win32.

O'REILLY™

TO ORDER: **800-998-9938** • **order@oreilly.com** • **http://www.oreilly.com/**
OUR PRODUCTS ARE AVAILABLE AT A BOOKSTORE OR SOFTWARE STORE NEAR YOU.
FOR INFORMATION: **800-998-9938** • **707-829-0515** • **info@oreilly.com**

Perl

Perl Resource Kit—UNIX Edition

By Larry Wall, Nate Patwardhan, Ellen Siever,
David Futato & Brian Jepson
1st Edition November 1997
1812 pages, ISBN 1-56592-370-7

The *Perl Resource Kit—UNIX Edition* gives
you the most comprehensive collection of
Perl documentation and commercially
enhanced software tools available today.
Developed in association with Larry Wall,
the creator of Perl, it's the definitive Perl distribution for web-
masters, programmers, and system administrators.

The *Perl Resource Kit* provides:

- Over 1800 pages of tutorial and in-depth reference documentation for Perl utilities and extensions, in 4 volumes.
- A CD-ROM containing the complete Perl distribution, plus hundreds of freeware Perl extensions and utilities—a complete
  snapshot of the Comprehensive Perl Archive Network (CPAN)—
  as well as new software written by Larry Wall just for the Kit.

Perl Software Tools All on One Convenient CD-ROM
Experienced Perl hackers know when to create their own, and
when they can find what they need on CPAN. Now all the power
of CPAN—and more—is at your fingertips. *The Perl Resource Kit*
includes:

- A complete snapshot of CPAN, with an install program for
  Solaris and Linux that ensures that all necessary modules are
  installed together. Also includes an easy-to-use search tool
  and a web-aware interface that allows you to get the latest
  version of each module.
- A new Java/Perl interface that allows programmers to write
  Java classes with Perl implementations. This new tool was
  written specially for the Kit by Larry Wall.

Experience the power of Perl modules in areas such as CGI, web spi-
dering, database interfaces, managing mail and USENET news, user
interfaces, security, graphics, math and statistics, and much more.

Perl in a Nutshell

By Stephen Spainhour, Ellen Siever &
Nathan Patwardhan
1st Edition June 1998 (est.)
600 pages (est.), ISBN 1-56592-286-7

The perfect companion for working programmers, *Perl in a Nutshell* is a comprehensive reference guide to the world of Perl.
It containseverything you need to know for
all but the most abstruse Perl questions.This
wealth of information is packed into an efficient, extraordinarily
usable format.

Programming Perl, 2nd Edition

By Larry Wall, Tom Christiansen &
Randal L. Schwartz
2nd Edition September 1996
670 pages, ISBN 1-56592-149-6

Programming Perl, 2nd Edition, is the
authoritative guide to Perl version 5, the
scripting utility that has established itself
as the programming tool of choice for the
World Wide Web, UNIX system administra-
tion, and a vast range of other applications. Version 5 of Perl
includes object-oriented programming facilities. The book is
coauthored by Larry Wall, the creator of Perl.

Perl is a language for easily manipulating text, files, and processes. It provides a more concise and readable way to do many jobs
that were formerly accomplished (with difficulty) by programming with C or one of the shells. Perl is likely to be available
wherever you choose to work. And if it isn't, you can get it and
install it easily and free of charge.

This heavily revised second edition of *Programming Perl* contains a full explanation of the features in Perl version 5.003. Contents include:

- An introduction to Perl
- Explanations of the language and its syntax
- Perl functions
- Perl library modules
- The use of references in Perl
- How to use Perl's object-oriented features
- Invocation options for Perl itself, and also for the utilities
  that come with Perl
- Other oddments: debugging, common mistakes, efficiency,
  programming style, distribution and installation of Perl, Perl
  poetry, and so on.

Perl 5 Desktop Reference

By Johan Vromans
1st Edition February 1996
46 pages, ISBN 1-56592-187-9

This is the standard quick-reference guide for
the Perl programming language. It provides a
complete overview of the language, from variables to input and output, from flow control to
regular expressions, from functions to document formats—all packed into a convenient,
carry-around booklet. Updated to cover Perl version 5.003.

Perl

Learning Perl, 2nd Edition

By Randal L. Schwartz & Tom Christiansen
Foreword by Larry Wall
2nd Edition July 1997
302 pages, ISBN 1-56592-284-0

In this update of a bestseller, two leading Perl trainers teach you to use the most universal scripting language in the age of the World Wide Web. With a foreword by Larry Wall, the creator of Perl, this smooth, carefully paced book is the "official" guide for both formal (classroom) and informal learning. It is now current for Perl version 5.004.

Learning Perl is a hands-on tutorial designed to get you writing useful Perl scripts as quickly as possible. Exercises (with complete solutions) accompany each chapter. A lengthy, new chapter in this edition introduces you to CGI programming, while touching also on the use of library modules, references, and Perl's object-oriented constructs.

Perl is a language for easily manipulating text, files, and processes. It comes standard on most UNIX platforms and is available free of charge on all other important operating systems. Perl technical support is informally available—often within minutes—from a pool of experts who monitor a USENET newsgroup (*comp.lang.perl.misc*) with tens of thousands of readers.

Contents include:

- A quick tutorial stroll through Perl basics
- Systematic, topic-by-topic coverage of Perl's broad capabilities
- Lots of brief code examples
- Programming exercises for each topic, with fully worked-out answers
- How to execute system commands from your Perl program
- How to manage DBM databases using Perl
- An introduction to CGI programming for the Web

The Perl Cookbook

By Tom Christiansen & Nathan Torkington
1st Edition June 1998 (est.)
600 pages (est.), ISBN 1-56592-243-3

The Perl Cookbook is a collection of hundreds of problems and their solutions (with examples) for anyone programming in Perl. The topics range from beginner questions to techniques that even the most experienced Perl programmers might learn from.

Advanced Perl Programming

By Sriram Srinivasan
1st Edition August 1997
434 pages, ISBN 1-56592-220-4

This book covers complex techniques for managing production-ready Perl programs and explains methods for manipulating data and objects that may have looked like magic before. It gives you necessary background for dealing with networks, databases, and GUIs, and includes a discussion of internals to help you program more efficiently and embed Perl within C or C within Perl.

Learning Perl on Win32 Systems

By Randal L. Schwartz, Erik Olson & Tom Christiansen
1st Edition August 1997
306 pages, ISBN 1-56592-324-3

In this carefully paced course, leading Perl trainers and a Windows NT practitioner teach you to program in the language that promises to emerge as the scripting language of choice on NT. Based on the "llama" book, this book features tips for PC users and new, NT-specific examples, along with a foreword by Larry Wall, the creator of Perl, and Dick Hardt, the creator of Perl for Win32.

Mastering Regular Expressions

By Jeffrey E. F. Friedl
1st Edition January 1997
368 pages, ISBN 1-56592-257-3

Regular expressions, a powerful tool for manipulating text and data, are found in scripting languages, editors, programming environments, and specialized tools. In this book, author Jeffrey Friedl leads you through the steps of crafting a regular expression that gets the job done. He examines a variety of tools and uses them in an extensive array of examples, with a major focus on Perl.

How to stay in touch with O'Reilly

1. Visit Our Award-Winning Web Site

http://www.oreilly.com/

★ "Top 100 Sites on the Web" —*PC Magazine*
★ "Top 5% Web sites" —*Point Communications*
★ "3-Star site" —*The McKinley Group*

Our web site contains a library of comprehensiveproduct information (including book excerpts and tables of contents), downloadable software, background articles, interviews with technology leaders, links to relevant sites, book cover art, and more. File us in your Bookmarks or Hotlist!

2. Join Our Email Mailing Lists

New Product Releases

To receive automatic email with brief descriptions of all new O'Reilly products as they are released, send email to:
listproc@online.oreilly.com
Put the following information in the first line of your message (*not* in the Subject field):
subscribe oreilly-news

O'Reilly Events

If you'd also like us to send information about trade show events, special promotions, and other O'Reilly events, send email to:
listproc@online.oreilly.com
Put the following information in the first line of your message (*not* in the Subject field):
subscribe oreilly-events

3. Get Examples from Our Books via FTP

There are two ways to access an archive of example files from our books:

Regular FTP

- ftp to:
  ftp.oreilly.com
  (login: anonymous
  password: your email address)
- Point your web browser to:
  ftp://ftp.oreilly.com/

FTPMAIL

- Send an email message to:
  ftpmail@online.oreilly.com
  (Write "help" in the message body)

4. Contact Us via Email

order@oreilly.com
To place a book or software order online. Good for North American and international customers.

subscriptions@oreilly.com
To place an order for any of our newsletters or periodicals.

books@oreilly.com
General questions about any of our books.

software@oreilly.com
For general questions and product information about our software. Check out O'Reilly Software Online at **http://software.oreilly.com/** for software and technical support information. Registered O'Reilly software users send your questions to: **website-support@oreilly.com**

cs@oreilly.com
For answers to problems regarding your order or our products.

booktech@oreilly.com
For book content technical questions or corrections.

proposals@oreilly.com
To submit new book or software proposals to our editors and product managers.

international@oreilly.com
For information about our international distributors or translation queries. For a list of our distributors outside of North America check out:
http://www.oreilly.com/www/order/country.html

O'Reilly & Associates, Inc.
101 Morris Street, Sebastopol, CA 95472 USA
TEL   707-829-0515 or 800-998-9938
           (6am to 5pm PST)
FAX   707-829-0104

O'REILLY™

International Distributors

UK, EUROPE, MIDDLE EAST AND NORTHERN AFRICA (EXCEPT FRANCE, GERMANY, SWITZERLAND, & AUSTRIA)

INQUIRIES

International Thomson Publishing Europe
Berkshire House
168-173 High Holborn
London WC1V 7AA
United Kingdom
Telephone: 44-171-497-1422
Fax: 44-171-497-1426
Email: itpint@itps.co.uk

ORDERS

International Thomson Publishing Services, Ltd.
Cheriton House, North Way
Andover, Hampshire SP10 5BE
United Kingdom
Telephone: 44-264-342-832 (UK)
Telephone: 44-264-342-806 (outside UK)
Fax: 44-264-364418 (UK)
Fax: 44-264-342761 (outside UK)
UK & Eire orders: itpuk@itps.co.uk
International orders: itpint@itps.co.uk

FRANCE

Editions Eyrolles
61 bd Saint-Germain
75240 Paris Cedex 05
France
Fax: 33-01-44-41-11-44

FRENCH LANGUAGE BOOKS

All countries except Canada
Telephone: 33-01-44-41-46-16
Email: geodif@eyrolles.com
English language books
Telephone: 33-01-44-41-11-87
Email: distribution@eyrolles.com

GERMANY, SWITZERLAND, AND AUSTRIA

INQUIRIES

O'Reilly Verlag
Balthasarstr. 81
D-50670 Köln
Germany
Telephone: 49-221-97-31-60-0
Fax: 49-221-97-31-60-8
Email: anfragen@oreilly.de

ORDERS

International Thomson Publishing
Königswinterer Straße 418
53227 Bonn, Germany
Telephone: 49-228-97024 0
Fax: 49-228-441342
Email: order@oreilly.de

JAPAN

O'Reilly Japan, Inc.
Kiyoshige Building 2F
12-Banchi, Sanei-cho
Shinjuku-ku
Tokyo 160-0008 Japan
Telephone: 81-3-3356-5227
Fax: 81-3-3356-5261
Email: kenji@oreilly.com

INDIA

Computer Bookshop (India) PVT. Ltd.
190 Dr. D.N. Road, Fort
Bombay 400 001 India
Telephone: 91-22-207-0989
Fax: 91-22-262-3551
Email: cbsbom@giasbm01.vsnl.net.in

HONG KONG

City Discount Subscription Service Ltd.
Unit D, 3rd Floor, Yan's Tower
27 Wong Chuk Hang Road
Aberdeen, Hong Kong
Telephone: 852-2580-3539
Fax: 852-2580-6463
Email: citydis@ppn.com.hk

KOREA

Hanbit Media, Inc.
Sonyoung Bldg. 202
Yeksam-dong 736-36
Kangnam-ku
Seoul, Korea
Telephone: 822-554-9610
Fax: 822-556-0363
Email: hant93@chollian.dacom.co.kr

SINGAPORE, MALAYSIA, AND THAILAND

Addison Wesley Longman Singapore PTE Ltd.
25 First Lok Yang Road
Singapore 629734
Telephone: 65-268-2666
Fax: 65-268-7023
Email: daniel@longman.com.sg

PHILIPPINES

Mutual Books, Inc.
429-D Shaw Boulevard
Mandaluyong City, Metro
Manila, Philippines
Telephone: 632-725-7538
Fax: 632-721-3056
Email: mbikikog@mnl.sequel.net

CHINA

Ron's DataCom Co., Ltd.
79 Dongwu Avenue
Dongxihu District
Wuhan 430040
China
Telephone: 86-27-3892568
Fax: 86-27-3222108
Email: hongfeng@public.wh.hb.cn

ALL OTHER ASIAN COUNTRIES

O'Reilly & Associates, Inc.
101 Morris Street
Sebastopol, CA 95472 USA
Telephone: 707-829-0515
Fax: 707-829-0104
Email: order@oreilly.com

AUSTRALIA

WoodsLane Pty. Ltd.
7/5 Vuko Place, Warriewood NSW 2102
P.O. Box 935
Mona Vale NSW 2103
Australia
Telephone: 61-2-9970-5111
Fax: 61-2-9970-5002
Email: info@woodslane.com.au

NEW ZEALAND

Woodslane New Zealand Ltd.
21 Cooks Street (P.O. Box 575)
Waganui, New Zealand
Telephone: 64-6-347-6543
Fax: 64-6-345-4840
Email: info@woodslane.com.au

THE AMERICAS

McGraw-Hill Interamericana Editores, S.A. de C.V.
Cedro No. 512
Col. Atlampa 06450
Mexico, D.F.
Telephone: 52-5-541-3155
Fax: 52-5-541-4913
Email: mcgraw-hill@infosel.net.mx

SOUTH AFRICA

International Thomson Publishing
South Africa
Building 18, Constantia Park
138 Sixteenth Road
P.O. Box 2459
Halfway House, 1685 South Africa
Telephone: 27-11-805-4819
Fax: 27-11-805-3648

O'REILLY™

TO ORDER: **800-998-9938** • **order@oreilly.com** • **http://www.oreilly.com/**

OUR PRODUCTS ARE AVAILABLE AT A BOOKSTORE OR SOFTWARE STORE NEAR YOU.

FOR INFORMATION: **800-998-9938** • **707-829-0515** • **info@oreilly.com**